RESUME OF A RESTLESS SOUL

A JOURNEY BACK TO SELF

DAVE BECKER

For Caroline and the boys

Don't have the inclination to look back on any mistake.
Like Cain, I now behold this chain of events that I must break.
In the fury of the moment, I can see the Master's hand.
In every leaf that trembles, in every grain of sand

—Bob Dylan, "Every Grain of Sand"

CONTENTS

INTRODUCTION

About two years ago, after a harrowing medical event shook the very foundation of my life, I felt a strong urge to start this project. I didn't want to leave this world as a stranger or be remembered only as the dad who made breakfast and mowed the lawn on Saturdays, the quiet guy working in his home office. So, I began to write. I wanted to share my entire story—tracing the winding path that brought me to where I am today and exploring the man I became along the way.

As I began to write, I realized this was more than just a personal account of my life. It was a way to ask and perhaps answer some of the questions that have quietly followed me through the years. How do people see me? What will be said about me when I'm gone? How will my children understand the life I led? These questions, rooted in legacy, self-reflection, and identity, became the heartbeat of this book.

To explore my experiences honestly, I needed to look beyond the surface of the curated version of myself that I presented at work, in social settings, and on social media. What emerged was the story of a man shaped by early travels, career changes, professional growth, and a series of bizarre and severe medical events. Eventually, I faced an unexpected identity crisis when the title and structure of corporate life were no longer there to define me.

My story begins just after college, when I entered the adult world with a deep thirst for adventure and exploration. What followed was a remarkable journey through various fields, including hotel management, landscape and garden design, private estate management, corporate wine sales, operations management, business ownership, and mentoring at-risk teenagers, among other roles. Each chapter of my professional life has been marked by curiosity, a drive to excel, and a desire to do meaningful work while pursuing a fulfilling existence.

I have never been someone who follows a straight path or quietly conforms to the expected, conventional route. When those in front of me collectively move in a particular direction, I instinctively seek an alternative way. This inclination isn't driven by spite or a desire to be difficult; it stems purely from my curiosity. This tendency often made me stand out in the corporate world, sometimes in isolating ways. I focused on outcomes rather than processes, actions instead of words, and results over rituals. I didn't share the same corporate language colleagues used; I had little interest in endless meetings, the peculiar social dynamic of corporate middle management; and I didn't play golf or follow football. I approached work with autonomy and urgency but often felt like a misfit in a system built for conformity.

This book is about the tension between who I was and who I was expected to be. It's about the freedom and fear that came with walking away from a stable career in my early fifties and the challenge of redefining success and self-worth in the aftermath of that choice.

At its heart, this story is about reinvention while centering myself—learning to let go of job titles and paychecks and rediscovering who I am as a man, a husband, and a father.

I feel nothing but gratitude for everyone I have met and worked with on the paths I have walked. Some of these people have contributed to experiences that were incredibly enjoyable, inspiring, and educational, and some did not. I have learned from all of them. In the story that follows, I have used only first names. In many cases, I have changed names to avoid causing anyone indigestion or unwanted attention. They did not ask to be in my weird little play; they just were, and I was in theirs.

CHAPTER ONE
SECONDS FROM NEVER

There is no point in dying,
having gone through your life not knowing who you are,
what you are, or what the purpose of life is.

George Harrison

After dinner, I stepped outside, overwhelmed by an intense coughing fit that seemed to erupt deep within me. As I gasped for breath, an unfamiliar sensation took hold in my chest—a peculiar discomfort reminiscent of swallowing something the wrong way. It felt like a small, jagged-edged chunk of something was slowly shifting sideways in my esophagus, nestled deep inside, igniting a fiery burn that radiated through my chest. Simultaneously, a rising wave of nausea churned in my stomach. The intensity of this discomfort sent shockwaves of alarm throughout my body, a warning signal I could not ignore.

Back in the house, I went into the bathroom, taking a moment to collect my thoughts while Caroline busied herself in the kitchen, clearing the dishes from the dinner table. The sound of clinking plates and silverware echoed softly in the background as she tidied up, and

I appreciated the quiet moment to assess what was happening with my body. My pulse raced as a cold sweat broke out on my brow. My head felt thick and heavy, swirling with confusion. The sickness in my stomach crept back up into my chest. Could it be pneumonia? I had experienced the terrible burning sensation in my lungs several times during bouts of pneumonia over the past few years.

It wasn't pneumonia. My lungs felt clear.

Breathe, Dave. Breathe.

A few minutes later, my body's general alarm became quiet again, my pulse lowered, and the sickness passed.

Caroline asked if I was okay as I wiped the sweat from my forehead and came over to help her with the dishes. "Yes, I'm fine," I said. I had been in the bathroom for almost fifteen minutes, but it felt like it was much longer.

I woke up late that night feeling uncomfortable and restless, drifting in and out of sleep. I sat up in bed and swung my legs over the side, feet on the cold floor, as a sense of alarm echoed within me again. A thick, sludgy queasiness returned to my chest, and it felt heavier this time. Confused and disoriented, I shook off the remnants of sleep and checked my phone for the time: 2:41 a.m., Sunday, February 11, 2024.

Swirling. Churning.

The sickness in my chest surged and ebbed repeatedly: congestion, heaviness, nausea, and now pain. I didn't recognize this feeling or understand what was happening to me. The internal alarms grew louder, nearly deafening.

I stood up, dressed in the quiet darkness of our bedroom, and sat on the edge of the bed where Caroline was sleeping, gently touching her arm. She awoke and I said, "I don't feel well, so I'll go get checked out."

"What's wrong?" she asked.

"Not sure. No big deal . . . Just wanted to get checked out. I will call you later." I stood up. "Go back to sleep," I whispered.

I went downstairs and briefly stood in the kitchen to assess the situation more carefully. I was sweating heavily, my body felt clammy, and the nausea was rising again. The most intense emotion I can recall was a sense of impending doom. A seriousness I had never experienced flooded my mind as I tried to process the situation in the dark, quiet kitchen. My mind swirled as it analyzed the event.

"What the hell is this?" I asked myself as I reached for a glass of water.

I felt a gentle push from an unknown source, like someone's hand was on my back. It snapped me out of my daze. I refocused my eyes and turned to walk toward the garage. I grabbed my keys and wallet, backed the car out of the garage, and slowly made my way through the turns of our quiet neighborhood streets.

Still unsure what was happening, I steered my car carefully on the empty predawn streets of North Scottsdale as I breathed through the sickness now pounding in my chest. *Where am I going?* I asked myself at every turn. *The Mayo* were the only words I heard in my mind. I drove five miles to the Mayo Clinic, navigating through the dark parking lots and around construction areas, and eventually found my way to the Emergency Department entrance.

The push on my back was more noticeable, undeniable. I felt as if my feet were barely touching the ground as I stepped quickly through the main doors, past the security guard, and into the lobby. I walked over to the glassed check-in area.

My mind was swimming; I was confused.

"How can I help you?" the bearded man behind the glass asked. I spoke without words. "I'm sorry, I can't hear you," he said, leaning in with concern. I tapped the center of my chest with my middle and index fingers. He stood up quickly, walked around the glass partition, and stood beside me. "Are you having chest pain?" he asked as he reached for a wheelchair to his right. I nodded, feeling embarrassed as I sat down in the chair. I didn't want the attention that was about to come my way.

He introduced himself, telling me he was a registered nurse and would assist me. He urgently pushed me through two doors into a small, dimly lit examination room to the right. He asked me to lie down on the examination table while he connected the ECG to my now bare chest.

"I'm sick," I groaned, eyeing the trash can by the door.

"Just give me a moment, my friend," he said as he worked quickly to place the electrodes on my torso. Then he spun around to the monitor behind him and carefully read the lines on the flickering green screen.

I tried to sit up.

He walked to the wall, slapped a red button, and quickly helped me back into the chair.

I remember the sound of my keys hitting the floor.

A cold, computerlike voice echoed, "Code Blue . . . Code Blue," through the still hallways and nurses' stations. I now heard the sound of many footsteps rushing down the corridor.

"I am not this person," I whispered to myself, my voice barely audible. "I'm not the kind of guy who dies from a heart attack in the middle of the night." The weight of despair settled heavily in my painful chest as I thought about my children, imagining the heart-wrenching moment they would learn that their dad was gone forever.

Images flooded my mind—memories of making breakfast on lazy Sunday mornings, the aroma of pancakes filling the air as we shared giggles over the movie we had watched the night before. I could almost hear their laughter ringing in my ears, a symphony of joy that now seemed painfully distant.

A deep sorrow enveloped me as I pictured the empty chair I would leave at their weddings and graduations—moments of joy and pride that my absence would taint. I could almost feel the warm little hands of grandchildren who would never get to know their grandfather, never experience the joy of being spoiled with his love and attention. Each thought pierced my sick heart like a dull-edged blade, leaving a trail of sorrow in its wake.

I'm so sorry, boys, I mourned silently.

I thought about my wife; she didn't deserve this. She shouldn't have to endure the pain of our lives being so harshly and prematurely ripped apart. I imagined her standing in our home alone, and immense sadness welled in me. This loss would also be difficult for my friends, parents, and brother. The weight felt immense, leaving me with a profound regret for unshared moments.

Am I leaving now?

Is it the end of me?

Is this what dying feels like?

"This shouldn't be happening! This is not how I am supposed to go!" I cried quietly to myself. "What have I done?" I asked myself as the shame rolled in like a cold, miserable fog.

"I am taking you to another room where some folks are going to help us, okay, Mr. Becker?" another man said, who was now the one pushing me. "Can you breathe for me?"

He pushed me through the doors of another, larger examination room so quickly I thought we would crash into something. Two other male nurses were in the room, waiting for us. The three men grabbed me, one instructing, "On three." They lifted me onto the hospital bed and began their work. More people entered. The activity in the room seemed to be in fast-forward, and I was in slow motion. I watched as several people worked on my body simultaneously. They pulled off my shirt; one shaved my entire chest while another set IVs in both arms. Another was working to connect me to a larger ECG machine, and another placed a pill under my tongue. Now covered in electrodes and wires, I heard the beeping start. Someone else was handing me a small white paper cup with pills they wanted me to swallow.

More people came into the room. "What's happening?" I asked with what breath I had.

A woman dressed in street clothes sat down on a stool to my left, and another man, wearing a long white lab coat, stood to my right. They were the only people talking to me. The woman spoke first and introduced herself as a cardiologist. The man to my right then placed his hand on my arm and said he was also a cardiologist, and they would help me.

I noticed their kindness.

Two nurses removed my pants and underwear, leaving me completely naked on the table in the brightly lit room. Many people surrounded me, frantically working, and the urgency in the atmosphere left no room for modesty or embarrassment. They quickly shaved my body, and I lost track of how many people came and went from the room. A blurred crowd of people in blue and green scrubs and white jackets swarmed around me.

The beeping grew louder.

They had complete control over my body.

A man stood in the hallway just outside my room, visible through the open door. He was different. He wore a slightly wrinkled blue button-down shirt.

He was watching.

The woman to my left leaned down and said, "Mr. Becker, you've had a few heart attacks this evening, and you are about to have a very serious one. All my friends here are preparing for when that happens. "Is that all right?" She spoke with an unusual warmth in her voice.

The man in the blue shirt stood quietly outside the door. Our eyes met. He was waiting for something. I am not sure why I found him so interesting.

One of the nurses asked what kind of car I drove. I thought this was an odd question, but I replied as best I could. "Genesis."

"Why are they asking me that?" I asked over the sound of the beeps and the electric clippers shaving my body.

A nurse spoke up from the foot of my bed as he adjusted some wires. "You dropped some of your things along the way, and we just want to make sure you are reunited with your personal property."

The female cardiologist seated to my left held up a green phone. "Is this yours, Mr. Becker?"

"Yes."

"You need to unlock your phone and show us your emergency contact information. Is that okay? Can you do that for us?"

"Why?" I said. "It's three o'clock in the morning; I don't want to wake her."

"Well, Dave, we will wake her because I want her to know what's happening, and I'm sure she would like to know." There was a growing seriousness in her tone.

"I'll call her," I said, reaching for the phone in her hand.

"Can you tell me her name, Dave?" she said, pulling the phone away.

"Caroline," I said in a croaky voice.

"Thank you. Now, can you tell me her phone number?" I did, and she stepped quickly out of the room with a nurse who had jotted it down.

My whole body stiffened like a board as the beeping became louder. My fists clenched, eyes wide, and I struggled to catch my breath.

The cardiologist beside me pressed firmly on my arm and said, "Okay, here we go, Dave. Just try to breathe through it. All you have to do is breathe." His tone was stoic and calming. I looked up at him and followed his now concerned gaze to a male nurse standing in the doorway. I became more aware of the people moving around me, intensely focused on their tasks.

A warm tear traced a path down my cheek as I succumbed to a dream born from pain. Suddenly, I found myself standing in a vast, snowy field, the air heavy with a quiet stillness that enveloped me like a thick blanket. The sky above was a tapestry of muted grays, casting its melancholy light over the scene. I felt a profound sense of peace, as if time had slowed to a gentle crawl. Snowflakes danced gracefully through the air. I watched as the tiny ice crystals, glinting as they floated in front of my eyes, landed softly on the cold, untouched ground around my bare feet.

It was silent; I could hear my breathing. I was cold. I wasn't scared.

"Are they ready?" I heard the cardiologist ask, with some impatience in his voice.

The nurse in the doorway looked back toward us and gave a sharp nod, and I started to move. My entire bed whipped through the wide doorway and out to the hall like some runaway train ride at Disneyland. I felt high, confused, and like I was spinning. "Hang in there, man. Almost there," I heard the pusher of my bed say. Two nurses ran beside my now accelerating bed-ride. It felt like the pusher was jogging as the lights in the ceiling flew by above me, as if I were in a movie. We turned sharply and pushed through a double door into a large surgical suite. I felt out of control of everything. The room was bright with light and filled with equipment, people, and sound.

I was disappearing under a waterfall of pain, eyes drifting from focus, closing, slipping from consciousness.

Someone said, "On three," and my body was lifted easily onto the large table in the middle of the room. I recall hearing the voices all around me.

"Am I here?" I asked myself because I was alone. "Can they see me?"

I am so cold.

My right arm was pulled firmly and extended toward someone behind a screen to my right. A voice said, "Mr. Becker, I am Dr. Granger, and I will work on you for the next little while." A nurse secured my arm tightly to the table as the doctor said, "We are in a little bit of a hurry, Mr. Becker, so I am going to just use a local on you and begin right away. Is that okay?" I nodded in my painful haze.

Seconds later, I felt a coldness in my right arm. I looked up at the giant monitors being positioned above me and saw a black line moving through the image of my chest, quickly finding its mark.

"You're there," someone said from right behind me. I felt his warm breath on the top of my head.

The surgeon replied, "I see it." I drifted away again, feeling like my body could not stay in this fight much longer. "Got it," the surgeon said.

"Wow! Big one!" the male nurse standing to my right said, looking at one of the monitors above me. A pinch in my wrist, and it was over.

The pain left as quickly as it had come, and my lungs filled with air again. I felt a massive sense of relief. It was over.

A moment later, I was being wheeled through the hallway on my bed again, more slowly this time. In a room in the cardiac ICU of the Mayo Clinic, the nurses worked hard to get me settled and hooked up to new beeping machines. "Well, you sure had someone looking out for you tonight, my friend," one of the nurses said with a smile as she reached across my body to place the new electrodes on my freshly shaved chest.

"What happened?" I asked. My voice was still shaky. I knew I'd had a heart attack, but my question was more about *why* it happened. I had no history of heart disease. I'd had my annual physical a few months prior, with no issues reported. I exercised daily, didn't smoke, and ate well, so why did this happen? Why were there no signs or warnings?

"The docs will be in soon; I'll let them explain all that to you, Dave. Now, settle back and get some rest. It's been a long night," she said as she closed the door. Soon after, there was a knock at my door, and a nurse leaned in and said that my wife would be in shortly to see me.

Oh my God, she must be terrified, I thought.

Caroline was led into the room by one of the nurses, who then turned and left, closing the door softly behind her. Caroline was tearful and white as a ghost.

I drifted in and out of sleep, caught in a haze of unending tests and relentless checks of my vitals. Once, on that first day, I shifted my gaze to the sofa, where Caroline sat in serene silence, illuminated by the warm afternoon light that filtered through the window. The stunning backdrop of the desert mountains loomed majestically to the north, their rugged contours framing her beauty in a way that made me think of home. I opened my eyes that evening to find the sun dipping lower in the sky, casting golden rays around the room. My son Max was sleeping peacefully in the chair beside me. He had rushed to catch a flight from St. Louis the moment he heard the news early that morning, determined to be by my side as I fought to recover.

I thanked God for such wonderful and caring people in my life.

Later that evening, after Caroline and Max left to return home for the night, I saw the man in the blue shirt again. He peeked through the privacy blinds in the corner of my room, which were designed to allow medical staff to see in without opening the door. A few minutes later, a nurse checked my vitals, and I asked her who he was.

"Oh, that's Bill. He's our chaplain," she said as she checked my IVs. "He was asking how you were doing. He was concerned."

I settled back into the crisp, white sheets of my hospital bed, the sterile scent of antiseptic swirling in the air as the rhythmic beeping of machines faded into the background. My mind raced as I attempted to reconstruct the events that had led me to this moment. Emotions surged within me. Amid the chaos, I felt a profound presence surrounding me. This indescribable warmth felt like God, angels, or some benevolent force was standing by me, offering steadfast support through every harrowing moment I had faced these past hours. It was a feeling I had known from another time in my life. Whispered memories from my past floated through my mind, and the words, "I know them," surfaced from deep in my soul.

Tears ran down my cheeks, not from despair, fear, or sadness, but from the overwhelming sense of gratitude that filled me. I found myself offering heartfelt thanks into the stillness of that cold, sterile room, my voice barely a murmur against the hum of machinery. With each word, I felt a profound sense of relief wash over me, acknowledging the unseen hands that had guided me through the darkness and led me to the help I desperately needed.

If I had postponed or second-guessed my need for care any longer, I likely would not be alive today.

As the day had progressed, information about the events of the previous evening flowed into my room. It was explained that I'd had a massive heart attack called a widow-maker. These are dangerous heart attacks because, often, they offer little or no warning and can strike anyone over the age of forty-five. It seems a blood clot or a big ball of goo shook loose, perhaps when I coughed, and traveled from the shadows of my vascular system, lodging itself in the left anterior descending artery, or LAD, causing 100 percent blockage in seconds.

The LAD is the largest of the coronary arteries. It runs down the left side of the heart and supplies oxygenated blood to that half of the organ, making it vitally important.

I learned that if you experience a heart attack like the one I had, your chances of survival are, at best, 12 percent if it occurs outside of a hospital or other medical facility. Even if you manage to reach the hospital in time, there is still a high risk of significant heart damage. I consider myself incredibly fortunate.

I absorbed information from the multiple doctors, nurse practitioners, physician assistants, and nurses that flowed into my room almost constantly over the next few days. They were all accommodating and informative. I even met the surgeon behind the curtain in the surgical suite who had inserted a stent into my heart. He stopped by to see how I was doing. He explained that he expected me to make a full recovery because only a tiny section of the heart muscle was lost during the heart attacks. He added that if I had not been able to get to the hospital as fast as I did, it would have been a much different outcome.

The clinic's staff thoughtfully reviewed my care plan and suggested minor tweaks to my lifestyle. I happily agreed to eliminate red meat and dairy and focus more on exercise. "Lose a few pounds and eat a Mediterranean diet." If I kept up the exercise, I would be as right as rain in no time.

As I lay in my hospital bed reflecting on my close call, I realized that I had escaped death from serious medical situations not just once, but twice in my life. I remembered the risky surgery I'd had five years earlier and the trauma that followed. This time, I heard phrases like,

"Someone is watching out for you," "It wasn't your time," and "You have more important things to do here."

CHAPTER TWO
SLOPPY LOGIC

Jump, and you will find out how to unfold your wings as you fall.
Ray Bradbury

The conversation usually begins with a leaned-in whisper to my wife at some gathering. Rarely are these questions asked of me directly. "Is Dave planning on going back to work?"

This question is usually met with one of several responses, depending on the specific situation that arises. A response like "Dave does work; he just doesn't work in corporate" might be one such reply if the person seems slightly nosy or judgmental. A more thoughtful response will be given if a friend is asking and genuinely curious.

My wife and I recently decided to change up our paradigm of dual corporate careers. After many years of holding two very demanding corporate jobs and raising kids in a large, blended family, we were worn thin as individuals and as a couple. Our lives had become exhausting. If we weren't working, we were talking about work. It felt like we were living to work, and it did not feel good. This way of living, of course, was driven by necessity. We needed money to fuel our hungry little machine: our family and our increasingly expensive suburban American lives.

Like many others, we found ourselves caught in the daily grind. I often had stressful nightmares about shoveling coal into a giant furnace as quickly as my arms could manage. The furnace angrily rocked back and forth like in the old-timey black-and-white cartoons, with big blasts of steam scalding me as I shoveled frantically. When one furnace filled up, another would whip open, hissing, blasting steam at me, demanding its fuel.

We were not happy, and neither was our family. Our friends had drifted away, obviously tired of our lack of emotional and social availability and ridiculous travel schedules. I couldn't blame them. We had trapped ourselves in an unforgiving earn/spend cycle. If we had extra money from a bonus or a slight salary increase, we quickly found an open furnace to shovel it into, believing it would bring comfort although it rarely did.

We had become too focused on our jobs, or at least I had. I lived and died by every snarky comment in meetings, harshly written emails, or late-evening work texts and water-cooler gossip about the next round of layoffs. I was securely on the hook. My job had become my oxygen; I would cease to exist without it.

In college, I was different from those with a clear career path. I didn't know what I wanted, and I was perfectly fine with that. I found excitement in the uncertainty of not knowing what was around the corner. I enjoyed watching the puzzle pieces of my life come together at each decision point. One thing led to another—like stepping stones through a beautiful garden. It was a thrilling and straightforward way to live as a young person. While I know this approach isn't for everyone, I truly cherished the adventure of it.

I had good friends who had known what they wanted to do for a living since their first year in high school. Their path was clear, almost predetermined. One friend wanted to be an architect, another wanted to practice medicine, and another knew she would be a teacher. I was envious of this at times. It was an elegant way of thinking, a practical and pragmatic approach to planning one's life. I appreciated how streamlined and focused their planning was, and I would imagine sometimes that it was less stressful than my approach but not knowing if that were true. They navigated their college years with purpose, ready to begin their chosen career after graduation.

I did not enjoy school, not because I found the work especially difficult but because I did not know what end it was serving. I did not pay much attention or apply myself as much as my friends, because I usually looked out the window, daydreaming and waiting for my real life to begin.

I didn't have just one passion, interest, or career goal when I was young. I found many things interesting, and my plans and desires often changed. I craved adventure and excitement, and I was determined to find it. I used to tell myself that I would never work in an office. "I will never be that guy!" I would confidently declare while wagging a finger at anyone willing to listen. I was always drawn to exploring the less-traveled tributaries of life, just a short distance from the mainstream. I had the most exciting experiences and met some fascinating people there.

I didn't have a specific plan for my professional life, either, and I didn't actively pursue higher positions or titles. Instead, I let things unfold naturally and moved from one experience to the next. I drifted down the slow-moving river of my life and appreciated where it took me. Some experiences were beautiful and enriching, while others were tough lessons that I staggered away from with red cheeks and a bloody nose. Throughout this journey, I gained unique experiences and learned valuable lessons that contributed to molding my character and personality. These experiences made me feel distinctive, and I sincerely appreciated that.

As I encountered the pressures of a more serious life, my approach to career development became more thoughtful and strategic. The thrill of adventure faded as my responsibilities increased. I found myself moving toward the middle of the river, drifting away from the exhilarating currents along winding riverbanks that I once enjoyed so much. Those currents had once carried me along on an exciting journey. As I evolved into a more mature version of myself, I actively steered my life in the direction I needed it to go.

We are all products of our choices in some measure. The architecture of my life evolved and developed as I grew, shaped by the increasing responsibilities of a family and the need for financial stability. I often wondered what my path would be if meeting the mortgage, paying that insurance bill, or having enough food for my family weren't such significant concerns. I think about where I would be today if I stayed in the mindset of just "going with the flow," seeing where life took me down that next great estuary of experiences. Who would I be?

The usual endpoint of this thinking is that I am exactly where I need to be now. My life has led me to this very moment, to this place. Only one question remains: What will I do with it?

Looking back on my personal and professional development

journey, I can't help but smile. During my early working years, I encountered many unique experiences. I didn't have a cushioned upbringing with a trust fund or come from a wealthy family that paid my bills so I could go gallivanting. I was a hardworking, regular guy who deeply yearned for a rich and unconventional life. Thankfully, at that time, I dared to seize the unusual opportunities within my reach. Sometimes, I fell so hard that it knocked the wind out of me and left me holding my hat with a blackened eye and quivering lip. At other times, I managed to climb to the top of the highest mountain, open my arms wide, and feel the presence of God.

How I lived, traveled, and worked as a younger man made me a little different and allowed me to extract more of the delicious marrow from life. I was passionate and curious. I treasured being viewed as one of the more interesting people in the room because of the stories I could share of jobs, people, and places I came to know as a younger man. I thoroughly enjoyed saying, "I've been there!" while watching a movie or listening to someone speak about their exotic travels at a social gathering or similar event. I felt unique, and I loved that.

Life then was vibrant and exciting.

I stepped out of my younger life to embark on something different yet equally rewarding: marriage, family, career, a home, and the responsibility of paying bills. I am incredibly happy that I made this choice. The challenges I faced, the personal growth I experienced, and the love from having a family have all been profoundly rewarding. This growth led me to adopt a new way of living. I realized that I needed to earn as much money as possible to support my growing family, and continuing to work as a wine steward would not suffice. I quickly transitioned into a more corporate lifestyle.

The days of wind blowing through my long hair while standing on the bow of a mega yacht were soon replaced with the dull hum of a small gray metal fan clipped to the corner of my cubicle in a sea of cubicles. My uniqueness slowly faded and changed into a more predictable and formatted way of working and living, one I accepted but never truly understood. My life of traveling to exotic, faraway places and working for and living with the ultrawealthy faded into the background. That time became a series of warm memories to cherish in the quiet moments between conference calls and changing diapers.

Even though I achieved some success in the corporate world later in my career, I never really felt like I belonged. My early experiences as a private-estate manager taught me to "just get it done," a mindset that often clashed with the corporate environment I encountered. I came from a process-less way of working where the only thing that mattered—and was worth discussing—was the result. The process of getting the job done was largely uninteresting and unimportant, rarely making its way into conversations. I was trained to be a problem-solving machine, pushing through any obstacles to complete tasks on time, with no exceptions or excuses. I was result-driven.

I found the midlevel corporate way of working was often focused more on the process than the actual result it was meant to produce. This way of working seemed counterintuitive as I sat through meeting after meeting, listening to people *talk* about doing but not actually *doing* anything. I was often the quiet one on the call or in the meeting room, listening to people talk back and forth, defending their process and tools, all in a new language—so many words to say so little.

I listened to this new way of communicating, this foreign language, attempting to understand its meaning as quickly as possible. Strange corporate phrasing and jargon-rich discussions filled the meeting rooms. I was lost.

"Settle people . . . we have a lot to unpack here. Let's pivot and make a hard stop to get our ducks in a row and flesh this idea out better before it turns into a real dumpster fire. If we want to take this to the next level, we need to move the needle quickly and grab the low-hanging fruit as soon as we hit the market, so let's reevaluate before the goalposts are moved on us again. We need to break down our silos and refocus on our core competencies to bring robust deliverables here before we get too far into the weeds. We can't just put a pin in this one. Let's get to whiteboarding this before we see another top-down reorg and even more people are thrown under the bus. Are we doing a deep dive or just drilling down a little? And who is putting the deck together?"

The word salad swirled around the room.

"What the hell are you people talking about?" I would mutter as I looked at my watch and back up to the nodding heads around the table.

Oh, you're saying we need to sell more wine? Good grief! Just write that on the board, and we can get on with it!

I always hoped to hear something about an actionable idea we could run with, but that was usually not the case. I waded through this marsh of midlevel management ramblings, posturing, and conjecture, often supported by endless trackers and countless data points.

I recall sitting at my desk or in meetings, quietly thinking, *I am happy you enjoy pivot tables, and I can see you spent a lot of time building this, but will you please get to the* fucking *point!* Unfortunately, the point was usually that we all needed to update this new pivot-table tracker weekly and send it back to the tool's creator, along with all the other trackers from the last few meetings.

It was clear that my company had fallen madly in love with its process, which, in turn, became the goal—to serve the process. Over the years, I leaned in, learned the language, pulled my focus back from a more productive horizon to concentrate on the process, and did just fine. I became skilled in Excel, PowerPoint, email, in-person and virtual meetings, corporate jargon, and other process accouterments we adopted with enthusiasm. I even donned the corporate uniform of pressed button-down dress shirts and slacks accompanied by a sports coat, to help blend in. I felt like a chameleon, hoping not to be discovered as unlike the rest and, God forbid, pushed out. I realized what a fickle beast corporate middle management could be and quickly learned how to fit in well enough to keep the paychecks coming in.

My goal was to survive.

In my twenty-plus years in the wine industry, I created a paradox within myself. I took something I was passionate about—fine wine—and combined it with something I did not enjoy: the corporate sales environment and that way of working. As I advanced in the industry, I eventually secured a role as sales director at one of the larger wine and spirits companies, which was not as lofty an achievement as it may sound, but it did secure a position for me right in the middle of a large pack, allowing me to dig in and earn.

As my career progressed, it became clear that I was no longer moving with the flow. Instead of exploring, learning, and growing, I struggled against the current. This constant battle led to fatigue and exhaustion, taking a toll on both my physical and mental health, which resulted in overwhelming stress. It was a difficult way to live. Sometimes, I just wanted to lie down and give up. Then I would walk through the front door of my cozy Victorian home, see my family, and know I needed to keep going.

Being a sensitive, pragmatic, introverted "thinker/planner" personality type, I dislike being in the spotlight or handed a microphone. It's just not my thing. You will know if I have something to say; until then, I will quietly do my work over here. I have always been comfortable being in the background and getting things done. I am equally comfortable leading a team, albeit in an understated manner. However, I must admit that I enjoy being alone more than being with people although certain exceptions exist. This quickly became problematic for me in the corporate environment, where a strong meeting culture was alive and well, and the ways of working leaned toward the extroverted "external processor" and the "For goodness' sake, someone give me the microphone already!" personality types.

I was not good at reading the herd's movements and often found myself either way out in front or off to the side, watching the dust cloud move away toward the sunset with the fading sound of hundreds of hooves. Now fold in some old codependent tendencies, a dash of insecurity, and a dollop of anxiety, and you have the recipe for a corporate stress bomb, which became an issue for me later in life.

I was surprised by the level of bullying that existed in corporate middle management. The meanness was challenging to adapt to, and I struggled to feel relaxed in this work environment. While it might be an exaggeration to say that this behavior was widespread, it was certainly present and often seemed to find me. I had to work hard to protect myself from emotional and financial harm while also trying to appear as a comfortable and happy team player. This working environment became the most challenging part of life in middle management.

Caroline and I both experienced the physical and emotional impact of the stressful lives we had created. We ate too much, drank too much, and exercised too little. We often rushed through meal preparation and opted for easy, less healthy dinner choices. On weekends, I just wanted to withdraw, quietly lick my wounds from the week, heal, and start planning for the next one.

I would look around the meeting room or airport bar and see all the other puffy, gray-skinned, button-popping, scotch-guzzling guys, and I knew I wasn't the only one caught in this vapid orbit.

When I powered on my computer in the mornings, I kept one eye closed, trying to regulate the flow of urgent issues waiting to scream at me from my inbox. Opening the floodgates too fast would surely blow a circuit breaker in my brain and cause an anxiety tailspin before my second sip of coffee.

My work had become a bad-news factory.

My company no longer embraced a creative process where discoveries were encouraged or exciting ideas were shaped and shared. Instead, it became a dull, black-and-white environment where conformity prevailed. My work life had slowly turned into a bleak, dystopian scene. I found myself sitting at my desk from sunrise to sunset, filling out reports, listening to conference calls, writing recaps of those calls, and creating lengthy PowerPoint sales presentations.

My work, and that of my team, had become the essence of mediocrity.

It wasn't always like this. The change happened slowly over the years I was in the wine business, too slowly to be noticed or measured. During that time, my company seemed to lose its passion. Instead of creating or acquiring new, exciting, or successful traditional brands, we were churning out dozens of cute-labeled brands and one-off SKUs to fight for the few open spaces on retailer shelves. The approach seemed to shift from thought leadership to being thought followers or chasers, which left me with a hollow feeling because, at the time, we were one of the more impressive wine companies in the industry. We were better than this.

We got caught up in promoting structureless, overly sweet, dark-purple-colored beverages with trendy labels or clever critter-themed packaging. Our focus shifted toward marketing, consumer analysis, sales trends, and customer profiling, causing us to lose sight of our original expertise in producing and selling high-quality, more traditional wine. Instead of emphasizing that expertise and allowing sales to ensue naturally, we attempted to push subpar products onto consumers and hoped they wouldn't notice. The leadership blamed the sales team for the declining trends. This approach significantly strained our sales managers and ultimately led to layoffs.

I no longer enjoyed my work. Then I fell ill. I experienced a life-altering medical situation that, in my view, was a physical manifestation of many years of enduring corporate stress, among other factors. Additionally, my wife had grown tired of my stress and constant complaints about work; she didn't want to witness her husband's slow, gray, boozy corporate death. We recognized that our current situation was unsustainable and needed to change.

I resigned from the company where I had worked for almost fifteen years, quitting my corporate career at fifty-two. I was saying goodbye to the wine industry, my professional focus for over twenty years. My wife and I quietly discussed this plan for several months, carefully planning the timing of my exit to maximize the benefits for us while ensuring that all my work was completed and ready for a smooth transition to the next person—because that's how I operate.

Like many others, my company focused on diversity, equity, and inclusion (DEI), bringing about many positive workplace changes. However, this shift posed unique challenges for middle-aged white men like me, who suddenly found themselves on the outside looking in. I could almost hear a big metal *CLANK* as the cold iron gates to the corporate way of earning money slammed shut. "If you leave, they won't take you back, you know," a work friend told me as I shared my plan over a couple of beers. "They are trying to get us old guys out, not keep us, and certainly not bring us back in." Those words hit me hard and forced me to realize the gravity of the situation, but I stayed on course, turned out the light, and quietly closed the door behind me.

There was no cake in the break room.

I did not expect the emotional turmoil, self-doubt, and identity crisis that this change would cause. I felt lost and terrified. I had yet to discover my identity without my corporate title and job. The situation reminded me of one of the contestants on the TV show *Survivor*. In one particular season, a neurotic corporate guy ended up on the island and, soon after arriving, was seen carving a Blackberry phone from a piece of driftwood he found on the beach. He pretended to be on conference calls, pacing along the beach with the makeshift telephone to his ear, desperately trying to reconnect with his corporate identity.

He was willing to look utterly foolish in order to gain comfort from his fading sense of self. That's how I felt.

For months after leaving my job, I would wake up early, have coffee, sit at my desk, and "work on something." I would create spreadsheets for everything, from the dog's care plan to itemizing every expense from the previous month, incorporating bar charts, bubble graphs, and, yes, even the occasional pivot table. I was conditioned to work this way. I needed a *process* to focus on.

The rapid distancing by many of my close work friends surprised me. People I had worked with every day for over twenty years would send me right to voicemail, adding to the feeling of absolute isolation. The announcement, *Dave has left the clan*, kept crawling across my mind. I had left, therefore I no longer fit into their world, demonstrating the imbalance I had created in my life and hinting at the imbalance in theirs. I had overinvested in my corporate job and underinvested in my personal life. Much of my identity had become tightly stitched to my corporate self, so when my corporate identity was no longer there, my core identity was not developed enough to stand on its own. Like a newborn fawn in the woods, my legs were too weak to support me, so I stumbled and fell. It took almost two years to establish an identity strong enough to separate from my work self.

We deliberately moved away from the traditional model of two corporate incomes and typical suburban living, opting for a different lifestyle. We believed my time, focus, and skills could be better used in other areas of our lives to create a more positive outcome. Fortunately, my wife's career had thrived, and her income was enough to support us comfortably as we sought a healthier work-life balance. We were ready to embrace a new way of living.

I took on the role of chief operating officer of our family. As the father in a blended family of six, we faced significant changes as the kids grew up and moved across the country, especially with our own upcoming relocation out of state. This new role felt like the right choice, and I was prepared to tackle the challenges ahead.

My wife used the newly created space in her life to invest more in her rapidly growing career, while I took care of everything else in our home life. Drawing on my background and education in restaurants and the culinary arts, I delved into cookbooks, followed chefs, and began preparing three meals a day that some might argue could comfortably fit on the menus of finer restaurants. We felt better, had more energy, and started losing weight. Overall, our home became a more comfortable, organized, calm, and healthy space, significantly improving our quality of life. The boys felt better supported and enjoyed stronger connections with us. Stress levels decreased rapidly, and we began to enjoy our lives again. We could now appreciate the lives we worked so hard to build. We felt more in control. It was working.

Before my youngest son's graduation cap had landed on the ground, we had the for sale sign in the front yard of our suburban home. We were leaving Portland, Oregon, and moving to a state we knew little about, Arizona. Although we enjoyed Oregon for many years, we had grown weary of Portland's rain, dreariness, and growing unfriendliness, not to mention the almost constant riots and demonstrations during that time. We needed change on many fronts, and this was another step in our strategic, multistep plan to rebuild our lives together more intentionally and healthily.

These massive changes to my life sparked some deep reflection and review of my professional path. I had been so focused on the stresses of the moment in my work over the past several years that I lost sight of how I got there and, more importantly, where I was going.

Reflecting on and revisiting my professional past has brought more meaning, value, and validity. I reflected on the hard work and care I put into the jobs I had done—well, most of them. I remembered the people I worked with over the years and took time to honor them, sometimes even reaching out to try to reconnect. I recalled the struggles, painful moments, hard lessons, opportunities, and especially the big wins, of which there were many. I found myself smiling and laughing out loud as I recounted my journey. The benefit for me in exploring my memories of these experiences was the reminder that they are part of me. I had entirely disconnected from my younger self. Reflecting on these experiences honestly and thoughtfully allowed me to feel complete as both a professional and a person. As a result, my life felt more meaningful and whole.

It was time I looked up and saw the world around me again—and I am so glad I did.

CHAPTER THREE
A CHARMED ISLAND LIFE

We must be willing to let go of the life we have planned
so as to have the life that is waiting for us.

EM Forster

After graduating from college, I relocated with a few friends to Martha's Vineyard, an island off the coast of Massachusetts. Using my newly acquired hotel and restaurant management degree, I quickly secured a front desk position at the Harborside Inn, a delightful ninety-guestroom waterfront resort. My friend and roommate, Travis, also joined the front desk staff. In contrast, our other friends Jeff and Dave, who had culinary degrees, found employment in nearby restaurants. The Harborside was an excellent place for young professionals to work, partly because it provided free employee housing. Upon our arrival, we unpacked our white button-down Oxford shirts and neckties from the bottom of our musty duffel bags, which still carried the faint odor of the dingy Providence apartment we had just left a few days earlier.

During our first shifts at the front desk, we quickly recognized the main challenge we would encounter over the summer. Her name was

Carla, and she was displeased to see us. Carla, a hot-tempered islander in her mid-thirties, was the front desk manager at Harborside. She was in charge and made a deliberate effort to assert her authority from the moment we arrived.

"As long as you know that I am youse guyses bawss, we will be fine," she said, in a crusty mélange of rugged New England accent with a twist of South Bronx dockworker.

"Here we go," I muttered as we placed our things in the back office.

Travis turned to face Karen, the sheepish-looking bookkeeper in a frumpy beige cardigan seated at a small desk in the back corner of the office, which was faintly scented with patchouli oil. "Is she serious?" Travis asked, whipping his hair back. Karen slowly cinched the top of her sweater, as if she felt a cold draft. She dutifully went back to her work, hoping to avoid the drama that was about to ensue.

"Is there a problem?" Carla asked Travis; her eyes were red and widening with a building rage, ready for a fight.

She had locked eyes with Travis, so I needed to act quickly. "No, Carla, all good here," I said with a smile, stepping between the two. "Hey Carla, is it possible to get that tour now? This place looks amazing!" I was hoping to avoid reenacting a scene from *Godzilla vs. Megalon* in the tiny back office on our first day.

"Hey, I'm Dave," I said, turning slightly and smiling as I extended my hand to Karen. She was still bracing for the confrontation between Carla and her new, badly wrinkled employee. "Nice to meet you. Karen, this is my friend, Travis. It's our first day." I glanced over at

Carla, whose breathing was starting to normalize and whose eyes were now a shade less red.

"What will he do about that shirt?" she asked.

"Sorry, Carla, we just got off the ferry and haven't had a chance to get organized; we will be in better shape tomorrow," I said, hoping to stay employed for more than fifteen minutes on our first day on the island.

Carla paused as she considered her next move with her strange new employees. I tried to lead the group out of the cramped space like a nervous tour guide on his first day. Travis seemed to enjoy provoking her, like a lit match near dynamite. "How many rooms do you have here, Carla?" I asked, gesturing for her to step out first. She did, followed by Travis, leaving behind a vapor trail of bong resin and body odor.

That summer, Travis and I acquired the joint nickname "Night and Day." We learned that this moniker had two meanings. Firstly, Travis often found himself causing trouble in nearly every professional and academic setting. I had developed a knack for diffusing these situations. As Travis likes to say, I was his "faceman." Secondly, we were known for being energetic partygoers after hours and turning back into polished professionals with white shirts and ties during the daytime—Night and Day.

Working at the front desk was relatively easy, so we quickly settled into a laid-back island lifestyle. We would come to work each day, maintaining a delicate balance between shaking off a hangover and being a smidge too high. We had a great time doing it. As the summer progressed, tensions escalated between Carla and us. She had grown tired of our foolishness, which became especially evident one morning when she saw us checking in our first guest of the day, a man named John Stone. We had just arrived at work and were a tad too stoned to handle business transactions or interact with the public.

"Checking in, Mr. *Stone?*" Travis asked in his best and oddly loud impression of Jeff Spicoli.

It was overwhelming for our stony little minds, and we both succumbed to laughter so intense that we couldn't even speak. Red-faced, snorting, bleary-eyed, bent over, and out of breath. We needed to rally quickly if we were to finish this critical front desk transaction and satisfy our now-seething manager. But, once again, she promptly escorted us into the back office and finished checking in the confused guest and his lovely wife.

During that summer, we had accumulated multiple offenses, which made me worry that we might soon be shown the door. One incident involved Travis playfully jerking his steering wheel into the center of Edgartown Vineyard Haven Road when he saw Carla's large black knobby-tired F-250 pickup truck approaching from the opposite direction. Travis's attempt to engage in good-natured center lane antics with his coworker and manager didn't go well, leading to threats of physical violence from Carla's husband, Tim, a giant man, and putting Carla even more on edge.

Martha's Vineyard is a small island, and if you get fired from a hotel or restaurant here during the season, word travels fast, and you will be on the list of those not to be hired. I was not about to tuck my tail and run back home. So, I leaned in and did what I knew how to do.

"You are late!" Carla said as we jogged through the Inn's front door.

"Sorry, Carla, this was entirely my fault; I forgot to put gas in the car," I said with a nervous laugh as I stepped into the back office to drop off my things. "It won't happen again," I assured her. We both tucked in our shirts and took our positions behind the glossy blue-painted desk.

Throughout the season, the infractions began to accumulate. I was allegedly seen by a couple staying at the Inn handing a large joint to one of the hotel's maintenance staff by the entrance. I gave it to him as a thank you for fixing my muffler hanger during work hours while my car was parked in the Inn's loading zone. I later learned that this was frowned upon by Harborside management. *Noted.* Additionally, management was informed that we occasionally enjoyed using the hotel hot tub in the evenings with guests, to help us relax after a long day at the desk. It's essential to note that we always ensured the cleanup of our empty bottles. We were tidy, if nothing else.

On another occasion, a young Irish housekeeper, new to the property, informed our now rather hostile manager that we had left some rolling papers in a guest's room. This guest had recently become our friend at the hot tub and had not arrived fully prepared for his vacation. We later learned that leaving such items was not considered hospitality and could even be considered a criminal offense. While I understood the concern, I took issue with being labeled as criminals; after all, none of us were hardened offenders! Using such strong language in a perfectly civil conversation seemed unnecessary, especially in such a delightful setting.

"How did you even get into his room?" Carla demanded to know.

"Becker has a master key," Travis blurted without considering the situation carefully enough.

"How the hell did you get a master key?" Carla asked with growing concern.

Travis laughed. "You have no idea what this guy can get his hands on, Carla." The truth was that the key was provided by my new friend in the maintenance department, but I left that detail out of the discussion.

Travis and I and the guest were sternly warned about our roles in this alleged nefarious incident at the Harborside Inn. I asked that the housekeeper be called in to discuss her role in the situation, but that request was quickly denied. Later that week, I shared my thoughts on the event with the housekeeper over drinks, hoping to resolve the matter. The water was soon under the bridge, and we became fast friends, enjoying several nights on the town together.

The first week of September arrived, and we knew it was time to move on before the management of our picturesque little workplace brought more severe charges. I notified James, the jittery, chain-smoking general manager, and explained that we would be on our way soon. When we returned to our staff quarters later that day, all our personal belongings, clothes, shoes, and unmentionables had been hastily shoved into large black trash bags and placed just inside the front door of the staff apartment, along with a note that said: "GO!"

This development may have resulted from newly discovered damage to the staff apartment while we were in residence. I had in mind a certain decorative whitewashed lattice panel, a charming and ubiquitous architectural feature in this part of the country. It screened the stairwell to the staff's second-floor abode. It had sustained some damage when a lady guest of ours, who may have been overserved, stumbled and fell right through it and onto the hood of a parked car just below, which left a real mess of splintered wood and white trim pieces swinging loosely in the late evening island breeze. Not to worry—Michelle was just fine. She rolled off the now-badly dented Toyota Camry hood and stood up quickly, as if straight out of a scene from *T. J. Hooker*. She brushed herself off with a good belly laugh that could be heard over the blasting car alarm in our sleepy New England town's otherwise quiet, dew-covered early morning. We later learned that the parked car's owner had complained, which may have contributed to our expedited departure.

Travis and I stuffed the black garbage bags into the car and drove to our next hotel, the Kelley House and Harbor View Hotel. This more upscale resort comprised two separate hotels, making it a natural upgrade for us.

The Harbor View Hotel was located on Starbuck Neck at the end of North Water Street, directly in front of the Edgartown lighthouse. The 127-room historic oceanfront luxury hotel was grand in every way. It was a beautiful old place, and the view from the lobby through to the expansive front porch was reminiscent of something you would see in an old Cary Grant film. The clientele was more discerning and required a higher level of service.

The Night and Day duo had just made the varsity team.

We learned about the reservation and front office systems and found them similar to those at our last place of employment. The front office manager, Troy, a twitchy thirtysomething man with bad skin, constantly pulled at his shirt collar as if he was doing a bad impression of Rodney Dangerfield. Troy and I got along well enough. Soon after arriving, I was offered the position of front desk supervisor.

News of our dealings and misunderstandings at the Harborside Inn had yet to reach our new employers, located half a mile down North Water Street, so we were starting fresh and turning over a new leaf, as they say.

Over the next few days, Troy trained me on the operational aspects of the front desk and the expectations for delivering excellent guest service at the Harbor View Hotel. My new manager shared some of his customer service tips, which I found very helpful. However, in a moment of inflated confidence, Troy revealed one of his favorite tactics. "You can say literally anything to anyone if you do it with a big smile," he said proudly, looking around to see if anyone was listening, as if we were trading secrets. "Here I'll show you. Love the hat, John." Troy said with a cheeky, fake smile as our maintenance chief walked by the front desk.

John turned, processed the comment made to him, and quickly raised his hand, showing Troy his middle finger and saying, in a thick Irish accent, "Feck off, ya twit." The backfire startled Troy, who quickly played it off as two friends just joking around, but it was painfully clear they were not friends.

Soon after settling into our positions, Travis and I had our new employee orientation. *How exciting!* The training was led by a woman named Gloria in the HR department. Gloria was a hardy islander. She was a no-nonsense kind of gal in her early thirties. She moved with an unusual sturdiness and authority to her gait, as if she were a direct descendant of an old whaling captain. We took our places in the classroom-style meeting room and were given our name badges with some ceremony.

"Welcome to the Harbor View, Mr. Becker," Gloria said with pride as she handed me my name badge. As in many destination resorts, the name badges displayed our home states directly below our first names, which is an excellent conversation starter for employees and guests.

Mine read *Dave* and, just below, *New Jersey*.

"Lovely. Thank you, Gloria."

Travis took his badge from the moist, puffy hand of the HR manager as she held it out and walked on to the next person. He delivered a sharp elbow into my side and held his badge for me to see. The bold black font on the white plastic badge read *Travis* and, just below, *Penisavalia*. A sinister grin slowly grew across his face.

"Don't!" I quietly pleaded.

"She doesn't even know how to spell Pennsylvania. Are you fucking kidding me?" he said, a tad louder than he probably should have.

Gloria spun around, and it was on!

The others in the orientation slid down in their faded burgundy fabric-backed conference room chairs like little kids in the back seat when Mom and Dad were about to argue. Ms. Gloria said, "E-x-c-u-s-e *me*?" to the group, not knowing who had the nerve to say this vulgar thing during such an exciting part of the ceremony.

Travis quickly held up his badge and said, "Do you see where you made your mistake?" She snatched it from his hand and tossed it onto her table, alongside her large colored binders, where it eventually came to rest against a giant plastic cup filled with Diet Pepsi.

"Should have kept it, man," I said. "Classic."

The rest of the orientation was darker and less friendly, but we managed to get through it.

While working at the Harbor View, we got to know some folks in the boating community, mainly through the bars in town. One such guy was Bob, the owner and captain of a beautiful forty-foot sloop named *Tesoro*. After having several beers at the Wharf Pub one night, Bob suggested I come down to the boat the next day because he had a sunset charter lined up and could use a hand.

"I like boats and sunsets, so yeah, sounds good," I said.

Helping Bob that next day quickly turned into a fun after-work crewing job. Each day, just before six o'clock, Bob would sail out of the marina with a group of paying tourists and take them on a delightful sunset sail through Edgartown Harbor. I worked for free, and Bob would supply booze, a cut of the tips, and some training. My primary responsibility was ensuring that his passengers were happy and well cared for, which involved replenishing their drinks and facilitating conversation when needed. I also threw lines and fenders to help with docking and took the helm if Bob was required to step away to work on something. I enjoyed sailing very much; it felt natural to me. It wasn't long before Travis joined me and helped crew. We were both very friendly and personable, always up for a good time. Bob enjoyed the vibe and energy we brought to his sunset cruises, which could sometimes be a little stiff.

Bob kept *Tesoro* in a slip at the docks in front of the Harborside Inn, our former place of employment, so it was a short walk down from the Harbor View after work. On the days when Travis joined the crew, he would usually raise his arms high and extend both his middle fingers toward the Harborside Inn office, just up the orange-marigold-lined walk, then whistle and shout, "Hey, Carla!" which usually startled the guests trying to relax by the pool, all with his newly corrected Harbor View Hotel name badge dangling precariously off his untucked white short sleeve dress shirt.

"Classy, man, classy," I would say as we tossed the lines onto the dock and shoved off.

That fall went by quickly. Following Troy's promotion to guest services director, he promoted me to his old position of front desk manager and asked me to take a weekly rotation as manager on duty, or MOD. A department manager would be responsible for the property each evening after the senior management team left for the day. I enjoyed my MOD evenings because I could have dinner in the main dining room and order anything I wanted from the menu, including the lobster or the hotel's famous rosemary-braised lamb shank. As a young man passionate about fine dining but needing more financial means to indulge in it, I found this perk exciting.

In exchange for enjoying a beautiful dinner, I would have to make myself available to handle any issues in the hotel that evening. Usually, this included some minor reservations or check-in issues, which I was well-acquainted with and could handle easily. Sometimes, a sign-off was required for a costly repair, or a staffing issue would arise.

One evening, I noticed a small group sitting at the table beside mine while I enjoyed my complimentary dinner and the remarkable view of the illuminated lighthouse and harbor from my white linen-dressed table. Among them was Harrison Ford. He was in town for a movie shoot and stopped by the hotel for dinner. We nodded, exchanged hellos, smiled, and continued our evening.

I was beginning to feel very comfortable in this environment, and luxury hotels started to make sense to me. As I gained more experience, I felt increasingly relaxed. I met some fascinating people at the Harbor View, including world travelers, celebrities, and other interesting individuals who were there for a holiday. That summer, some noteworthy island residents and local celebrities were invited to join us for an event at the hotel. I observed our new general manager, who had just come from Boston, struggling with some VIP island guests. He seemed awkward and uneasy, constantly blotting his moist forehead with his handkerchief. He pulled me over and smugly explained how important it was for this event to go well, as if I hadn't realized it.

Then, Walter Cronkite and his wife stepped onto the hotel's front porch. The GM did not miss a beat as he extended his damp hand, told Mr. Cronkite what a huge fan he was, and shared his favorite newscasters, trying desperately to make a connection. It was cringeworthy.

After a moment, I stepped in, hoping to keep our guests from making a run for it. "I'm Greg's friend. It is so nice to meet you finally, and we are glad you are here," I said as I reached to open the front door for them.

My boss, trying to salvage what he could of the situation, asked, "Who is Greg?"

Mr. Cronkite said, "Greg is the skipper of my *Wyntje.*"

My boss had difficulty understanding the reference, so I explained that Mr. Cronkite was an accomplished sailor who owned a beautiful yacht named Wyntje. I knew this because I would pass by her each evening during my boozy sunset cruises.

"She is some boat, sir," I said as I opened the big door for them.

Walter smiled proudly and said, "Yes, she is. Oh my yes, she is." He turned back as they stepped into the lobby and asked, "What's your name, son?" I told him.

I became very good at making people comfortable in this environment, developing a skill that would serve me later in my work life. I began to feel like I was pulling away from the pack and achieving professional growth. I enjoyed that feeling.

Around this time, the senior managers believed my abilities could extend beyond front office work. I was soon promoted within the organization and given additional responsibilities. In turn, I bought a couple of new white shirts and some ties and ditched the old, wrinkly, and stained ones from the Harborside Inn. I was enjoying my first experience as a manager. Employees were now coming to me for answers and help. I traded my white name badge for a gold manager's badge, which added a little spring to my step, and I liked it.

In the fall, I was invited to join the sales team for the two-property resort. I packed up my desk space in the small office just off the lobby and moved to the sales office in a large cottage near the rear of the property. My new role would involve selling conference space and hotel rooms to companies and organizations. I was familiar with this from my studies at Johnson & Wales College. I had become proficient there in calculating conference and group rates, coordinating among multiple departments, and planning banquet events. I was eager to apply these skills in real-life scenarios.

At the end of the season, just after the Christmas holiday, the Harbor View was to undergo a massive remodel. The old gal would be closed for several months while she was stripped down to her studs and rebuilt. I was excited to be in a salaried sales position, which allowed me to continue working even with the hotel closed.

The season elevated to a magnificent crescendo during the preconstruction employee party. Once everything of value had been removed and secured, the property owners opened the hotel for the remaining thirty or so employees, and *just* the employees, for an entire night—all guestrooms, bars, pool, everything. We had been tasked with one glorious job: to drink and eat everything on the property before the doors were shuttered the following morning. This sort of employee gathering would most likely not be approved today. During the evening, many of us danced on tables in the restaurant while drinking from bottles of rum and wine. The music was loud, the booze was flowing, the clothing was scarce, and there were no rules.

I'd learned my new boss, Ed, the sales director, was consistently the victim of pranks, and this evening was no exception. Troy, Gloria, and I gathered as much clear plastic wrap from the kitchen as possible and tightly wrapped Ed's tiny white Suzuki Samurai, accented with sporty brown-and-gold striping, from top to bottom, front to back. We added layer after layer until it was close to half an inch thick—quite an achievement for a pack of drunken hotel managers.

Watching Ed trying to open his car door later that night was priceless. We, of course, had a camera ready. I found it humorous that the HR manager was the one who led our booze-fueled caper that evening. Later that night, we found Gloria passed out on an old sun lounger at the pool's edge with a neatly ironed beige dinner napkin carefully draped over her face, the words *HR Dept* sloppily written on it with a black marker. As I looked on, a near-empty bottle of vodka dropped from her hand and rolled noisily across the Pebble Tec deck before finally splashing into the pool, where much of the remaining hotel furniture was now floating.

This was well before Instagram, TikTok, or even cell phones with cameras, so there was little hard evidence of the magnificent debauchery that occurred that crisp winter Sunday night. It is now the stuff of island lore, a story no doubt still being told late in the evening at the Wharf Pub, David Ryan's, and the Navigator—if they are, in fact, still there. Our group at the Harbor View all became excellent friends. Wintering over a few times on a small island will do that.

The next morning, the trucks and crews arrived on the first ferry to dismantle the property and restore the old Harbor View to its original grandeur. I lived in one of the guest cottages on the property, and that morning, I took a stroll with my overnight guest in search of coffee and some Tylenol. We watched a group of construction workers standing beside the pool, holding clipboards and wearing orange vests and hard hats, as they waved their arms around. Gloria's empty vodka bottle was still bobbing in the pool, tapping softly against a partly submerged dining room chair.

Good night, Harbor View. Thanks for a really good time.

Travis headed out to Vail with friends to enjoy the Colorado powder for the rest of the winter. This plan was accelerated when the chief of police instructed Travis to leave the island and never return. This notice was given shortly after he was discovered in his robin's-egg-blue

Chrysler K-car at a strange little accident scene. He had misjudged a corner and rolled his car through someone's manicured privet hedge on the way home from the pub. When the dust settled, Travis's car was found leaning precariously against the exterior bedroom wall of a charming white Cape Cod–style home. The image of the homeowner, standing in his bathrobe, taking in the bizarre scene in the swirling red and blue lights as Travis sat quietly on the curb in handcuffs, remains etched in my memory. Luckily, being a very slow-moving accident, there was only minor damage and no injuries.

I was promoted to sales and conference services manager for the two properties that winter. As the remodel was underway, our team worked hard to sell meeting space for the newly renamed Harbor View Resort and Conference Center. Before the remodel, the two properties had been sold to Winthrop Holdings, a Boston real estate holdings company. This new role was my first introduction to corporate ways of working.

Ed and I often traveled off the island for sales trips to Boston, Brookline, Quincy, or Braintree to promote our soon-to-be remodeled hotel. The company requested that we share a hotel room to decrease expenses during the off-season. Since we didn't know each other well outside of work, sharing a double room was uncomfortable for us, especially Ed. He would sleep fully dressed on his covers each night, as if he might need to spring into action at any moment. I felt somewhat responsible for this behavior. We had played so many pranks on Ed over the months that we may have left him in a constant state of readiness to flee or protect himself from the next embarrassing situation we might create for our amusement.

As we spent more time together, he relaxed and even forgave me for my role in cocooning his car in Saran Wrap and then posting the picture of him trying to open his car door on the Wharf Pub community bulletin board, looking like a wobbly raccoon caught in the headlights. He also forgave me for when Gloria and I hung a large Christmas wreath on the rear bumper of his car while he was in a meeting. As he left, we pressed our faces against the cold window and watched him drive up the hill and around the corner onto Main Street. The little metal bells dragging on the pavement made quite a yuletide racket, throwing the occasional spark as he drove away from the office each evening through Edgartown's quiet, wintry streets. We were all surprised that Ed remained unaware of this noisy holiday appendage dangling from his bumper. I finally broke down and told him about it one night at the pub during an event where we had been asked to be guest bartenders, and all tips would go to folks in need on the island. I was perhaps swept up in the charitable atmosphere of the evening.

"Dave, I'm your boss, for crying out loud!" he sheepishly reminded me with that awkward smile.

I offered a Cheshire cat grin. "Sorry, Ed, but in my defense, HR did approve it."

Despite all the challenges, we formed a successful sales team. Ed is a kindhearted, somewhat awkward soft-spoken man, fifteen years my senior. He has a cheerful disposition and is quick to laugh. Like me, he felt out of place in the new corporate sales environment. Nevertheless, we met the goals set by the Winthrop team. We secured enough business to keep the old place busy for several months after the remodel.

The senior management team from Winthrop visited the property periodically to assess the progress of the remodel. After one particular tour and discussions at our sister property, the Kelley House, now a part of Faraway Hotels' Martha's Vineyard location, I set out for the ten-minute walk back along North Water Street, one of the more picturesque streets I have known. The CEO of Winthrop waved me over outside the lobby of the Kelley House as the rest of the group fussed about, pointing at things. "Walk with me," he said as he started the stroll up the short hill and around the corner onto North Water Street. We walked together, discussing the island, the property, my background, and my ambitions. I remember him as a straightforward man who was easy to talk to. He invited me to the corporate office to work with his national sales director, Susan. He sang her praises as a strong sales leader and someone who could "get it done," as he put it. He suggested I make that trip alone.

A couple of weeks later, I arrived at the office in downtown Boston, near the waterfront, and met with Susan. She was an energetic lady with short, spiky, reddish-brown hair and an electric personality. We set off on sales calls she had arranged around the Boston area. I appreciated that Susan provided me with new ways to prepare for and approach sales calls. I tried my hardest to perform well, and by all metrics, I did. Soon after, Ed moved on from Harbor View, and I took over as the lead on the sales effort for the property.

Despite fast promotions, more money, a decent travel and expense budget, use of a company car, and two offices—a small one in the corporate building in Boston with a spectacular city view, the other on Martha's Vineyard—not to mention the several nicely pressed shirts and ties in my closet, I felt like I was missing something. I recall stopping by the liquor store in the Edgartown Triangle shopping center after work one evening, wearing a white shirt, a navy blue blazer, and khaki slacks, to pick up a bottle of something, some rolling papers, and likely a cigar.

The salty old islander behind the counter said, stroking his red beard in a circle, "You already got most of the vices, huh?" Those words echoed in my mind during my drive home and for several days afterward. I was twenty-one but felt like I was going on forty and wasn't happy. I was still a young buck who just wanted to run. I needed a change. It was time to step in a different direction.

CHAPTER FOUR
FALLING UP

I don't know where I am going from here,
but I promise it won't be boring.

David Bowie

On weekends, I worked with my good friend Anders, who owned a small tree-service company on the island. Anders had lived on the island for a long time and seemed to know everyone, and everyone knew him. Our primary focus was on lot clearing, brush cutting, and tree removal. I enjoyed this work, especially after spending the week in my hotel sales job.

On Saturday mornings, he would pick me up promptly at 7:00 a.m. in his old green dump truck, which had white lettering for his company on the doors. Before I closed the truck door, Anders would pass me a lit joint and a thermos of Gevalia coffee. "Good morning, sunshine," he would say while turning up the volume on the small boombox he kept on the dashboard. Anders was a beast, both at work and at play. He stood six feet, one inch tall and weighed 230 pounds. He was six years older than I, was solid muscle, and was fearless—an honest, tough, hardworking Nordic man. We would close the pub on Friday nights and still make the 7:00 a.m. start time on Saturdays when the work needed to be done.

Anders taught me how to work. "If you are sitting down on the clock, you must be sick or have broken your ankle; which is it?" he would shout as he dangled from a rope high in the tree above with an idling chainsaw. I quickly learned to endure tiredness, discomfort, and pain to complete the job. He was tenacious and would take on jobs that many would not. He made good money and paid me well—always cash. We would arrive at the job site for the day, and I would unload the tools and fuel the saws while he spoke with the property owner.

We would start early and run the saws for seven to eight hours. It was hard work, but I loved it. At the end of each day, we would neatly place all the equipment in the back of the dump truck and climb into the cab for the ride back down the island. There was something very satisfying about this kind of work for me. The smell of fuel and chain oil on my hands; the dirty old work truck; the thick, oily, sawdust-covered jeans and boots; and the sweat-soaked hat all contributed to the experience. After a day like that, I could walk away and tell myself I did some real work today. We worked and talked like men, and it was good. I half expected a bald eagle to land on my flannel-clad shoulder. I never experienced that same feeling after a day in corporate hotel sales.

One evening, Anders came by to pick me up for what would likely be another long night at the pub. When I climbed into the cab, a lit joint was passed to me as he told me about a job he just landed. It was a big waterfront estate job. "I need someone who can garden," he said. This guy wanted big tree work, landscape construction, and cutting in new garden beds. "Big job. You in?"

"I got a job, man," I said.

He parked the old Chevy truck in the yacht club parking lot, around the corner from the pub. As we climbed out, an Edgartown cop slowly rolled up to us, noticing the blue cloud of smoke following us out of the truck.

"You guys gonna be a problem tonight, Anders?" the cop asked coldly.

"No way, man, just having one beer, that's it! *One* beer!" he yelled as he closed the truck door, raising his arms to express his exaggerated sincerity, as he often would.

"Yeah, right. Anders, I'm watching your truck tonight," the cop said as he pulled slowly past.

"Yeah, whatever, Chris." Anders extended his middle finger jokingly. "Oh, hey, Chris! I left a package in your car yesterday; you get it?" he yelled at the brake lights of the cruiser, now stopped twenty feet away.

Backing up slowly, the cop came alongside us. "Yeah . . . I got it," he said in his coastal New England accent. He put his cruiser back into gear with a clunk. "Hey Anders, you shouldn't leave packages in police cars, you know; it gives people the willies." He casually dropped his left arm out the window, showing us his middle finger as he rolled around the corner and up past the Among the Flowers café.

"Fuckin' guy . . . giving me the finger right here in the middle of the street like an animal, shameful!" Anders said with a snort at a couple of confused tourists standing nearby. We walked the block to the pub.

We talked about the job that evening with our elbows on the bar. It was spring, and he was getting busy and wanted me full-time. "Come on!" he shouted, disturbing the vacationers quietly sipping their fruity cocktails at a nearby table close to the end of the bar. "I'll set you up on this new estate job for a while, and you can stay there until we are done; I'll get Tommy to cover the up-island tree work. It's a cush deal, man!" He downed what was left of his third beer.

A police cruiser slowly rolled by.

I knew I wanted a change, and this was starting to feel like the right move.

"Alright. Okay, I'm in!"

Things were changing; big pieces of my life were moving when they had recently been stuck, which felt good. A few days later, I gave notice at the Harbor View and thanked my Winthrop sales colleagues for my two great years there. They were kind and professional, and I would miss working with them. They were indeed an outstanding bunch.

Little did I know that deciding to help with this landscape project would lead to a once-in-a-lifetime job opportunity lasting the next several years. Eventually, that job would take me to California, marking the beginning of a challenging and complex chapter in my life.

Anders picked me up in the green dump truck that following Saturday morning. "Let's go meet this guy for that estate job," he said, passing a joint over and turning up "Moving in Stereo" by the Cars on the radio that was duct-taped to the top of the dashboard.

"What do you know about him?" I asked, taking another pull off the joint and turning to exhale out the window as we rolled slowly through town, receiving strange looks from the tourists on the sidewalk.

"Not much," he said. "He's got money; that's all I need to know!"

We stepped out of the truck's cab, waving away the wispy cloud of smoke. After putting some Visine in our bloodshot eyes and popping some chewing gum, we walked across the street to a grassy lot to meet the property owner. The man stood in the middle of the lawn, wearing a white polo shirt, Nantucket Reds pants, docksider shoes, and a large cigar pinned between his forefinger and middle finger. "Fellas," he said, extending his hand.

"What are we looking at here? What can we do for ya there, Norm?" Anders asked in his heavy "Southie" Boston accent from behind strikingly dark sunglasses.

"Trees, fellas! Lots of trees!" the property owner said, waving his arms in big circles. "I don't even want to see that house next door. And I don't want to wait twenty years for them to grow." He puffed his cigar and grinned. "Do I have the right guys?"

"You sure do, there, Norm," Anders said.

"It's Norman, but yeah, good to hear."

"What kind of budget are we working with here?" Anders asked.

"Whatever it takes, fellas. Whatever it takes. Let's see how this goes, then we will talk about the next job." He favored us with a boyish grin.

"I like the sound of that, there, Norm!" Anders said as the man walked toward the main house through a cloud of cigar smoke.

"This guy wants big and now! We will give him big and now, buddy!" Anders said wildly, smacking me in the arm and knocking me sideways. "Monday, we go to Weston Nurseries in Hopkinton."

We completed the project by installing dozens of large conifer trees along one side of the property in a natural, forest-style planting, featuring blue spruce, cypress, bald cypress, arborvitae, and cedars. We did good work. The trees looked like they had been there for years; it was a beautiful installation job.

A few weeks later, the owner returned and called Anders to discuss the project. When we arrived at the site, we were once again stoned. We didn't care much about it. Anders's company had secured several large jobs, and we were busy. This client was just another individual in need of work. However, I felt that this situation might be different in some way.

The owner was happy—almost giddy—with the work we'd done for him. "You guys don't mess around, huh?" He laughed.

"No, sir, we do not," Anders said. "We are a get-shit-done crew!"

"Let's walk up to the house; I want to show you some things,"

Norman said as he turned onto the street. We walked with him in a cloud of sweet Macanudo smoke.

We made our way up the steep driveway, past the guest house, and to the main house and yard. He waved his arms around enthusiastically while rattling off projects. "All this goes! And I want retaining walls—stone walls—but nice Chilmark fieldstone, you know?"

"Sure, we can do that," Anders said.

"All English gardens over here and here," Norman said, pointing to the lawn of the main house.

"That's Dave's thing, English gardens," Anders said with a big, stoned smile.

"Good. I want the best gardens in town; you read me, fellas?" Norman said with that grin, almost checking our gumption.

"Sure, we can do that," I said with a smile.

He stood halfway up the driveway and turned to his left, examining another open space between his property and the neighbor's. "Trees! And I mean *big* ones! Right here and up to there, between the houses."

"How big do you want?" Anders asked, jotting down some scribbly notes on a coffee-stained yellow legal pad.

"How big can you get them, Anders?"

"As big as you want!"

Norman laughed as he walked away. "Make it happen, guys. Make it happen!"

Anders said. "We just got a shit-ton of juicy estate work, buddy."

The following month was very hectic for us. I put in fifteen to sixteen hours a day on that job alongside the crew. "Set up the lights!" Anders would shout from the truck as he pulled into the driveway at 5:30 p.m., still wearing the blue FedEx uniform from his day job. There were days during crunch time when we had the guys working on that job site nearly twenty-four hours a day, quietly planting herbaceous perennials and annuals all night long under the lights. We did our best to do the loud work during daylight hours. We occasionally saw a flashlight aimed at us from a neighbor's yard in the middle of the night, with the sound of barking dogs. Still, we didn't stop for anything or anyone.

We were taking a massive swing on this job. We would either piss off the owner and get fired, or we would get more work.

We found some gorgeous Hoopsii blue spruce up in Hopkinton. They were perfect—absolute specimens. They ranged in height from twenty-eight to thirty-four feet, weighing well over five tons each. If the plantings were successful, these would be the largest trees ever transplanted on Martha's Vineyard. They would need to be moved to the island each on a separate tractor trailer. Cha Ching! This was a giant swing.

We found an excavation company capable of doing this work and had them on-site to meet the trucks. The hydraulics on the excavator whined as it lifted the massive trees into place, one by one. They were gently rocked into their well-prepared soil cradles, backfilled, and straightened. Cable stays were set, and the trees were watered heavily. After each tree was carefully put in place, its lowboy tractor trailer would pull away down the street, heading back to the ferry, as the next one pulled up to the end of the driveway, ready to be offloaded by one of the massive excavators standing by. The entire project was meticulously planned down to the minute and executed flawlessly. We cleaned the site perfectly. It looked like we were never there. It was as if someone had pushed fast forward on nature, and voilà! Massive trees overnight!

It wasn't cheap, but we managed to do it.

Norman flew back from California to meet with us. "J-e-s-u-s, this could get weird, huh?" Anders said with some concern as he took another hard pull off the joint. We rolled into the driveway and saw him standing with his back to us, hands on his hips, looking up at the monstrous conifers now separating him from his neighbor.

"Here we go," I said as we climbed out of the truck's cab. My heart was racing.

We all stood there quietly for a moment.

"Fellas, I said big. These are monuments!" the owner said with a serious face.

Later, we both joked about wanting to jump back in the truck, toss the massive invoice out the window at him, and speed off in a cloud of weed smoke and diesel exhaust, leaving this expensive situation in the rearview mirror—because running away feels good sometimes. I am glad we didn't.

We stepped closer and watched him as he examined the evergreen behemoths. Norman turned, nodding slightly as he processed what he was looking at. "Not many people could pull this off," he said with a widening grin. This is impressive work, fellas. Holy cow! You did this?" There was a touch of amazement in his voice.

"Yes, we did," I said. "It wasn't easy, but we got it done."

He vigorously shook both our hands and thanked us. "You guys are something else, you two," he said. I did inform him that the neighbor to the east wasn't thrilled to see the trees go in and had a few choice words for me earlier that week.

"Who, Ted? Eh, that's alright; he'll come around." Norman turned and spoke to a woman standing twenty feet behind us. "Helen, would you please send Ted something nice and thank him for his patience, alright?" The woman nodded silently and wrote something on her notepad.

I remember being so impressed by this. It made me wish for a similar experience—where I could turn to someone and ask them to do something for me without getting the middle finger or a swift punch in the ribs. Sure, I had developed a small amount of clout at the Harbor View, but as the youngest manager on the property, my instructions sometimes were met with a good measure of huffs and snorts. It did not help when Travis and I were in a front office meeting and he would laugh loudly while I was reviewing a plan for the team, announcing to the group, "The hardest part of all of this is taking Becker seriously—because I know what he did last night . . . bah ha ha!"

"You may want to send that guy over there something, too, Helen," Anders said, pointing to the neighbor on the other side. "I wouldn't expect a Christmas card from him either, there, Norm." Norman laughed, giving his nod of approval.

We walked the rest of the project and enjoyed watching him explore his new English gardens, stone walls, and massive trees. "Magical," he said as he peered around corners to see the fabulous little pocket gardens, with hundreds of perfectly flowering annuals and perennials.

"You did this?" he asked, turning to me.

"I did, yes, sir. I hope you like it."

"Very much, yes, I do. Very much," Norman said with that big sideways grin.

I was working on his property a few weeks later, ensuring everything was going okay and adjusting the cables on the new trees, when Norman came up to me.

"Hey, Dave, got a minute?" he asked.

"Of course, sure," I said as I removed my gloves and brushed myself off.

"I want to make a change around here," he said, examining the glowing end of the freshly lit Macanudo. "I want you to work for me. Are you interested?"

"Yes, I am. What are you looking for?" I knew he already had a head gardener.

"Good. I'll have Helen find you." He strode to the main house and disappeared through the front door.

Becky, the estate's head gardener, pulled into the lower driveway about thirty minutes later, said hi as she bounced by me to the main house, knocked on the door, and went in. A few minutes later, red-faced, she walked by me, quietly this time, got into her rusted mocha brown Subaru, and drove away.

Helen strolled down the driveway in an odd, almost theatrical way, like in an off-Broadway production of *The Sound of Music*. She was the estate's property manager. She was an older islander, probably in her mid-sixties at the time, and she was the one who paid us, so she was on the list of good people to know.

"Oh, Dave, got a minute?" she said.

"Yeah, sure, Helen. What's up?"

"I hear you have impressed the boss."

"That's great to know."

"Well, it seems you are now our head gardener," she said with a big smile.

"You have a head gardener; she just walked by," I said with some feigned polite confusion.

"Well, we *did* have one, but she is gone. Out with the old and in with the new and all that. Welcome to the estate," she said, extending her hand to me. I shook it.

"We will talk tomorrow and get you set up with everything you need." She walked back up the driveway in her black yoga pants and long sweater.

I spent the next few weeks acclimating to the new job and work environment. I continued to help Anders on weekends and occasionally as I could, but my focus was on my new estate job. My head was spinning. In a few months, I'd transitioned from resort sales management to a more challenging job in tree work and lot clearing and then to serving as the head gardener on a billionaire's private estate. It's amusing how life sometimes works, if you relax and let it unfold how it wants to.

This environment was very different for me, but I enjoyed it. It felt good. I enjoyed getting to know the rest of the staff on the property: the boat crew, the chef and kitchen staff, and the housekeepers. When Norman was most active at this property in the summer, it was common for the place to have a staff of nine or ten. The home operated like a small, very high-end luxury hotel, bustling with staff and activity, especially before guests arrived. Initially, my job was fairly straightforward; I was responsible for the grounds and all areas outside the house. Anders was also getting more involved in the property as the summer approached. He was tapering off his tree work, focusing more on FedEx, and working on the estate with me. We were a great team. There was little that the two of us could not accomplish.

As the summer progressed, I fell into a rhythm. During the busy season, we worked every day. The property was becoming increasingly complex from a gardening perspective. We installed some breathtaking English gardens that summer. It was an excellent opportunity to become a better gardener and designer when I had unlimited budgets and a small army of people to help when needed. We would walk into the garden centers and nurseries, and they would rush to help us, which was a new experience for me.

At the beginning of my time on the estate, I reported to Helen. I got to know her as a quirky old gal and islander, but she was always nice to me. She was a kind person. Sure, there were times when we butted heads a little; she would call Anders and me Tweedledee and Tweedledum, and I never knew who the latter was in the reference. She would often step out the front door and into the gardens, searching for the prize blooms for her vases. She'd look over at me and raise her shears high in the air, giving me a devilish grin as she snapped the blades open and closed. This way of working was problematic because I needed my prize blooms to stand tall when the boss arrived, especially in the main house gardens that bookended the entrance. These gardens were designed to envelop you as you approached the front door.

I spent weeks coaxing the delicate perennials into a heavier bloom cycle so guests would see the best the gardens had to offer when they arrived—the big show. I also kept schedules for the best organic fertilizer programs, pruning, weeding, and watering.

The gardens were, well, pretty badass!

Helen was unresponsive to my plea not to cut the best blooms, so I needed a better plan to discourage this behavior without upsetting the person who paid me.

"I got it!" I said, spinning around and racing back down to the garage. I whipped into the equipment room and opened the irrigation control panel. I found the label for the main house's front door garden on the panel and pressed "System On" and then turned on zones six and seven. I wheeled back out of the garage, and halfway up the drive, I was just in time to hear a shriek followed by a few colorful words and a slamming door. *Brilliant!* I did this for the rest of the summer. Anytime I saw Helen walking toward one of the gardens with shears, I would turn the pertinent zone on, full spray. It worked every time. The prize blooms remained intact, and our local florist had a nice bump in sales, thanks to Helen. Win-win.

Who is Tweedledum now?

The energy on the property a few days before the boss arrived was electric. Every team worked around the clock to ensure the place was exactly as it should be. Anders and I scrambled to make sure everything outside was perfect—not one weed, deadhead, broken limb on a tree, fallen leaf on a walkway, spent lightbulb, or even the most minor patch of dirt on the hand-brushed driveway. The expectation was perfection. That is what we were paid to provide. I enjoyed learning more about what the other teams did. For instance, Helen and the housekeepers would scour the house to ensure it had been cleaned to exceptionally high standards. Someone would hear about it if it took the owners more than one match to light a fireplace.

In anticipation of the guests' arrival, the chef and her dedicated kitchen team embarked on an intricate process of menu design and provisioning, working diligently for several days. Every kitchen surface was meticulously scrubbed and organized, ensuring a pristine environment ready for the flurry of culinary activity that lay ahead. The dining room sparkled with gleaming accents, set to an impeccable standard that could grace the pages of a magazine. This exquisite home, a visual masterpiece in its own right, has been celebrated in *Architectural Digest* magazine on multiple occasions, showcasing its stunning architectural details and stylish design.

The captain and crew thoroughly inspected all small boats and watercraft to ensure they were clean, fueled, serviced, equipped with the necessary safety gear, and ready for use. The largest boat, measuring well over ninety feet in length, was meticulously cleaned, provisioned, and serviced. This stunning motor yacht looked regal at the end of the dock, set against the picturesque backdrop of Edgartown Harbor.

Charts were laid out and prepared for any cruise the owners might wish to take during their stay. *Looking to have lunch in Nantucket? No problem. How about dinner in Oak Bluffs? Just let us know what time you'd like to leave, sir.*

I loved watching the teams scramble and do their work. They were true professionals and a great group of people who became close friends.

The overarching theme on the property, which came down from the top, was "Just get it done!" No one seemed to care about how much a project or task cost or the time and effort required to accomplish it—*just get it done*. The massive trees we planted were our test, and we passed with flying colors.

It is hard to imagine this methodology or way of working having any application in today's corporate environment. We worked in an environment where meetings, conference calls, emails, smartphones, iPads, and memos outlining timelines, budgets, objectives, and goal setting were not part of our workflow. There was no approval process. Each team on the estate had its tasks and expectations in neat order. We all knew what had to be done and just did it. There was no other option. If you didn't meet your objective and expectations, you would most likely be off the team in the snap of a finger. No written warnings, no HR department, no exit interviews, no reports, just right out the door, like our Subaru-driving gardener friend. You would be quietly and quickly replaced with someone who *could* get it done. Plain and simple. We were all paid very well and enjoyed many perks that would be considered unusual for most work environments. I quickly realized this was something special. So, I leaned in and crushed it.

Some examples of the perks and benefits we often enjoyed included using almost anything on the property when the owners and guests were away. It was encouraged. We all needed to ensure that everything worked perfectly and that we knew how to use it effectively. If the owner or one of his guests felt like jumping onto a motorcycle, WaveRunner, or into one of the tricky antique cars and struggled to use it, whoever was closest needed to be able to jump in, with proficiency, and help them. So, we all enjoyed becoming "proficient" at using all the toys.

While guests were on the property, we needed to be aware of everything happening around us. The staff would quietly communicate with one another about any conversations or comments from guests they might have overheard. For example, if a kitchen staff member overheard a guest asking if anyone had fished off the dock, they would quickly inform me. I would prepare fishing rods and gather the necessary tackle for the outing.

I would place the rods and tackle just outside the front door, so when the guest stepped out with their coffee to enjoy the morning sun in the gardens after breakfast on the veranda, they would find everything they needed for some good old-fashioned dock fishing on a perfect Edgartown summer morning. Afterward, I would go down to the boat and speak with the captain about the request. He would immediately instruct his crew to prepare a Boston Whaler if the guest wanted to venture into deeper waters to catch bluefish or albacore. Owners and guests were given what they wanted, sometimes even before they knew they wanted it.

We did not take time off during the summer when owners and guests were around, no vacations or PTO. You were expected to be there. It was common for us all to work fifteen-hour days or longer, seven days a week, during the season. It was the job. During the off-season and between guests, we could take some time to catch up on rest.

Every day was different and challenging in its own way. If the owners were on the property alone for a few days, it would usually be a relaxed weekend. If they hosted high-profile guests, you could bet it would be long hours and little sleep, especially for the interior staff.

Some guests included governors, US cabinet members, Fortune 500 CEOs, ambassadors, diplomats, and the president of the United States and the first lady. On more than one occasion, the US Secret Service was on the premises, conducting thorough searches before high-profile visits.

There were moments when the staff and crew got on each other's nerves. The work environment was often quite intense, leading employees to feel both physically and emotionally exhausted. Once, after several weeks of accommodating high-profile guests, which involved numerous dinners, outings, events, and cocktail parties, the staff felt tattered and worn out. After the last of the guests left, Anders, some interior staff, and I headed to the pub to blow off steam. Some boat crew and kitchen staff opted for cocktails on the aft deck of the owner's yacht at the end of the dock.

The boat's captain asked Carol, the new chef, a hot-tempered gal from Providence, RI, to come down onto the swim platform to see some "barracuda" swimming by. Carol, perhaps not knowledgeable about the indigenous aquatic life of the cold waters of coastal New England, did not see the ruse. She leaned over the water to try and take a picture, and the captain gave her a playful shove, sending her, her disposable camera, and half a glass of Napa Chardonnay straight into the water, a trick that some of us had fallen prey to in the past.

She had apparently missed the announcement that these were harmless albacore tuna, not the dangerous sea predators she had been led to believe. One could imagine her fright.

Anders and I walked up the estate driveway after a few beers and a late lunch at the Wharf Pub. We met Carol coming down the driveway, soaking wet and carrying armfuls of personal items from the kitchen. "Fuck this place! And screw you guys!" she said as she stormed by in her rage, her long red hair sticking to her face. I remember the squishing sound her shoes made as she walked by us.

"We may have chosen the wrong party, man," I quietly suggested.

"Seems like it, huh?" Anders said. "How about dem barracuda?" he asked with a smirk as she walked by, giving us the finger.

Carol stopped by my house later that evening to pick up some weed on her way to the ferry for her drive back to Rhode Island. She had reached her breaking point, which I understood. This kind of work was not for everyone.

"I'm not sure I can give you the staff discount anymore, Carol," I jokingly said as I pulled my hair back into a ponytail.

"Jesus! You are just like them!" she yelled, still coughing from the bong hit she had just done. I felt bad. She tossed the cash onto the sofa, snatched the plastic sandwich bag from the upside-down Frisbee on the coffee table, and stormed out, never to be heard from again. I understood how she felt and was sorry to see her go. She was a very talented chef, and I am sure she landed squarely on her feet soon after she left. A new chef arrived a few days later, and it was business as usual.

CHAPTER FIVE
CHAMPAGNE AND WOODSTOVES

Wealth consists not of having great possessions
but of having few wants.

Epictetus

I recall an interesting discussion with Norman one summer morning. We were talking in the lower driveway by the garage about changing the guest house gardens when he suddenly recalled it was his friend's birthday. "It's Henry's birthday next week, David," he said, sounding proud that he'd remembered. "What can we do for him? I want to send him something unusual. A plant or a tree. Something that will give him a chuckle!" He grinned and squinted as he puffed on his Macanudo. "I got it!" he said with a widening grin, raising both arms. "Send him a redwood tree! Can you do that?"

"Of course, we can, sir," I said. "But my concern is that it wouldn't live long, which would be a shame."

"Fine, okay. Find him something cool and send it, okay? Something cool, David! And it has to live!" he said with a chuckle as he turned back up the driveway in a cloud of white smoke.

Anders and I returned to our favorite off-island plant wholesaler, Weston Nurseries, where we scoured a thousand acres of outstanding plant stock for something that would fit the bill for such an important project. "We want something rare," I said as we rode in the utility ATV with our friend from the nursery, poking around in the back forty for a hidden gem.

"I got it!" our Weston man said as he turned the wheel sharply and sped us to the back edge of the massive property. He stopped the ATV near the end of a long path near the property's southern boundary. The cloud of dust we'd been kicking up enveloped us. "Check this out, fellas!" We walked over to a magnificent rhododendron. She was tall, standing close to six feet, and full—a beautiful specimen. It was called a PJM rhododendron. The nurseryman gave us its history.

Ed Mezitt cultivated the PJM hybrid rhododendron in the 1930s in Hopkinton, Massachusetts, and it was later named after his father, Peter J. Mezitt, the founder of Weston Nurseries. After graduating from Cornell University, Ed rejoined the family business with a single focus in mind. He wanted to create a better rhododendron. It is one of the more popular plants in this part of the country. Still, it often struggled through the sometimes brutal winters of New England, as did its colorful cousin, the azalea. Ed knew that if he could solve this issue, it would ensure the success of his family's business.

Ed received some plants from a friend working in China that winter. Among them was a vigorous, showy azalea covered in dense purple flowers from which Ed collected pollen samples. Later that spring, while working on his prized Carolina rhododendron (*Rhododendron carolinianum*) in his backyard gardens, Ed remembered the pollen he had collected from the Chinese specimen and crossed the two plants to create a hybrid that is now known as the PJM rhododendron, hands down the most tolerant and versatile rhododendron ever grown. These beauties thrive in most conditions that New England gardeners wrestle with, from the coldest, windiest conditions to the sunniest spots in their gardens, pushing the most magnificent, dense clustering of flowers one could ever hope for—a gardener's dream plant.

"This plant is from the direct lineage of the old man's original cross project way back when and has special value to us," he said as we circled this beauty. We checked the health of the new growth and looked for any apparent issues.

"It's perfect," I said. "Can we get it to Kent, Connecticut, and put it in the ground?

"Kent, Connecticut!?" our nurseryman said with a snort and a giggle. "You serious?"

"Yep. We need this planted in Kent by next Thursday. It's a birthday thing."

Feeling a swell of pride, he said, "Damn right, we can do it! But you will need your checkbook!"

"That's not a problem, brother," Anders said.

"You two are something else. This is one for the books for sure!" he said as he pressed the ATV's accelerator and drove us back to the office.

We rendezvoused with the nursery crew a few days later and

caravanned southwest to Connecticut. Anders and I were in the lead vehicle, the crew truck followed behind us, and the tarped flatbed with the boxed specimen brought up the rear as we motored down I-90 to I-84. Eventually, we arrived at a gate at the end of a gravel drive on a beautiful stretch of quiet country road just outside Kent. After a brief chat, the guard told us someone would meet us at the house and waved us through.

The trucks pulled up in a line in front of the main house. I walked over to the front steps of the gorgeous country estate to meet the woman standing there. I introduced myself, and we spoke briefly about my employer's gift. "How wonderful!" she said, peering back into the house, looking for her husband. "He will be so surprised! I believe he is on a call, but hopefully, he will be down soon."

She and her assistant walked with me to a spot in the garden not far from the wide circular white-graveled drive. "This is a nice spot, don't you think?" she said.

I turned to Anders and the guys, who were busily preparing the rhododendron to be off-loaded, and whistled, pointing to the spot. The nursery crew boss looked up at the sky to track the sun's direction, quickly looked back at me, and gave a big thumbs-up. "This is a good spot," I said. The crew sprang into action, planting the specimen and watering it before I knew it. As we pulled around the driveway and headed back out, Dr. Henry Kissinger stepped out of the front door with his wife to admire his gift. He gave us a big smile and a wave.

I became more comfortable with this way of working and quickly got into my groove. I was good at this. Soon after I started at the estate, I began managing the cars and garage. Helen had been caring for the vehicles before my arrival, but she was busy in the house and did not know much about cars. I was happy to take on this challenge. The "driveway cars" were surprisingly unadventurous and low profile and included a minivan, a classic Jeep Cherokee, and a newer Jeep Grand Cherokee—just regular island cars. I learned that this was by design. The homeowner liked to live comfortably but was not flashy by any measure and preferred to avoid drawing attention to himself or his guests, if possible. This summer home was designed to be more relaxed than his primary residence in California.

There were some real gems in that garage, including a beautiful 1936 Ford phaeton convertible in showroom condition. My favorite was the hunter green 1928 Cadillac convertible with a tan leather interior. I had never seen a car like this before. It was massive, barely fitting in the garage, and covered in ornate chrome features. It looked like it had just rolled off the set of *The Great Gatsby* movie. It was a most impressive vehicle.

Also in the garage were some choice motorcycles, including two fully equipped BMW 1100 touring bikes and a new Harley-Davidson Sportster. The expectation was to ensure everything was spotless, ran perfectly, and started on the first try. Others on the property told me of times when the owner would come to the garage to take a spin in one of the old cars after dinner with his guests. It wouldn't start, which led to a colossal ass-chewing the next day. I was not going to let that happen on my watch.

The one way I could ensure the condition and readiness of the vehicles was to drive them. I would be the first to know if something was wrong with the cars and would be quick to find someone who could fix it. If a mechanical concern arose with these old cars, we would fly in a specialized mechanic from Hyannis to make the repair. So, once a week, I took each vehicle for a good run to blow the cobwebs out. In addition to increasing the readiness of these vehicles, it gave me a unique insight into how they operated. To enhance my understanding of primary automotive care, I enrolled in a course that enabled me to diagnose issues more effectively and engage in more detailed discussions with mechanics. This plan paid dividends almost immediately.

It was not uncommon for me to be seen cruising down the streets of Edgartown, Martha's Vineyard, in a rare antique car worth well more than the house I grew up in. And I must admit, I looked pretty damn good doing it, or at least I thought so. Norman saw that I was becoming comfortable driving the enormous Cadillac. As a very private man, he asked me to drive it in the annual July Fourth parade through Edgartown, as the parade officials had asked of him.

"Absolutely!" I said.

I spent all morning polishing up that gorgeous beast; every inch of that chrome shone like new. Anders jumped into the passenger seat, and we were off to the parade with a small cooler of chilled Newcastle Brown Ale tucked neatly by his feet. We were right up front, just behind the high school marching band. We waved as we tooled down North Water Street, smiling for pictures. I spotted Norman standing on the corner by the bank, behind some tourists; he tipped his red cap, smiled at us, and winked as we rolled by.

I live in a postcard, I thought as we slowly turned the corner onto Main Street.

"Jesus, keep those beers down there, fellas, or send a couple back here, why don't ya?" a man said from behind us. Anders turned back to see an old Edgartown fire truck, with the town's fire chief standing on the passenger-side running board, throwing candy into the crowd.

Small island towns—gotta love 'em!

One of my favorite outings each week was on Norman's Harley Sportster. I used to quietly idle out of the garage on a Saturday morning, turn right, then left, and open her up on Katama Road. Chest down, hips back, pushing through all the gears at full throttle, I'd let those beautiful, loud pipes sing. While putting the bike through its paces one morning, I tore past my boss, who had been out for a run. He must have slipped by me when I was in the garage prepping the bike.

"Oh shit!" I backed off the throttle and slinked back to the barn, a pristine three-bay garage. I backed the bike in and wiped it down. *Okay, this could be bad.* It wasn't that I shouldn't ride the bikes; I was expected to. However, I wasn't expected to take them out on a hard, loud burn, waking everyone on the road to South Beach on a sleepy summer Saturday morning.

A few minutes later, the boss walked up the driveway in his white V-necked jogging sweater and entered the garage. "Have fun?" he asked with that sideways grin.

"Yes, sir. That is a nice bike." The hot metal still made a loud *tink tink* sound as it cooled. "I just wanted to take it out and see how she was running."

"Well, how did it go?"

"Ran like a dream, sir."

"I could hear that."

As he turned to walk out of the garage, he stopped, looked back at me, shook his head, and laughed. The Sportster was smaller than my Magna 1100, a big pig of a bike, but it handled far better. Harley-Davidson makes a great bike, and I am grateful to have ridden one for a few years in such a beautiful place.

By the early fall of my first season at the estate, I was now reporting to a man named Ron in Los Angeles. Ron oversaw everything in Norman's personal life, including his homes, staff, art collections, wine cellars, cars, properties, and private jets. He also ran the corporate executive dining room in the California office. He was a very talented man.

I was impressed by Ron's extensive knowledge of household management. He could stroll through a home and engage in a detailed conversation with a housekeeper about how to make a bed properly or discuss which polish would bring out the best shine from a coffee table. Then, he could turn to me and discuss landscape construction projects, garden design, and automobile maintenance at the same level of detail. He would be equally comfortable walking through a construction site with a contractor and discussing framing plans. He could step into the kitchen, offer suggestions for tonight's menu, and pair a perfect wine with the duck entrée the chef was considering. I knew I was going to learn a great deal from this man.

Ron helped me understand how to work for a man like Norman. One such lesson was when I asked Norman if he would like me to get new tires for the Jeep Cherokee up at the main house. Norman leaned down with his cigar, poked at the tire with his index finger, and said, "We can get another season out of these," and walked into the house.

Ron noticed the worn tires and asked me about it during his next visit. "Do you have a plan for these tires, Dave?" I told him I had asked Norman about them the week before, and he said to wait until after the season. Ron was disappointed. "A couple of things here, Dave. We don't ask Norman about these things; we just do them." He explained that sometimes people with this kind of personal wealth will find satisfaction in being frugal with small things like this. "This is a safety issue, and we pay you well to ensure nothing bad happens." I learned my lesson, and we never had to speak of it again.

Ron was happy to hear about my interest in food and wine. That winter, he asked me to join him in New York City to attend the New York Wine Experience, hosted by *Wine Spectator* at the Marriott Marquis. I felt a little nervous because I was only twenty-two and had no credit card. How could I book a room at an expensive hotel in Manhattan without a credit card? Before the anxiety spun out of control, Ron called and said, "I have you set up in one of our apartments for a few days while you are at the wine event." He explained that he would put me in touch with the person in New York who would arrange my stay. I was relieved. A few days later, his assistant mailed me a white business card with a woman's name and phone number and included a handwritten note from Ron: *She is expecting your call.*

The apartment I was invited to use that weekend was nothing less than astonishing. It was one of two guest apartments in that building. The Corinthian, the city's largest apartment building at the time of its construction, comprised an entire city block on Thirty-Eighth Street in Manhattan. Upon my arrival, the doorman greeted me and supplied me with the key to the unit. I took the elevator to the forty-fifth floor and found the number. I swung open the door and was gobsmacked by the view. A large flower arrangement and a gorgeous gift basket of gourmet foods, accompanied by a card, were in the living room. I set my dirty old backpack down, showing care for the snow-white carpet, and read the card:

Welcome to New York, Dave. We are happy you are here.—Ron

The *Wine Spectator* event was remarkable. I felt a budding passion for wine, but had yet to experience the world's finest wines. The event drew over 1,700 guests, featured two hundred wineries, and showcased more than twenty thousand bottles of wine. Ron and his assistant met me in the lobby of the Marriott Marquis, and we strolled through the massive ballroom, shaking hands with some of the industry's finest. I remember being impressed by Ron's knowledge of wines and how so many in the industry seemed to know him.

Lunch centered around the finest wines from Australia, guided by the renowned wine writer Len Evans. Another tasting event showcased Château Haut-Brion, a premier cru first-growth Bordeaux, presented in a vertical format, allowing us to taste several consecutive vintages together. The flavors, textures, and aromas of the wines from this magnificent château captivated me completely. I was enthralled. It was on this day that my love affair with French wines began.

We found our seats for the highly anticipated Opus One tasting led by winemaker Tim Mondavi later that afternoon. The tasting was a vertical of ten Opus One vintages, just one more once-in-a-lifetime wine opportunity from that weekend. We took our seats and eyed the glasses and tasting mats before us. I turned and said hello to the older woman beside me as I arranged my mat and glasses, carefully pushing the glasses into the center of the circles on the paper mat. We got to chatting; she was so lovely. Her name was Margrit, and she explained that she was from Switzerland but had lived in California for many years. She was an artist.

She introduced her husband, Bob, who sat beside her and was also kind. We chatted for a while. They came to see their son present his wines at the event. They were so proud.

"When will your son be presenting? I don't want to miss that!"

"He is starting now," Bob said proudly, pointing to the stage as the crowd hushed.

"Tim is your son?" I asked as I quickly put this together in my mind. I was sitting beside Robert and Margrit Mondavi—wonderful people. I was in heaven. I was so grateful for the opportunity to experience such things.

It was at this event that I was introduced to champagne. I had a basic understanding of the wines, but had no idea of the depth and complexity this sublime bubbly wine offered. Ron handed me a perfectly chilled glass of 1985 Dom Pérignon Rosé as I returned from making a phone call. "Pay attention to this," he said with a wink. Holding the flute up to the ballroom lights, I notice the pale salmon hue as the small-bead bubbles dance eagerly from the bottom of the glass. I unabashedly stuck my nose deep into the glass, eager to know more about it. The wine revealed its layers of delicate aromas, beginning with some soft herbaceous notes followed quickly by floral cherry and vibrant ripe red fruits, then a vanilla warmth coated my nostrils, inviting me into the most magnificent, doughy, almost biscuity mouthfeel.

I kneeled next to the table and began to write in my journal, barely noticing the representative from the producer standing next to me. "It feels like stars are dancing on your tongue, no?" She said this with the most delightful French accent as she explained the art of assemblage and the careful harvest of the Pinot Noir and Chardonnay grapes used to make the wine.

During the event, I filled my journal with detailed notes about all the wines I tried. I delved into the subtle nuances, viticulture practices, and different wine styles while recounting conversations with winemakers. I couldn't get enough; I craved more of this in my life. In that moment, it felt as though I had rediscovered a passionate connection with wine that I had forgotten from another time. I remembered that wine was integral to who I wished to be. I was deeply in love—enraptured.

Reflecting on this wonderful wine memory recently, I considered picking up a bottle of the 1985 Dom Rosé, but the nearly $1,400 price tag prompted reconsideration.

Ron left for LA the following day, and I had time to kill before my flight, so I joined a cigar tasting in one of the event's breakout sessions. Our boss loved cigars, so I thought I might as well learn about them while I was here. I sat down and started chatting with the folks around me before the presenters took the stage. I had two booklets in front of me, and someone two down to my right reached around the back of the man next to me, touched my shoulder, and asked if he could have my extra booklet for the presentation. "Yeah, sure, man," I said, extending the small spiral-bound book to the reaching hand. I looked up and immediately recognized him as the actor Matt Dillon. I was a little starstruck and shyly handed the book over as the presenters started.

During one of the breaks, I stepped out to use the restroom. Matt Dillon stepped up to the urinal two down from me and started chatting about the cigar tasting, asking what my favorites were, and we talked for a moment. "Oh, I guess I liked the AVO No. 6 the best. How about you?" I said, adjusting my body positioning to maximize our privacy in this potentially awkward setting. I am sure I sounded like a doofus.

The winter passed quickly, and spring brought more responsibility for me. Helen was moving on, and I was asked to take a lead role on the property as manager and interact more with the owners, their guests, and the rest of the staff. I enjoyed my job and welcomed the challenges it presented. Ron asked if I would move to the property. He liked the idea of having someone living on the property year-round. I agreed and moved into the newly constructed tennis house. The tennis house residence was on the second floor and had partial harbor views. It was beautiful.

I had been living in a small log cabin down a mile-long dirt driveway near the harbor. I did love that place. I could not see any other houses. The only sound I could hear was the wind moving through the pines that enveloped the tiny cabin. A friend of a friend had reached out the summer before to ask if I would live in the cabin and mind their property while they were away for a year, traveling in Europe. I paid no rent but was expected to do daily walks through the twelve-acre waterfront estate to ensure everything was secure and there were no issues, which there rarely were—a pretty easy gig.

The only heat source was a chunky old Vermont Castings woodstove, which enhanced my appreciation for firewood. I educated myself on the ins and outs of heating your home with wood. I became proficient in setting the woodstove to burn slowly all day while I was at work, then cranking it up when I needed to quickly push the cold out of the cabin in the evenings and on weekends.

While living in the cabin, I learned about burn rates for firewood and what would provide the most efficient fuel. Oak has a burn rate of about twenty-nine BTUs, maple is about twenty-five BTUs, and pine is closer to seventeen BTUs. Pine and some other conifers are loaded with resin or sap and can muck up chimneys, so I sourced properly seasoned hardwoods for my stove. I would take my old work truck, a Ford F-250, affectionately known as Zorlac due to an old skater bumper sticker, to Anders's property up island. We would then cut up some oak that we felled the previous summer and bring it back to the cabin. I would crank up some Allman Brothers through my JBL Northridge tower speakers, crack open a cold beer, take off my shirt, and hand-split a couple of cords in the splintered late-summer sunlight of my quiet, forested yard. I found this way of living very comfortable—it made sense to me. The cabin allowed me to recharge my batteries after a day of work at the estate. It was an honest and straightforward way to live. The solitude nurtured my soul. In the silent evenings in that cabin, I waded deeply into the works of Emerson and Thoreau. I explored their ideas on self-reliance, solitude, and the search for a deeper connection with nature.

I bought a used Adirondack chair from a roadside sale one Saturday morning, gave it a quick sanding, brushed on a coat of white paint, and placed it in a small clearing in the pines, not far from my cabin. I cut two small rounds from a maple log by the driveway and rolled them over to my chair in the woods. I set one next to the chair to be used as a side table, and the other, the shorter of the two, worked as a footstool. This place in the woods became a portal of sorts, allowing me to step out of the hurried pace of the workday and slide into a more peaceful space where I learned to be with nature, in it, part of it.

I thought of Thoreau, living by his pond for those two years in a setting perhaps similar to this one. Leaning back and looking up, the tops of the pines swayed lazily and whispered to me as the breeze brushed across them. I examined the idea of a simpler existence, a life not so bound to the material things we cling to so tightly but rather to moments like this, in my little clearing. Moments free of talking, expectations, electronic distractions, judgment, or material things we surround ourselves with. Money served no purpose in this place in the woods, other than to possibly add some padding in the autumn nest of a blue jay. Thoreau's words, "The mass of men lead lives of quiet desperation," suddenly made sense to me. I got it. Many of us scrape and claw our way through life, hoping to earn more money and acquire more possessions, but it is not in these things that we find true fulfillment or happiness. The richness or wholeness we so badly crave comes from somewhere else, from places like my little clearing in the woods, albeit sans pond.

The dichotomy that developed in my life, between working in an environment of such massive wealth and my creaky little Adirondack chair in the woods, became more pronounced, a divided reality. The realization that we need very little took shape in my mind as I breathed the crisp September air. I sat for hours some days, listening, thinking, breathing, reading, searching for clarity. Always alone. I explored the music of Bob Dylan, Neil Young, James Taylor, and Joni Mitchell in that place, whose music seemed to pry my mind open and shout *Do you see now? Do you understand what we are talking about?*

I learned to enjoy being alone there, to take solace in it. I sat in the quiet, breathing, letting my mind drift, almost aligning with the sway and energetic rhythm of the place, much like the movement of the pines in the breeze. Sometimes, a small handful of mushrooms would enhance the experience further, drawing me further into my peaceful little reverie and providing a deeper, more authentic connection to nature. Here, I began to feel at peace with myself and covet moments where I could be alone, especially in nature.

Nature can be a teacher if we sit quietly, alone, and listen.

The tennis house was posh and very comfortable in a different way. It was close to town, so a stumbling distance from the pub is always good for a young man who enjoys such recreation. The tennis house was so called because it was built adjacent to one of the first Argentine paddle tennis courts constructed in the US. While traveling, Norman was introduced to the game and instantly made plans to build a court at his Edgartown home. Remember, this was in the mid-1990s, well before the explosion of pickleball's popularity. It was an impressive clay court with high walls all around. It was a fast-paced game that allowed playing the ball off any of the walls. The court had lights so that a game could be played at any time. The staff often held little tourneys when we had no guests on the property. Some of us became skilled at the game, especially Anders, an absolute monster on the court.

The estate quickly became my home. I was often alone there, especially in the offseason, which was fine with me. The rest of the staff would move to another of the family's homes or take a little time off to travel or work in restaurants, but I would stay, even when things became difficult.

One morning in mid-August 1991, Anders and I were preparing the property for Hurricane Bob, which was forecast to hit the island. I was in the garage working on something when Norman came in to talk to me.

"Say, this storm will be pretty bad, huh?" he said.

"Yes, sir. They say it will hit us head-on late tomorrow. Most of the flights and ferries will be canceled by tomorrow morning, I imagine."

"Well, since I have my plane here, it's probably best I head out soon, huh?" He chuckled.

"Yes, sir. I just talked to Ron, and we are suggesting you leave soon, or you may be stuck here."

"Hey, why don't you jump on with us and go to LA for a few days until this blows over?"

"Thanks, Norman, but I should stick around here to watch things. I'll stay on the property to ensure everything is okay."

"I appreciate that, David," he said, turning toward the door. "Let me know if you change your mind, okay? I'll be ready to go soon."

Hurricane Bob hit the island the next day, leaving a path of destruction. Anders and I stayed on the property and watched the storm from the third-floor balcony. We maintained radio contact with the yacht crew, who had the boat on the hook, deep in the inner harbor, sheltered from the wind. We watched in disbelief as the 115 mph winds scooped small boats from the harbor, pushing them into a big pile in front of the yacht club. We saw Boston Whalers somersaulting over the water before smashing against the town dock. I recall standing in the bathroom on the third floor, watching the water in the toilet shift back and forth in the bowl, as if we were on a boat, as the heavy gusts hit the side of the big house. The one thing I remember most about that storm was the eye passing directly over us. It went from feeling like Armageddon to a beautiful sunny afternoon in minutes. The temperature rose a few degrees, and the wind lay down. Moments later, the heavy clouds moved back in, and we were getting hammered again. We took turns patrolling the property to check for damage. If a limb or tree fell across the road or driveway, we got the saws out in the driving wind and rain, cutting it up to ensure emergency access to the estate was open.

The property was well-maintained and sustained only minor damage. The yacht crew also ensured the boat's safety and reported minimal damage. We were fortunate—very fortunate.

In late October of the same year, we were hit again by a massive storm known as a nor'easter. Most of the tourists and seasonal residents had gone, so it was quiet. The storm was forecast to become quite powerful as it converged with other dangerous weather systems. The big nor'easter had merged with a massive low-pressure system and absorbed the remaining energy from Hurricane Grace. I listened to the weather report on the marine radio in the garage of the estate the day before the storm was set to hit the island, noting the urgency in the report, which bordered on panic. The forecast predicted this would be the most powerful storm to engulf the island in over a century.

Once again, Anders and I worked quickly to prepare the estate. We covered the harbor-facing windows with plywood and secured anything that could potentially break free and become a projectile in the predicted disastrous winds. We were accustomed to high winds and knew how to prepare for them, having recently experienced a significant hurricane. However, the most alarming aspect of the forecast was the expected catastrophic storm surges associated with this megastorm. The marine forecast predicted storm surges, extremely high tides exceeding twelve feet above normal, and dangerously high waves. The monotone NOAA marine forecast warned that ocean waves in deeper water could reach heights of up to forty-two feet in some areas. As I looked out the garage window while the forecast was being reread, my eyes tracked upward along the trunk of a young maple tree. I estimated the tree to be about twenty feet high and pictured waves twice that size.

The following afternoon, when the fists of this gargantuan weather system were smashing into the island, I was returning from Oak Bluffs with more supplies for the house. The skies turned dark, forming a terrifying, swirling mass of grays, with a haunting blackness building on the horizon to my left. My 1982 Jeep Renegade was being pushed across the beach road by heavy gusts; the canvas soft top flapped so loudly that my ears hurt. Just then, a large wave lifted over the break-water on my left, rising like an angry beast, and crashed down on the hood of my black Jeep, sending it sideways onto the shoulder of the road. My engine stalled, and steam began to rise from under the hood. I was in a precarious situation, trapped in the middle of the exposed beach road—open ocean on my left and a tidal pond to my right.

As twilight came on, I sat quietly, shifting my attention to the ocean over my left shoulder. The water receded, revealing the rocky beach in the dim light of dusk only for a moment, before rushing back in as a powerful, greenish-black wall of water. Holding my breath, I turned the key, willing the engine to start. The fierce winds howled around me, lashing against the sides of my stalled Jeep, causing it to tilt precariously to the right. Out at sea, a dark blanket of storm clouds gathered on the horizon, and distant waves resembling moving mountains quickly formed miles from shore. The road beneath me had transformed into a shallow lake, submerged under about six inches of churning, foamy water. "Come on, come *on!*" I urged the stubborn engine, my heart racing. "Start, damn it!" I shouted at the hood, desperation creeping into my voice. As hope began to wane, the engine finally erupted with a most satisfying roar. Relief washed over me as I swiftly released the clutch, carefully maneuvering the Jeep down the flooded road and back into the safety of Edgartown.

I made my way back to the estate through the floodwaters. I had never seen anything like it; in some parts of town, the water was so high that it started to come in through the doors of my Jeep. At one point, the seawater inside the vehicle splashed up over my ankles. I reached down to pull the floor plugs and let the water drain out while I drove through the darkened streets toward the estate.

I pulled the Jeep to the top of the driveway, killed the lights, and set the emergency brake in the pounding rain. As I closed the door and secured the latch, my finger traced an eight-inch scratch along the left side of the hood, a reminder of the moment when the debris-filled wave made contact. I walked into the dark main house, locked the door behind me, and leaned my back against the door for a moment.

The storm hit us hard. Hurricane Bob had already damaged many trees on the island, and when this colossal storm struck, it brought down thousands more, resulting in massive power outages throughout the area. Some locations, including Anders's property farther up island, were without power for over a month.

This storm became widely known as the weather event that caused the sinking of the *Andrea Gail*, a fishing vessel that went down with all hands, which inspired the book and movie *The Perfect Storm*, released some years later. In all, thirteen lives were lost, and over $200 million in property damage was caused by the storm. It was the only weather I have experienced that genuinely frightened me; it was brutal and unforgiving.

Every fall, after the owners and last guests had departed for the season, the crew would relocate the boat to Florida for winter maintenance. I would tag along and assist the crew on those weeklong trips down the Eastern Seaboard, which I thoroughly enjoyed. We stayed about thirty miles offshore for most of the journey, providing ample time to appreciate the peaceful horizon. We took turns on four-hour watch shifts throughout the day and night as we journeyed to Florida.

She was a stunning boat—a custom refit luxury Burger motor yacht with an interior that matched the main house's quality, style, and décor. It was sublime. Every few days, we would take on fuel and supplies, pump out the tanks, stretch our legs, and shake off the fatigue. One of our favorite stops was the marina in Atlantic City. We would rush to get the boat tucked into her slip, cleaned out, and washed down, then secure her before heading into the casinos.

There was always an exciting feeling when stepping off a boat like this, especially in a place like Atlantic City. Casino-goers and tourists would glance over to see if they recognized us, imagining whom they thought we might be. Some would even take pictures. Oh, how disappointed they would be if they knew we were just a bunch of tired staff and crew—employees heading into town to blow off some steam and lose our paychecks at the craps table.

Some of the most peaceful moments I can remember were while on the flybridge in the middle of the night. During one such night, I looked at my watch; it was 3:07 a.m. We were thirty miles offshore with a sky full of stars and nothing on the radar. Shooting stars streaked across the sky as Pink Floyd's *The Dark Side of the Moon* played softly over the hum of the big diesel engines, the evening sea peacefully splashing against the hull. Gilmour's words were etched into my soul as we steered through the night.

"Getting tired of this sleigh ride, man," my watch partner and friend Kenny said, after a long evening of struggling against the relentless push of a swollen following sea. The big boat was shoved from behind every few minutes by round, lazy swells, sending us sliding down the front of the wave and requiring constant, stiff corrective steering. Kenny, a seasoned fishing boat captain from Edgartown, finally succumbed to fatigue. As the sea began to calm and the large swells subsided, he dozed off on the bench beside me, his soft snores punctuating the quiet darkness while I tried to keep the boat steady through the now tranquil waters.

As I stood gazing into the vast expanse before me, fleeting glimpses of profound meaning surfaced and receded like dolphins in the surf, illuminating my mind with flashes of insight. My thoughts wandered to a time when I felt less secure about who I was, a less confident version of myself. I vividly recalled the bitter feeling of not fitting in during my early high school years and the fear of not belonging in the world. Growing up, it often seemed like very few people, including my family, truly understood me. Although I was generally well-liked, I was aware that I was different, struggling with anxiety and self-doubt like many young people do. Introverted, thoughtful, and naturally quiet, I often felt isolated.

The words of Mr. Gilbert, my old junior varsity soccer coach, struck me like a cold pine board: "Becker, you stood in the good-looks line too long, when you should have been over here in the man-up line." The team laughed and pointed while my face turned red as a ripe tomato in the sun. That night, I slept on a tear-soaked pillow, as I had many times before.

My mind drifted back to those moments when I would gaze longingly out the classroom window, dreaming of what life might hold for me once I was free from that place. I was quietly waiting for my life to begin. Deep down, I knew I would be fine once I entered the world. I just felt convinced of it.

Those feelings of rejection, misunderstanding, and judgment were replaced by a calm understanding that I truly belonged somewhere. There was a place for me. At that moment, I felt the page in my story turn. The beauty of *this* place felt like a warm hug from God, almost taking my breath away as I wiped a tear from my cheek. A smile spread across my face as I experienced one of the most beautiful moments of my life—entrusted to steer a billionaire's luxury yacht, surrounded by good and capable friends, through a star-filled night while listening to one of the most powerful and moving albums I had ever known. I had a once-in-a-lifetime job, deep friendships, love in my heart, money in my pocket, and I was seeing the world in a way that most people do not. It felt like my life was beginning to open and blossom, like a tender rosebud in the morning sun. I wondered if Mr. Gilbert would still believe I had been standing in the wrong line if he could see me now. I thought of my clearing in the woods, as the words of Dylan and Thoreau washed over me, and my connection to the universe felt deeper, wrapping around me like a comforting blanket as we motored along with the night's currents.

I found myself grappling with the enormity of the night sky, each star a tiny pinprick of light on the infinite canvas above, as if a divine hand had drawn back the curtain just enough for me to witness the mysteries typically concealed from our weary mortal eyes.

I don't go to church; it's just not my thing. At the risk of sounding cliché, I am not a religious person, but I am deeply spiritual. I have never been drawn to reading the Bible or listening to others share their interpretations of God and how, in their view, He wants me to live my life. Don't get me wrong, I highly appreciate religion and the place of churches in our communities. I completely support their efforts and the comfort and support they provide to so many people. I've just never understood the concept of human agency within God's divine ways. I think this may be because I have always felt God's presence in my life. I've experienced His closeness many times, and I know Him as much as anyone can, I suppose. It feels strange to have someone stand between God and me, trying to explain what He represents or what His message is for me. It's like having a stranger between you and your kindhearted grandpa, speaking on his behalf. He's right there; I can ask Him myself. We're good.

Years later, I experienced a profound interaction with God. At that time, we were living in New York State on a large property in the mid-Hudson area. It was a quiet place, surrounded by trees, sun-warmed meadows, and a small mill pond on the south side of the house. I recall it being a particularly stressful period for us. We had just discovered that we would soon become parents, and money was tight. Our jobs were challenging, and we'd recently moved from Los Angeles, leaving most of our friends and family behind. As a result, we felt alone, isolated, and lost. Like many extended families, we were dealing with tensions and complicated, strained relationships that seemed to be reaching a breaking point. We felt scared and uncertain as we navigated the rapidly changing circumstances in our lives. It was as though we were walking on ice in dress shoes during a windstorm, bracing ourselves for the next slip and the painful fall that was sure to come.

I remember it as a dark, damp spring day, with intermittent cold rain falling from an endless blanket of dark gray clouds. I was home alone that day; my wife was working in the city, and I wasn't scheduled to work at the winery until the next morning. While making a fire to help push the chill out of the place, my anxiety began to rise. A deep sense of worry washed over me as I paced in our small living room. Thoughts of being unprepared to be a dad, strained relationships, and insufficient money crashed into me like a wrecking ball. I was panicking. This felt different, more intense. I was terrified, spiraling quickly into despair.

"What is the fucking point of all this!?" I cried.

Suddenly, something shifted. The room felt warmer and more serene, and everything seemed to slow down. The music I had been listening to just moments before faded away. That was when I felt Him—the presence of God, I believe. In that moment, I realized it wasn't just my imagination; He was truly there. I stood still, trying to grasp what was happening.

Then, I felt what seemed like His heavy hand on my shoulder. My breath caught in my throat, and I began to sob. My body became limp as the toxic stress flooded out of me, replaced by an overwhelming sense of love and tranquility. I felt as if I were floating.

It was then that I heard His words—not so much heard them as felt them: *Everything is going to be okay. You are not alone. You are never alone.* And just like that, it was over. I became aware of the music again as I stood there, crying and shaking, desperately trying to process what had just happened.

I have never shared this experience with anyone until now. It is a profoundly personal memory that I have quietly treasured for many years. I will keep that memory in a small box labeled "Beautiful Things."

The rest of my winters on the Martha's Vineyard estate were active with off-season projects. Anders and I stayed busy with garden overhauls, tree planting, and property upgrades. Some days were less busy, so after crunching out our projects, we would wander down to the Wharf Pub for a late lunch and stay to close down the place at midnight. Winters on the island were very quiet, so everyone who wasn't home with kids gathered at the pub. We played darts, drank beer, and played trivia games with friends before returning to the cold, damp evening and heading home.

To help break up the winter, I would often take January or February off to travel. While working on the estate, I visited many fascinating places, including Bermuda, Amsterdam, Belgium, France, England, Scotland, Mexico, Hawaii, Canada, the Dominican Republic, and Haiti. One quiet winter, Anders and I went on a road trip in my newly acquired white Ford Ranger pickup truck. We did a full lap around the country before returning home broke and smelly after thirty days.

During an off-season trip to Central America in the early nineties, I traveled from San José, Costa Rica, to Sapoá, Nicaragua. The long bus ride ended just across the Nicaraguan border when soldiers with automatic rifles boarded our bus to check our paperwork. As the only white person on the bus, I was quickly removed and made to stand by the side of the dusty road in the midafternoon sun. Fortunately, I had the foresight to secure my valuables, extra cash, and passport in a safe at my hotel in San José before embarking on my journey to Nicaragua. I had only taken some money and photocopies of my passport and driver's license, which were sufficient for moving around safely in that part of the world if using ground transportation.

I stood between two soldiers while a third one rummaged through my backpack, laying out the contents beside the road. They took the money pouch that was around my waist, tucked under my shirt. They sifted through my paperwork, counted my cash, and placed it on the ground. Then the bus left. My Spanish wasn't strong, but I gathered they had issues with my passport photocopy, and ultimately, they seized it. I got back most of my cash, minus a roadside "fee" for their services, and they told me to be on my way.

I walked a mile or so to the nearest town, close to the border, and found a small market. I bought some water and tried to devise a plan to get out of Nicaragua with no passport or documentation and less money than I had started the bus ride with. I knew the only way out would be to pay the border guards to let me cross, which was risky. As I set my money on the counter, a nice-looking, air-conditioned tour bus stopped in front of the tiny roadside market. I watched as a dozen or so older white people stepped off the bus with cameras around their necks. I immediately recognized this as an opportunity. I started to chat with the friendly, silver-haired English-speaking passengers. I learned they were a Canadian bird-watching tour group that had spent the morning observing their feathered friends at the nearby lakeshore.

They were making a quick market stop before heading back across the border and down to Parque Nacional Guanacaste in Costa Rica.

A small group of us were chatting outside the market when I explained my little dilemma. Even though there was considerable risk, they invited me to join their group on the drive to the national park in Costa Rica. I was stuck in a country that was going through a tumultuous time without any documentation. The Chamorro government was in the process of taking control from the Sandinistas. General Humberto Ortega, the chief of the Sandinista-controlled army, would not go quietly into the night, which led to significant civil and political unrest in the otherwise beautiful country.

I stepped onto the lovely, spotless, air-conditioned tour bus and found a seat in the back. My new friends were kind, offering me food and engaging in friendly conversation during the short drive to the border checkpoint. One of the guys on the bus loaned me his floppy bucket hat to use, which we all agreed would be less noticeable than my dirty old John's Fish Market hat.

"It's all about blending in, young man!" one of the old-timers said. I could tell they were enjoying the thrill of the adventure, and honestly, so was I. Not every day do you get smuggled across an unfriendly border by a group of Canadian senior citizens on a bird-watching tour! God bless our neighbors to the north!

As we approached the border checkpoint—the same one I had crossed just hours earlier—my heart raced with anxiety. I slid into my seat, pulled my hat down, leaned against the window, and remained quiet. The same soldiers from before patrolled around the bus, and eventually, one stepped on board to speak with the driver. They exchanged documents and chatted briefly. Though the soldier scanned the passengers, he never moved away from the front of the bus. Out of the corner of my eye, I noticed another soldier standing just outside my window, an M16 slung over his shoulder.

"Shit! Did he see me?" I muttered to myself. I slumped farther and turned from the window, pretending I was asleep.

After what felt like an eternity, the soldier finished his business with the tour operator and stepped off the bus. The door closed, and we started to move again. Soon, we found ourselves back in Costa Rica. We arrived at the entrance to Parque Nacional Guanacaste, and I said goodbye to my new bird-watching friends. I then set off to find Hacienda Los Inocentes, a traditional cattle ranch, which I had read about; it was just a short bus ride away and didn't require any border crossings.

Once in a while, someone from our little winter pack of island friends would drift too far into the pub scene and tumble into a tricky early morning reality. After one such occasion, I bumped into my good friend PJ on the corner of Main and North Water Streets while on a coffee run. He told me his story. After leaving us at the pub the night before, he stumbled out, hoping to walk home or at least to a nearby friend's place, to crash on the sofa and sleep it off. As expected, he reached a nearby comfortable sofa late in the evening. However, this couch did not belong to a friend or acquaintance.

He explained that he woke up to the sound of cartoons on the TV from the next room. He rubbed the sleep from his swollen, pink eyes to see kids sitting on the floor in an adjacent room, watching *The Fantastic Four* and eating Cheerios. A kind woman was handing him a cup of coffee. "How are you feeling?" she asked. "You are Phil's son, right?" After taking a few hearty pulls from the steaming cup and politely thanking his hosts for their hospitality, he packed up what little dignity he could salvage and headed back downtown to find us, grab some grub, and shake off the strange night.

"Why don't people lock their doors here, Becker?" he asked with some frustration.

I laughed. "Yeah, because it's *their* fault, PJ . . . That sounds right."

"Well . . . man, what if I were a thief? he asked, clinging desperately to his flimsy point. "What if I stole something from them?"

"Then they would meet you at the line for the first ferry off with the cops and ask you for their stuff back, I suppose. We live on an island, brother—you can't get that far." Trying to dig the toe of his shoe into the sidewalk, he recognized his mistake, and we laughed.

Living on a relatively small New England island in the winter makes for a unique experience. The community here has a special closeness often absent in larger towns and cities on the mainland. People genuinely look out for one another, fostering an environment with less meanness. A quiet tolerance for each other's quirks and imperfections contributes to the island's distinctive charm. Sure, people got on each other's nerves and probably a little too deep into gossip sometimes, but it was a quiet and comfortable place to winter over. And though the island's character would eventually wear thin for me, I have not felt that sense of community since and now miss it terribly.

We would keep ourselves busy and entertained during the brief downtimes between stays by the owners and their guests. One such time was when I met a couple of guys at the pub one evening who were headed out the following day to try their luck in the annual Monster

Shark Tournament, with teams from all over the East Coast trying to win its coveted prize. The guys had chartered a boat for the two-day event but were short a crew member because one of their buddies had to leave the island that day for a pressing personal matter. "We are down a man!" Steve, the team leader, told me, leaning into the bar. "Hey, can you fish with heavy gear in deep water?"

"Hell yeah. I can fish anywhere!" I said.

The following day, Tuesday, July 25, 1995, at 5:30 a.m., we met on the dock in Oak Bluffs and motored out on the chartered *Downeaster* for the two-day tourney. Each team was allowed to bring back only their best two sharks for the weigh-in, which would be recorded as a combined gross-weight total. We managed to land two enormous blue sharks on day one, each weighing well over three hundred pounds when hung up at the scales and measuring over ten feet in length. The larger of the two sharks was over eleven feet long, requiring adjustments to the scale to accommodate its size. Our 622 total pounds held up for the second day.

Long story made very short, we won the damn thing and took home the first-place trophy! The second place was taken by a team that hooked a chunky mako shark weighing over 450 pounds.

I received a steady stream of memorable quotes from the movie *Jaws*, filmed on Martha's Vineyard. As I left the bank, I heard, "You're going to need a bigger boat!"

"Taxidermy man is going to have a heart attack when he sees what we brung him!" someone said later as a cold beer was slid down the bar at David Ryan's in my direction. Joe, the bartender, had placed copies of the *Gazette* article about the tournament on the bar for everyone to read, resulting in several free beers for me. It was a good day!

We found other ways to keep ourselves occupied and entertained on the long, gray days of the New England winters. Ron would occasionally update Norman's Rolodex and FedEx it to us at the house, where we would set it on the corner of his desk in the upstairs study. One quiet rainy afternoon, a couple of us stood in the kitchen after the updated Rolodex arrived and started thumbing through it. The names we saw were fantastic. While examining the card system, my thumb stopped on *E*, then Eastwood, Clint. Our mouths were agape.

"Clint Eastwood's home number is right here," I said, tapping it with my index finger to amplify the magnitude of the discovery.

"Oh, we should just call the number!" someone yelled. So, I reached for the kitchen phone by the window and dialed the number. A woman with a Spanish accent answered with the name of the home. I quickly set the receiver down.

"That was Clint Eastwood's housekeeper!" I said.

"Call another one!" someone burst out. We quickly found ourselves drawn into the moment's temptation, but remembered our better selves and became the discrete professionals we were expected to be. I set the small wheel full of cards on the desk upstairs and quietly closed the door behind me.

The phone rang as I was walking through the kitchen one morning. I picked it up and pressed the green blinking light labeled *Line 1*. After providing the standard greeting for the property, I heard a voice on the other end of the line say, "This is the White House switchboard calling for Norman ____." I was a little nervous when responding to the caller and asked her to repeat what she'd said. As she started to speak again, she was interrupted by a man cutting in on the line.

"Hey, buddy! Did you get our gift?" It was immediately clear that I was speaking with then-President Bill Clinton. I quickly informed the kitchen staff of the caller's identity, and they notified our boss. I could hear from around the corner, "The President is holding on line one, sir," which felt surreal. It helped me frame my employment differently—the president of the United States was holding for my boss.

On a Sunday morning, another call came in, but I did not answer the phone this time. Luciano Pavarotti was calling to wish the lady of the house a happy birthday and to thank her for attending his performance in New York two evenings earlier.

Whenever we felt bored or trapped, anyone around would book a Cape Air flight, affectionately known as "Cape Scare" by locals—and head up to Boston. There, we would hit a few bars before making our way to the North End, where we would indulge in some of the most delicious Italian food. After our meal, we usually stopped by Mike's Pastry on Hanover Street for cannoli. We'd then stumble back to the airport and catch a quick flight home. Sometimes, we would receive sideways glances from the pilots as we poured our drunken selves into the small Cessna.

"Hey, it's just like we are in that show, *Wings*!" One of us would inevitably say, which was always met with heavy eye-rolling from the cockpit. We were happy idiots. Life was good, and we drank it in.

One such evening, some friends asked me to join them in Boston to catch a show on a rainy fall night. Since I had nothing else going on, I got in the standby line at the ferry this time and was on my way. A few hours later, our hands were on the edge of the stage at the old Channel night club in Boston, looking up at Johnny Winter. I had been to some fantastic shows before and been very close to stages, but when Johnny plugged his 1963 Gibson Firebird V into that amp, a heavy clunk moved like a massive sound wave through our chests, and I knew this would be special. My friend Ben, a musician himself, pulled his hair back out of his face, turned to me, and said, "Hold on, man!" Johnny, a few feet away, pulled that long white hair back in a ponytail, repositioned his black cowboy hat, gave his band a sharp nod, and proceeded to belt out the most incredible "Highway 61 Revisited" we had ever heard. The old Fort Point waterfront building could barely contain the enormous sound his band pushed into that space; you could almost feel the century-old beams vibrate and twist under the strain as the entire crowd moved, jumping up and down as if they were one organism in that dimly lit, beer-soaked room. The building, with its tumultuous past, seemed almost to move with us, part of the music.

CHAPTER SIX
THE MALFEASANT BUTLER
AND A GRACEFUL EXIT

Without deviation, progress is not possible.

Frank Zappa

In 1995, after living on the island for six years, I began to feel restless and bored. The island started to feel small. Life had become predictable. I had thoroughly explored this island lifestyle, right to its salty and frayed edges. As I walked down the street, the excitement of discovery gave way to a routine filled with friendly and sometimes less-than-friendly nods.

Living in a small island town might seem charming from afar, but for someone in their twenties craving challenges and new experiences, it can feel confining. It's difficult to explain, but living on an island where you can only drive eighteen miles in any direction before hitting the ocean creates a sense of being trapped or limited in your ability to explore. This feeling has a genuine psychological impact. The locals call it "island fever," and I was experiencing it intensely. With a permanent population of only about fifteen thousand residents on Martha's Vineyard, the year-round inhabitants often feel understimulated during the off-season, making privacy a rare commodity.

I knew everyone's business; they, in turn, knew mine. I can't count the times I walked into the post office or bank and had the person working the counter say, "Heard you guys had a late night," or "When did you get that dent in your tailgate?"

Ron sensed this and approached me with another opportunity. He explained that Norman had recently purchased another home in Bel Air, California, and was about to start a large-scale remodeling project. He asked if I would move to the Bel Air estate and manage the exterior projects while staying involved with the goings-on at the Vineyard estate. Without much thought, I packed my bags and headed west.

A new stepping-stone had appeared just as the old one became wobbly, inviting me to continue forward.

A car and driver picked me up from LAX and took me to the Bel Air property. Ron had a car ready for me in the driveway when I arrived that struck me as a tad out of place. It was a large black Ford Bronco with a lift kit, massive mud tires, and a throaty V8 engine. It was a good-looking truck, but not aligned stylistically with the other vehicles on the property. Don't get me wrong, I was thrilled to be able to use it; after all, a free car is a free car!

Ron was expecting my call that afternoon and picked up the phone with a giggle. "Well, how is the company car?"

"It's perfect, Ron," I said with a grin. "I love it. I would imagine there is a backstory to this. Care to share?"

This vehicle had initially been provided for Norman's new wife's son, who, at the time, reportedly misunderstood his family vehicle maintenance-and-safe-use agreement. So, the truck was pulled back into the estate's fleet to be repurposed, and another, less stimulating vehicle was provided for the young man: an unremarkable gray sedan.

I focused on settling into my new home. As Ron explained, this was "the varsity team." Our boss had just purchased the house, which would soon undergo extensive construction and remodeling. I had been tasked with assembling a crew and redesigning the property's expansive, once-lavish Italy-inspired grounds.

The main house was massive, encompassing well over sixteen thousand square feet. Nestled just off Bel Air Road, it featured a long, winding driveway that curved to the left, descending a hill to an open roundabout parking area adorned with elegant Italian stone pines. Designed for utmost privacy, the house was completely hidden from the road and had no close neighbors.

The main entrance was grand, showcasing enormous oak and iron doors imported from Italy. These doors opened on an expansive marble foyer at least forty feet across, complete with a high domed ceiling and a stunning view of West Los Angeles sprawling below. The residence was truly palatial—unlike anything I had ever encountered before.

The grounds were a labyrinth of stone-lined pathways that meandered through acres of exquisite Italian gardens, accented with Gothic marble statues and fountains. I later discovered that this home had been featured in several movies, including *Charlie's Angels* and a Bruce Lee film.

Javier, in his late fifties and originally from Latin America, was not pleased to see me arrive. He had enjoyed comfortable solitude, almost stuck in time, in this grand home for years, and the thought of sharing it with an ambitious and energetic young guy tasked with "making significant changes" did not sit well with him.

"Young man, there is a certain way of doing things here. We have rules," he said coldly, as I dragged my bags through the enormous front doors. Javier spoke eloquently, as if on Broadway, articulating his lines sometimes grandiosely.

His black Belgian Malinois paced stiffly around the edge of the cavernous foyer, eyeing me.

"So, it's just the two of us here?" I said.

"I count three, young man," Javier said as he nodded to the dog I would learn was named Toro, now heeled perfectly at his side. "Some would say that it is two to one." He gave a hearty laugh that seemed more bitter than joyful.

Javier showed me to the staff quarters and stood in the doorway while I set down my bags. "I think I am all set, thanks, man," I said as I looked around my new living quarters. He turned quietly and walked down the hall and back toward the kitchen.

The staff wing of the home was located on the northwest side of the main kitchen and consisted of four bedrooms similar to those in a comfortable hotel and laid out as simple yet tasteful two-bedroom suites connected by a shared door, each with a private bathroom. Each suite had a balcony that offered a view of the expansive Tuscan-inspired gardens. Ron had informed me that I would have a roommate who also lived in the staff wing. Javier was the butler who, as it was explained to me, "came with the house." I don't recall exactly how long he had lived in the home, providing service for the previous owners, but it was well over twenty years.

The staff wing had not been remodeled yet, so while it felt dated, it was still very comfortable. I opened the French doors to the small balcony, which was shared with the vacant staff room next door. "An impressive view, don't you think?" Javier said as he darkened my doorway once again.

"Oh, I didn't see you there. Yes, it is amazing!"

"Just try not to mess it up too badly, young man," he said with a peculiar laugh, reminiscent of villains from old black-and-white movies. I couldn't shake the feeling that he envisioned tying me to the train tracks.

Javier was always hovering, watching, almost guarding the mansion's place in time in a creepy, territorial way. I would step into the kitchen to put something together for dinner, and he would silently stand in the doorway and watch me like a ghost, then step back into the dimly lit corridor and vanish.

The owners, who lived in Beverly Hills, rarely visited the property, so it was just Javier, Toro, and me. I was concerned he was entering my private living space when I wasn't there. A few weeks after I arrived, I decided to test my theory by wedging a paper matchstick in the top corner of the door each morning as I left for work. I placed it carefully between the edge of the door near the top and the side jamb, keeping it concealed. If the door were to open, the matchstick would silently fall to the ground. After picking up the matchsticks several times over the following weeks, I spoke with Ron about my discomfort with this living arrangement. He assured me that he would discuss with Javier the importance of respecting my privacy and my position on the property. The hierarchy was straightforward: Javier managed everything inside, while I managed everything outside—we were equals in this unconventional workplace.

Javier kept unusual hours and social schedules, almost vampire-like, spending most of his time in his quarters down the hall and around the corner from mine. Then, around 10:00 p.m., dressed in black jeans and a black buttoned shirt, he left, not to return until 2:00 or 3:00 a.m. I found this odd because he did not drink alcohol or have any friends to speak of. I learned of his nocturnal activities a week or two after my arrival, as he was happy to share with me. He went to a strip club almost every night for hours by himself. This was not the type of strip club that attracted bachelor parties or corporate guys who had indulged a bit too much at a work dinner. Instead, it was the sleazy kind, in a dimly lit, neglected parking lot next to the freeway, where money is discreetly exchanged in dark, grimy corners.

Yes, this person was sneaking around in my living quarters while I was out.

Toro was trained never to leave his owner's side and would happily take a chunk out of your leg or arm if instructed by his odd, old-timey-movie-villain master. If that wasn't enough, Javier kept a 9mm pistol tucked into his belt when he walked around the house—a less than ideal roommate. This situation was not like living on the serene island estate I was accustomed to; it would take some getting used to. The months passed quickly, and I remained focused on my work, yet I struggled to adapt to life in Los Angeles. I was not enjoying living in this cold, empty mansion with an emotionally unwell—not to mention armed—sociopathic butler and his attack dog.

I started finding black dog hair on my bed, so I confronted Javier. "Excuse me, Javier?" I said when I saw him in the kitchen the next morning.

"Yes, young man," he said without turning away from making his toast.

"Say, it looks like someone has been going into my room while I'm working outside during the day," I said, trying to avoid directly accusing him.

He slowly turned, clearly annoyed by my question, and said, "Well, young man, I need to check every room in this house to ensure the windows are secure."

"I understand, but I would prefer to be responsible for my living quarters," I said, irritated with the conversation.

"If there's something wrong in there, I need to know about it. It's my job," he said, returning to his toast.

"Javier, I will manage my own living quarters. I do not want anyone in there. If there's a concern or an issue, simply call me, and I will come in and take care of it. I am a property manager, too."

"Have it your way, young man," he said coldly as he walked out of the kitchen and back to his room.

"Oh, Javier, my name is Dave, not 'young man,'" I said with a polite smile.

I discussed the situation during my catch-up call with Ron later that day. "Ron, could you please explain to Javier that there's no reason for him to enter my living quarters when I'm not there?"

"He goes into your room?" Ron said, surprised.

"Every day."

"Just lock your door, Dave," Ron said, eager to move on to another topic.

"I do, Ron. He has a key and lets himself and his dog in when I'm not there."

"I'll talk to him," he said.

I know Ron reached out to Javier shortly after and helped set that boundary, which I appreciated. However, the atmosphere in the house changed almost immediately.

For the next few days, Javier carried a black shotgun with him as he lurked around the massive home in the evenings, whistling as he meandered through the vast and shadowy hallways with Toro.

My peaceful island life had been replaced by something much more hostile.

I locked my room every night during the rest of my stay at this property. Some nights, after Javier returned from his nocturnal activities at the strip club, I would wake up with an unsettling feeling. When I glanced at my door, I could see the shadowy outline of black boots standing just outside in the dimly lit hallway. The sound of a dog sniffing loudly through the crack under the door was especially disconcerting. I would wait for the dog and his odd little master to move back down the hallway before trying to fall asleep again. I felt unsafe there.

I had another conversation with Ron about it.

"Are you kidding, Dave? I did talk to him, ya know."

"I know, Ron, so did I. He is creeping me out."

I could tell he wasn't quite sure where to take this situation, so he suggested I get my own place nearby if things didn't improve.

Living there was a surreal and odd experience, but it wasn't all bad. Often, when I pulled out of the nearly twelve-foot-high main gate and steered onto Bel Air Road, a Tour to the Stars bus would be rolling by slowly, with about twenty cameras pointed at me through its windows. I learned quickly from living in such a high-wealth, high-profile area that these tour operators often fabricate stories about those who live in these massive homes to stimulate their customers and boost their gratuities. Since they saw me coming and going quite a lot, driving nice cars, I am sure they told their clients I was someone famous.

This was over thirty years ago when I was arguably more attractive, with long blond hair, a dark tan, and a bright white smile. I was just so curious to find out who they thought I was. One evening, I had a thought while sitting on the massive marble veranda, sipping a Château Lynch-Bages, and soaking in that fantastic illumination of West LA. I imagined buying a ticket on one of these tours, driving by the main gate, and hearing what the tour guide had to say. *Brilliant!*

Like most of my tipsy veranda contrivances, this plan never came to fruition.

Every morning, as I headed out to LA Fitness at the bottom of the hill with hot coffee splashing in my lap, I encountered flashes from cameras and people waving at me. I could think of worse ways to start my day.

I sometimes gave them a show with a big wave and a thumbs-up as I revved my jacked-up Bronco and turned onto Bel Air Road just behind their blue star-spangled bus. At other times, I would pretend to cover my face and wear dark sunglasses and a hat, as if I didn't want to be photographed. The faces pressed against the bus windows, and the cameras clicked away. They ate it up. *So funny*. Then, they would roll up the street to aim their lenses at Elizabeth Taylor's gorgeous home or President Reagan's famous estate, far worthier stops, to be sure.

One of the challenges of living and working this way was that I could not share these fantastic experiences with anyone. I lived in a sprawling hillside mansion in Bel Air, but couldn't enjoy it with friends or family. It would be inappropriate for live-in staff to have guests, so I sat alone on that magnificent veranda every evening, sipping superb wine, with just the cold stare of a guard dog and his owner skulking silently in the shadows behind me, watching.

"Javier, please keep your dog from eating my food," I asked the shadowy figure behind me as I dumped my now half-eaten sandwich into the kitchen wastebasket. "When I step away, he takes my food."

"Little can be done about that, young man. Why don't you call your good friend Ron, and ask him what he suggests?" he said coldly, leaning against the wall of the corridor behind me.

"Javier, I asked you nicely to control your dog. Are you saying you are not going to do that?" He stepped back into the dark corridor, like a vampire.

As live-in staff, I witnessed the family in those private moments hidden from public view. I sometimes saw and heard very personal things. I saw these people up close, living their lives and feeling sad, angry, happy, troubled, stressed, joyful, and sometimes tipsy. I heard arguments, private business information, and personal discussions. I was expected to practice absolute discretion. These observations were not to be repeated or shared—ever. That is why I changed the names when telling this story and have not revealed the true identity of my former employer, his family, their guests, or the names or specific locations of his private homes. He was always fair and professional with me, and I will always be the same with him. I hold a tremendous amount of respect for the man.

On Martha's Vineyard, we occasionally got some lookie-loos at the airport, with two vehicles idling, ready by the gate to the private jet entrance in a place known for being a vacation destination of the rich and famous. When the jet was taxiing to its assigned spot on the tarmac, we would verify the tail number then code our way through the gate and drive, in pattern, out to the plane, being mindful of the wing, and park the cars close to the airstairs. The flight crew would remove the bags from the cargo hold and load them into the back of the waiting vehicles. Once the bags were off, the passengers would step down and right into the cars to be whisked directly back to the estate. Smooth and fast.

The drivers of the cars, I, or other staff or crew that day, might glean information on what the owners or guests were interested in doing during their stay. Once the cars reached the top of the drive, the interior and exterior staff quickly delivered bags to the guest rooms and main suite. The drivers' information regarding the guests' interests would be conveyed to the correct staff member: food or dinner reservation requests to the chef, boating requests to the captain. Garden, car, motorcycle, tennis, delivery, or errand requests would come to me. If someone in the car mentioned how much they love fresh peonies, I would run around the garden, finding the best peony blooms, cut them, and hand them off to someone in the kitchen, who would quickly arrange them in a vase and take them up to that guest's room or the owner's suite.

If I were in the mood, I'd take one of the old cars for a drive around town on a gorgeous autumn evening after the owners and guests had left for the season. What a feeling that was! With the top down on that beautiful 1928 Gatsby Cadillac, I would slowly cruise through the picturesque town, smoothly shifting through the gears as I turned onto Water Street just as the sun set, sharing the last moments of its warm autumn light. I would give a little wave and nod to the tourists standing in front of Mad Martha's, their ice cream cones dripping as they fumbled to capture the perfect photo. I was driving the most stunning and expensive car I had ever seen in one of the most charming towns imaginable. It was divine.

I paid for very little. Someone else provided me with places to live and cars to drive and covered my expenses and utilities, so I could stay completely focused on supporting my employer, his guests, and his property without the distraction of worrying about such real-life things. My employers were incredibly patient with me, even when I took one of the young estate housekeepers with me on vacation to Maui and wound up staying that winter to surf and work at the Hard Rock Cafe.

"Get it out of your system, Dave, and just let me know when you are ready to come back," Ron patiently said.

I had worked in private estate management for nearly seven years for the same employer, the last two years, splitting my time between Bel Air and Edgartown. Doing this type of work can be as challenging as it is rewarding, but it does cut you off from the rest of the world. You are a support mechanism, helping to make someone else's life more comfortable while putting your own in the quiet background. You need to know when to step out of that, or the next thing you know, you will have a guard dog, a 9mm tucked into your belt, and the only friends you will have are paid in singles in a dark, windowless building down on the seedy end of Pico Blvd.

This realization became the catalyst for my decision to leave. I wanted the freedom to travel, have a girlfriend, and enjoy a social life. There was so much more I wanted to see, and I wasn't ready to commit to one job for the long term—a choice I would later reconsider.

Transitioning out of living and working with the mega-rich would prove more difficult than I imagined. While I craved independence, it came with a significant cost. I had become accustomed to a very comfortable lifestyle, and this way of living and working may have caused me to lose touch with social and financial realities. I was sure many peers were not experiencing life and work as I was.

I recall catching a train to Penn Station in New York City during the Christmas holiday. After visiting my parents in New Jersey, I had plans to spend the weekend in the city, seeing a show and enjoying dinner with friends before returning to the island. I sat in the back of the commuter car and spotted a guy I knew from college named Andy, who was closer to the front of the train. Instead of walking up to him and saying hello, I hesitated and watched. Perhaps I was unsure if it was him.

I could sense his sadness. He sat quietly, gazing out the smudged window, watching the damp gray and brown landscape rush by as we approached the tunnel that would lead us into the bustling Penn Station in Manhattan.

He wore an inexpensive, well-worn blue suit that badly needed pressing. He looked much older than I remembered. His face was drawn and sullen, and I imagined he was on his way to a job he didn't care about during what should have been a warm and joyful holiday season. I didn't know him well, but I felt a connection. Instead of reaching out to him, I fell into deep reflection. In that moment, I realized how fortunate I had been. My life had been rich and filled with exciting and extraordinary experiences. Watching him, I felt a profound gratitude as our train entered the dark tunnel.

He stepped off the train and disappeared into the faceless crowd. I should have said something to him. My self-focus at that moment paralyzed me, and I regret that.

Eventually, I started to grow discontented with what I was doing. The drive to excel in my job was waning, and I found it increasingly difficult to envision myself working and living in the same situation for another year. While enjoying a new relationship, I also noticed a strong desire to travel emerging within me.

My mind often drifted and dreamed of travel and new experiences, pining for change. This is a familiar feeling for me. I can be intensely focused on a task or job, often for extended periods. Then, without notice or reason, I snap out of it, look up, and think *Okay, Okay. I am done with this*. I knew I was not built to do the same thing, day in and day out, for long periods of time. I also knew that if I stayed much longer, I would become more uncomfortable and most likely start to get in my head and spiral into emotional and professional decay, not to mention the real fear of being shot by my roommate in some dark corridor deep in the bowels of that cold mansion we shared. I even considered telling my friends back on the island, "If I suddenly go missing, the butler did it!"

I recognized and valued the unique opportunities I had been afforded but knew it was time to move on. I returned to the Edgartown estate to assist with some end-of-season projects. While there, I wrote a professional resignation letter and called Ron to have a difficult conversation. We spoke for a long time. Ron had become a friend and understood my reasons for needing to leave. I sent my resignation letter to Norman's office in Los Angeles and said goodbye to an incredible experience. Norman responded with a thoughtful note to thank me and wish me well. After that, we met at the Bel Air property a few times and said our goodbyes.

A few weeks later, I was wrapping things up in Bel Air and getting prepared to move out and move on. I am incredibly grateful to my former employer and his team of outstanding professionals who allowed me to live so close to their extraordinary lives. I will never forget it. You are all amazing people, and I am forever grateful for the profound experiences and lessons I learned while working with you. Maybe not as much with Javier, but at least he gave me some good stories to tell!

Before the year 2000, fewer than three hundred billionaires lived in the US. I am fortunate to have worked closely with one for many years. I will always be grateful for the experience and will cherish the memories for the rest of my life.

CHAPTER SEVEN
LAST I HEARD, HE
WAS IN TANGIER

Nothing behind me, everything ahead of me, as is ever so the road
Jack Kerouac

Feeling an urge for adventure before making my next career move, I carefully laid my world map on the kitchen table. I grabbed a bottle of Freemark Abbey Napa cabernet and turned up Peter Gabriel's *Secret World Live* album. As the layered, percussion-driven music and rich, soulful vocals filled the room, I lost myself in the African- and Latin-influenced sounds and dreamt of faraway places.

With building anticipation, I began to explore the map, my index finger tracing over countries and coastlines until it landed on a place that barely registered in my mind: Indonesia. The name sparkled with exotic promise and mystery. "Okay, there we have it," I murmured to myself, with a mix of excitement and resolve as I folded the map, a sense of fate enveloping me.

Without hesitation, I picked up the phone and called my friend

David, a travel agent, back on Martha's Vineyard. I booked a ticket out of LA for three weeks later, my heart racing with the thrill of the unknown that awaited me.

This trip was shaping up to be one of the most significant travel adventures I had ever embarked on. Bali was almost nine thousand miles from Los Angeles, the furthest I had ever traveled. With my pack slung over my shoulder, a coach ticket in hand, and a pocket full of cash and traveler's checks, I walked into the airport for my 10:30 p.m. flight on that cloudy Tuesday. I felt a sense of trepidation as I made my way down the jetway for my nighttime flight to the other side of the world. From past experiences, I knew that overcoming my apprehension over such an adventure usually paid off. I always returned from these types of trips feeling fulfilled. So, I found my seat and settled in for the long journey ahead.

Since high school, I have sought opportunities to venture out into the world alone, without a net. It was during these times that I experienced the most profound personal growth. There is something refreshing and challenging about stepping out of an airport on the other side of the world, knowing nothing about the place or its people, culture, currency, or language. I loved that feeling of adventure and exploration. It was freeing, pure, and exciting.

After wandering through the mostly deserted terminal during our brief early morning layover in Honolulu, I returned to the plane, filled with anticipation for the journey ahead to Bali. There's something profoundly humbling about an overnight flight over a dark ocean; it makes you feel remarkably small against the vastness of the world.

After fourteen hours of darkness, surrounded by restless fellow travelers shifting in their seats, I caught a tantalizing aroma of freshly brewed coffee drifting back from the galley, cutting through the stale, recycled cabin air. I have come to cherish that moment while traveling; it is filled with rich possibilities and the exhilarating promise of new adventures—much like the excitement that builds as the curtain rises at a Broadway show or when the stage lights come up at a concert.

The flight attendants flitted up and down the aisles, their movements synchronized like a well-rehearsed dance, whispering behind the curtain separating the galley from the passenger cabin. Gradually, the overhead lights brightened, flooding the cabin with a soft, warm glow that unveiled the weary faces of passengers awakening from a fitful slumber. Eyes still heavy with sleep, they began to stir, stretching stiff limbs and letting out deep yawns that echoed softly in the cabin. With a gentle clatter, they opened the overhead compartments, rummaging through their belongings in search of toiletries and fresh changes of clothes, readying themselves to face the adventures that awaited them in the day ahead.

We were almost there.

I asked my travel agent friend to book the first night's hotel stay so I could have a place to go and settle in after the long flight. I would decide where to stay after that as I became more comfortable with the area.

As the flight crew tidied up after the breakfast service and the plane began its initial descent, a strong sense of confidence and adventure washed over me as I returned my tray table to its fully upright and locked position. I was charged up and ready to go. I felt like I could handle anything! I was completely free. I pictured the adventures waiting for me in this faraway and mysterious place.

There was something scintillating about disappearing into the world with very few people knowing where I was going; hell, I didn't even know where I would end up. Surrendering to the natural, energetic flow of the world is exciting to me. It sweeps out the cobwebs and dusty corners in my mind, helping me reset; no schedules, no expectations, no plan—just a good old-fashioned walkabout.

It was 8:30 a.m. when the plane pulled up to the gate. After collecting my backpack from the conveyor belt in baggage claim, I had my passport stamped, and I stepped outside to flag down a taxi. It amazes me how places have their unique smells. The first thing I noticed about the air in Bali was the faint yet ubiquitous smell of wood smoke. The place smelled like a campfire, with a hint of clove cigarettes lingering in the heavy, warm air. I found this unusual outside a city airport, and I suppose I was expecting the smog I left in LA. This was pleasant and inviting, evoking a genuine sense of adventure.

I stepped into my hotel room, dropped my pack on the white tile floor, and quickly changed into my swimsuit. I walked about a hundred feet to the ocean. It was midday, and the sky was overcast, creating a peaceful feeling. As I stepped into the sea, I noticed the water was the same temperature as the air. If it weren't for the line where the sea and air met on my skin, marking the transition between the two different pressures, it would be hard to distinguish between them. I took a deep breath and gazed at the pale gray horizon, spotting small fishing boats in the distance. These narrow boats resembled large canoes, each with a flat canvas canopy and brightly colored outriggers on either side.

As a young man on a cash-only budget, I was cautious about how I spent my money. When it was gone, it was gone. This reality motivated me to stay on budget when almost nine thousand miles away from anything familiar.

The following week was spent exploring the area around Sanur Beach in Bali. I found some fantastic places to hang out and have a couple of beers with other travelers in the evenings. One such place was Agung & Sue Watering Hole in Sanur Beach. I enjoyed local dishes like *gado gado*, *nasi goreng*, and some fantastic curries, all for a few dollars US.

A group of us travelers would meet at Agung & Sue Watering Hole every couple of days to exchange stories of where we had been. We would drink beer or tea and talk for hours. One of the German couples I had become friendly with suggested that I visit Nusa Lembongan, a small island off Bali's southeast coast.

I planned the adventure for the following day, and after a quick discussion with Agung, the café's colorful proprietor, I got the transportation details: "Go to the beach, turn to the left, walk a while until you see the big boat, then wait by the tree. Be there by 7:30." *Copy that.*

Agung's definition of a big boat was not aligned with my understanding. After some arm-waving, pointing to the sea, and an awkward exchange of money, I stepped onto the medium-sized, outrigger-style boat with an outboard motor—a slightly larger version of the fishing boats I had seen just offshore that first morning. I'm not sure what I expected, but something akin to a small ferry would have been closer to what I had in mind. According to my journal notes, it was a wet and lumpy ride, with three- to four-foot rounding swells. I enjoyed being on the water, whether it was smooth or rough.

We made landfall about two hours later by sliding the bow onto one of the most exquisite, powdery white sand beaches I had ever seen. It was lined with coconut palms gracefully leaning out over the sand, as if reaching for something.

"This place looks just like my screen saver," I said as I climbed out of the large canoe. I grabbed my pack and walked up to the beach. My friend Jimmy, the chef from Norman's estate, had also suggested that I check out this island and instructed me to find Agung, who owned a place near Shipwrecks, a well-known surf break. By this point, I had realized that many Indonesian men are named Agung; it was the most common name for boys, much like John in the US. However, this didn't deter me. I was determined to find Agung and his excellent beachfront property.

As I walked up and off the beach, looking for a road, a young guy, maybe seventeen or so, came racing up behind me on a small, noisy dirt bike. He hopped off the bike and came running over.

"Transport, mister?"

I am looking for Agung's place," I told him.

"I know Agung! He is my uncle!" he said enthusiastically.

"Great! Let's go."

I turned and imagined the sound of a needle sliding across a record when I saw his motorcycle. It was a small Yamaha 100cc trail bike with considerable wear and tear. When I looked doubtful, he made hand gestures, acknowledging my size and the large backpack slung over my shoulder.

"No problem, mister, no problem," he kept saying. I remember thinking my breakfast was bigger than his motorcycle, so I felt there might, indeed, be a problem.

We both laughed. I liked his youthful ardor. "All right, fuck it. Let's do it," I said as I stepped over the sun-warmed and torn black seat and kept my pack slung over my shoulder. The springs compressed, and the old metal creaked. We sped off as quickly as that little bike could handle, down the jungle paths, dry palm fronds gently slapping our shoulders. The shocks could not withstand the strain and would produce a harsh, metal-on-metal clanking sound every time there was a bump in the path, of which there were many. I envisioned us as some bizarre, noisy, and slow-moving comet, with sparks and plumes of smoke trailing behind us.

I stepped onto the front porch of Agung's guest house and gave a friendly nod to the surfers hanging out, playing chess, and drinking *kopi tubruk* coffee. As I stepped inside, I met Agung just as he was coming out. He stopped and looked up at me, then circled me until he was in front of me again. His English was excellent.

"You are the biggest man I have ever seen," he said quietly. Then, realizing he may have been rude, he quickly apologized.

"Don't worry, brother, I come in peace," I said, making a peace sign with my fingers and giving a friendly laugh.

The following morning, I got up early, having not slept well. "Those fucking roosters!" I grumbled as I stepped into my board shorts. I walked down the path to the beach and saw several young Aussie surfers paddling out to the Shipwrecks surf break a few hundred yards offshore. The beach itself was empty. It was 6:00 a.m., and the sun was rising. I waded into the bath-warm water and swam for a while along the beach. I floated on my back in the salty crystalline sea, watching the sunrise as it slowly revealed its ravishing amber hues. That moment was a real gift.

Pulling on a T-shirt as I stepped onto the porch, I said good morning to the other travelers hanging out and watching the sunrise. I felt this group was a little closed off, so I found a small table in the corner and ordered breakfast and coffee. I was always equipped with a good book or two when I traveled and a leather-bound journal to write my notes in, so I always had something to do. The Aussie surfers sat around, talked about shipwrecks, and played chess.

It wasn't long before I met a local fisherman with a boat. For just a small handful of rupiah, we set off for a day of fishing and snorkeling. It was a perfect way to escape the heat that blanketed the beach all day like a hot, wet towel. Over the next few days, I spent time on the boat with Captain Adi, exploring the hidden mangrove coves and stunning beaches of the Nusa Islands. In the mid-nineties, the only people around these islands were surfers and a few adventurous travelers. There were no hotels, fancy resorts, or vacation homes—just modest thatched-roof bungalows and small, brightly colored outrigger boats dotting the crystal-clear waters of the powdery white beaches. At times, the combination of the purest, whitest sand and the clearest seawater I have ever encountered created the illusion that there was no water at all. Only when sunlight glinted off the surface or a slight ripple disturbed the calmness did the presence of water become evident.

One morning, we decided to explore a small mangrove cove and go snorkeling. Adi had a great idea to cover more area, so he had me dive into the water and hold onto one of the outrigger supports with my left hand. Once I was settled, he put the motor in gear, and we moved gently forward, the water flowing around me like a slow-moving river. The variety of sea life I encountered was breathtaking. We glided like this for about a mile through that pristine, aquarium-like cove. It was the best snorkeling experience I've ever had by far. I spent the equivalent of fifteen dollars US for two and a half days of boating, snorkeling, and spearfishing with my new friend.

The only concern I recall during our motorized snorkeling expedition was the fear of losing my swimsuit. What a sight that would have been—good grief! This wasn't the first time I felt anxious about suddenly being naked in an inappropriate setting. While living on Martha's Vineyard a year or two earlier, I drove down to South Beach after work on a midsummer Saturday afternoon for a run and a quick swim. I ran about a mile down the beach, away from the beach-goers with their Frisbees, coolers, and blankets. It was a peaceful spot where I could enjoy the natural beauty of the marram grass–covered dunes and the sea, alone. I loved it there; it truly captured the essence of the island.

After finishing my short run, I removed my shirt and sneakers and dove into the surf. It felt wonderful—until I realized I'd lost my shorts when I entered the now-rough water. I was naked! Standing au naturel on a high dune, with my right hand pressed against my brow, shielding my eyes from the sun, I appeared to salute my idiocy as I scanned cresting waves for my navy blue swimsuit.

The walk back to the car required that I go straight through the populated beach area by the parking lot where my Jeep was parked.

There was no way around it. I walked quickly through the busy beach, hoping not to be noticed, stepping around blankets and navigating through the beach bags, coolers, umbrellas, and chairs. I did my best to hold my T-shirt and running shoes in such a way as to cover my dangly bits.

"Hi, Dave," I heard a voice say from my immediate right. It was Ann, my favorite bank teller, who was enjoying a day on the beach with her three kids, watching my bare white ass step over their blanket. *Lovely*.

I walked quickly across the hot pavement, through the crowded parking lot, and jumped into my car. I drove home bare-assed naked in my topless Jeep Renegade. I mean, I thought, why put the shirt on? That would be a whole other level of creepy—like a giant toddler running away from his mother at bath time.

So, I climbed the stairs to our apartment, past the now-mangled white lattice, and walked through the front door. Travis looked up from his sandwich and burst out laughing. "Looking good, Becker!" He said with a wide grin.

"Just don't," I said as I strode up the stairs two or three at a time to my room, covering my junk like a humiliated Sasquatch crossing the road in the headlights of a tour bus.

A few days after my arrival on Nusa Lembongan, I was relaxing on the alang-alang porch, enjoying a few beers to escape the oppressive afternoon heat, when I leaned over and challenged the Australians to the next chess game. They seemed surprised and a bit confused about why I was horning in on their surfers' chess hang. My request was met with some quizzical looks. My mind swirled with unhinged theories.

What is their deal? Why are these dicks staring at me? Now one is pointing at me? What the fuck! They are messin' with the wrong guy! I should kick their asses to prove a point, like in those old prison movies. Go all Cool Hand Luke *on these dicks. That's what I'll do. Fuckers!*

Considering my size and quiet demeanor, I thought *Walking Tall* would be a better theme for this situation. I would need a stick of some kind, a club even. Being unfamiliar with the indigenous hardwoods of this region, I would need to make sure I chose something that would stand up to its desired purpose. I looked around, thinking a piece of driftwood could double as club. Being hasty in procuring the material for a proper club and settling for, say, the viny, rubber plant–like thing nearest to hand (the botanical name escaped me), could lead to embarrassment because it would be like striking someone with a barky wet noodle. *Leave a mark? Sure.* Still, it would not deliver the intended message and may even be met with a giggle, a snort, or just swatted away. I wondered how long Buford Pusser took to find the perfect piece of wood from which to carve his club. I didn't think anyone giggled when Buford landed his magnificent stick across someone's shoulders. I found this oddly concerning.

Me, attacking with my club: Thwap!

"Knock it off, idiot!"

"Fear me!" Thwack-crack,

"Piss off, you wanker!"

Just then, as I was scanning the area for suitable materials for weapons, one of the chess-playing staring guys came over, gently took a praying mantis off the side of my hat, and showed it to me.

"Look at this, mate; you had this little guy on your lid. Cool, right?

Sometimes I behave like a dog that has been kicked too much.

A few minutes later, an Aussie guy waved me over, and I sat at his table. He was older, maybe thirty. Initially, he could have been more friendly. However, by the end of the game, we were fully engaged in conversation. I like to believe it was because I was winning, but we had a great time, nonetheless. I plugged in my little travel speaker and turned up the Beach Boys' *Pet Sounds* album, and we all drank beer, told stories of places we had been, and laughed.

This situation was familiar to me. Like many, I often feel uncomfortable in new social situations, and working my way in can be difficult, as I feel different or not wanted. I felt this many times in meeting rooms and corporate events later in my life. What I learned about myself was that I would sit on the outside and cast mild judgment on people who seemed not to be interested in knowing me or including me, as if it were somehow their responsibility to make an effort to bring me in. In such situations, I often felt hurt, so I would pull back and tell myself they were not worth knowing, and that I should sit alone and read or write. I jotted down notes and doodles in my journal, even making fun of them in my writing. Sometimes I wanted to lash out at them. Why did I do that? Such strange and antisocial behavior.

I have since learned that this was my unconscious story coming to the surface. *I am not good enough nor smart enough nor lovable. I am not worthy.* We all have stories from our early developmental years that come rushing up when we feel vulnerable as adults, just like mine did. The reality was that they didn't dislike me; they were doing their own thing and didn't think to include me. Perhaps they were working through their own unconscious stories.

I recall times early in my corporate career, years later, when I was absolutely paralyzed by fear and anxiety in a meeting, for no apparent reason other than I didn't know the answer to a question. One such instance was during a training meeting in New York, where approximately thirty sales managers from my company gathered for a sales negotiation workshop. I was new; it was my first week in the company. We sat around a U-shaped table while the instructor paced rigidly in the center, talking.

The instructor abruptly asked about a specific grocery industry category-management technique, as implemented by a specific retailer. He directed the question at me, fully aware that I had been working on this project just weeks earlier as an employee of that same grocery chain. He stood directly in front of me, clearly expecting an answer. It felt like a setup for a spike, but it didn't unfold that way. All eyes were on me, and suddenly the room felt brighter, with the walls closing in.

What is happening? The silence was deafening, interrupted only by the hum of the fan on the overhead projector. *Why is it so hot in here? Oh no, I think I might puke!* The instructor was oblivious to my growing panic and continued to wait for my response. My heart was pounding. *Why am I holding my breath?* My mind went into fight-or-flight mode, ultimately retreating deep within itself and misfiring. I turned into a statue.

Panicky thoughts surged through my mind, and my heart felt like it was about to burst out of my chest. An avalanche of negative thoughts crashed over me: *I will get fired in my first week because I'm an idiot.*

I should know this answer—why can't I remember? I'm stupid and shouldn't even be in this room with these experienced sales managers. My chest hurts! They can see right through me! They hate me and think I'm ridiculous! I could feel my pulse pounding in my temples. There was a loud hum in my ears.

After what felt like an eternity, the instructor finally answered his own question and relieved me of my anxiety. The attendees returned their attention to him, and the meeting moved on. The lights dimmed, my stomach settled, and my racing heart calmed. The tension in the room eased, and everything began to feel normal again.

I had experienced my first meeting room panic attack. After the meeting, an older manager from New York City, who had been sitting across the room, approached me to talk.

"Hey, are you okay?" he asked.

"Oh, yeah, sure. I am fine, thank you. How are you?" I said, hoping to get the attention off of me as quickly as possible.

"I could see you were struggling there for a minute. It sucks when that happens. Try to be patient with yourself, son. You are doing just fine." He gave me a friendly slap on the back. It was over. It was then that I realized I needed help with this. If I were to work in this environment, I would need to get this under control. After returning from the meeting a few days later, I scheduled an appointment with a psychologist. I worked for many years with this excellent doctor in untangling this big, messy ball of rubber bands in my mind, comprised of stress, anxiety, self-doubt, and depression, all fueled by the pressures of being a new father in a strained marriage, with a new career and money issues, not the least of which was a home we couldn't afford. It was too much, and I was cracking. I have little doubt that if I had not gotten help at that time, I would have continued to suffer, and my life would look very different today. Dennis—thank you.

I have struggled with this throughout my life. I tend to be an isolationist, a loner, and a quiet observer. Past emotional injuries may have contributed to this tendency but perhaps not. I deeply value friendships and community, yet I feel an equal, if not greater, pull toward solitude. Since childhood, I have dreamed of living alone on a boat, sailing to the world's farthest corners, or residing in a cabin far away from people, cars, and houses. Over the years, I have found a more comfortable balance to satisfy this inner conflict by carefully examining the reasons behind my social anxiety. I have learned that it is possible to live without crippling anxiety and depression, and that help is available.

By day eight on Nusa Lembongan, I was growing tired of having nothing to do, and my days had become so dull and sluggish that it was time to move on. That night on the porch, I had a few beers with a couple from South Africa and learned about another island that, in their opinion, was well worth the visit. They told me about Sumbawa, a quiet destination between Flores and Lombok in the middle of the Lesser Sunda Islands. I made plans and let Agung know I would leave in the morning.

Later that evening, after dinner, a couple of the Aussie surfers I had played chess with stopped by my room to tell me about a bar in the jungle they were aiming to find. "I like where this is going!" I said, putting my book down and slipping my shoes on. We trudged along the dark jungle path, armed only with Bic lighters and a map of smudgy blue lines scribbled on a beer-soaked napkin late the previous evening. We eventually emerged from the dense tropical greenery onto a dirt road, and there it was. A glowing Bintang Lager sign beckoned from a small thatch-roofed building, standing next to the dusty road like a boozy little oasis, from which we heard the sound of laughter and English speakers.

We walked along the sandy path leading to the front door, passing pieces of artfully placed gray driftwood, a tattered hammock, and large, porous stones carved into white scalloped clamshells, which lined the walkway to the open screened door. Upon stepping inside, the sounds of laughter and clinking glasses grew louder. About ten or twelve travelers and locals were in the small roadside bar with a welcoming, laid-back vibe. We found some chairs around a small table and settled in comfortably.

We gathered with travelers from every corner of the globe in the secluded jungle bar, hidden beneath a canopy of lush greenery along that lightless jungle road. The atmosphere buzzed with warmth and camaraderie as the travelers shared their stories of exploration. With each tale told, laughter filled the air. Before long, we found ourselves emptying several bottles of cold lager, reveling in the new friendships that flowed as freely as the Bintang.

I learned more about Sumbawa, my next stop, by chatting with two young French women who had just returned from there a few days earlier. While they puffed on their Gauloises cigarettes, they shared valuable information about this lesser-known and intriguing island, including recommended places to stay, ferry schedules, and areas to avoid. I was excited about my upcoming visit. Along with the transit details, they mentioned that the atmosphere on the island can sometimes feel a bit strange.

"What do you mean?" I asked.

"It's just got a different energy, yes?" one of the girls said, in a thick Parisian accent that I found very attractive. "It's wonderful, but a couple of days is enough."

"Tell him about the dreams," the other girl said, glancing at her friend sheepishly and almost a little embarrassed.

"We both had strange dreams while out there," the first girl said, less mysteriously. It was just weird, man, ya know?"

Later, we stumbled out of the jungle well after 2:00 a.m., our bellies full of beer. After a few hours of sleep, I returned to the outrigger, heading back to Sanur. I made a quick stop in Denpasar to repair my camera before heading to the airport to catch the plane to Lombok.

It was a short flight, followed by a ferry ride and then a bus trip. Apart from what I'd heard from the South Africans and the girls in the bar, I knew nothing about this place. As I watched the scenery pass by through the dust-covered bus window, I wasn't sure I could even point to it on a map if I had to. About an hour into my journey, the bus came to another squeaky stop in a small village. This seemed as good a place as any, and I picked up my pack and stepped off the bus. I walked into a *swalayan*, bought a big bottle of water, and asked the man working at the counter for a good place to stay. He pointed down the road to the south. I walked about half an hour before the jungle opened, revealing the most beautiful beach. A small wooden sign pointed west along the beach and read, "Seaside Cottages."

"Well, that sounds perfect," I said as I picked up my pack and walked.

During the third night, I experienced the dreams my Parisian friends warned me about. Reading my journal entry from that trip to Sumbawa brings back the strangeness of that night. The actual entry from the next morning reads:

I sank into a depth of sleep I had never experienced before—a subaqueous, almost euphoric state. My body felt too heavy to move, almost paralyzed. I felt high, as if I had been drugged, floating, drifting, and falling.

Something was rustling outside my window. Darkness surrounded me, and the word that surfaced in my mind at that moment—"evil." Then I heard a voice.

"We know you are awake," the voice from outside said. "We need to show you something," it whispered. I felt something moving closer, speaking too softly to hear, mumbling. A dark presence washed over me, and adrenaline surged as I snapped out of the trance.

I sat up in bed, sweating, my heart racing. *What the fuck was that?* I jumped up to check the windows and door but found nothing. I turned on the lights and spent the rest of the night pacing in my tiny room, waiting impatiently for dawn to break. I stomped heavily around the bungalow, banging my hiking boots against the walls to make as much noise as possible. I considered going outside, but I had no idea what was out there, and I was all alone, knowing that no one knew where I was at that moment. So, I stayed inside and waited.

I was back at the bus stop before sunrise.

During my conversations with local people after my experience, I learned the significance of the offerings they place outside their doors each morning and evening. I had noticed these offerings, known as *canang sari*, but I had paid them no mind, thinking they were merely trinkets for tourists. Each morning, while I was in Bali and Nusa Lembongan, someone would place a small handwoven grass tray, about three inches in diameter, outside my door. Depending on the desired outcome, these trays typically contained a mixture of flowers, rice, betel leaf, lime, and a stick of burning incense. Some offerings were made to express gratitude and devotion, while others aimed to promote harmony and balance or ward off evil spirits. I noticed that no offerings were placed by my door while I was in Sumbawa.

Later that day, I returned to Bali and reconnected with a local man I had befriended during my stay. His name was also Agung, and he lived with his family in the suburbs of Denpasar. I was invited to join Agung and his family for dinner that evening at his home, during which he informed me that his uncle had passed away recently and that they would be having a funeral the following day. I was invited to attend the *Ngaben*, or funeral ceremony. I was honored to be invited to such an important family event and quickly accepted the invitation.

I met Agung and his family at the street corner he had mentioned the evening before. I wasn't sure what to expect, but it certainly wasn't what I encountered. Over a hundred people had gathered, talking and dancing. The sound of gamelan music filled the humid air as the crowd of family and well-wishers began to move down the street, following the deceased, dressed all in white and lying on a platform inside an ornately decorated and colorful bamboo tower.

Several men carried long poles, lifting and moving the tower much like pallbearers do with a casket in traditional Western funerals. As the tower was paraded through the streets, the sounds of music and cheering grew louder. The men carrying the tower spun it around, made dramatic changes in direction, and continued down the street.

Agung leaned over and said, "This is done to confuse the soul so they don't try to return."

We walked with the crowd for about a mile until we reached a small field near the banks of the Ayung River, where a roaring bonfire blazed. Standing close to the fire with Agung and his family, we watched as the tower approached, moving in erratic circles down the dusty road.

The men carrying the tower were moving quickly toward us, and I felt uncertain about what to expect. "Should I be standing here?" I asked Agung. Just then, the men tipped the tower onto the roaring fire, engulfing the deceased only feet away from where I stood. The tower erupted into flames. I recall the distinct smell of burning flesh as the music grew louder. The experience was surreal and discordant yet strangely natural at the same time. It seemed I was the only one who had not witnessed this before, so I tucked my Western discomfort away and, allowing the moment to wash over me, I danced. I felt genuinely privileged to witness such a significant and moving ceremony. It was an experience I'll carry with me for a long time.

Being a time well before the age of smartphones and Google, I was used to traveling by gathering information from people I met. I enjoyed traveling this way. When traveling today, folks can look down at their phones to gather information without engaging with the people around them, simply because they don't need to. Everything they need is on that tiny screen in their hand. If they want to know all the great places to eat nearby, they look down at their phone. If they need to know how to get to the airport or find that ancient hilltop stone church they read about before their trip, they look down at their phone. If they need to know tomorrow's weather report, well, you get the idea. I am certainly not trying to devalue the convenience of modern technology while traveling; these devices are amazing. But they create a different travel experience than before the advent of smartphones.

Traveling like this today always makes me feel more like an observer, quietly collecting specific experiences. I sometimes feel like I'm on a strange international scavenger hunt, following the clues on my phone until I stand in front of something of interest or what someone else has found interesting on Tripadvisor. Then, I look up and click a couple of pictures to add to the photo evidence of my trip. A quick post to socials then look down at the phone to find the next point of interest, get the step-by-step directions, and start walking. I do not enjoy this type of travel experience—not one bit.

It is hard to get lost while traveling with a smartphone. However, getting lost in a foreign place sometimes leads to the most exciting experiences. You may find the most amazing things, people, and places during such times. You may find a bit of yourself along the way. There is, however, an argument that traveling this way without smartphones, Uber, Google Translate, Expedia, or Tripadvisor is less safe. This may be true, and the times have certainly changed since those early days of my travels, but my point remains that striving for a deeper connection with the places we visit will often offer a more vibrant experience.

Years ago, we traveled by fully engaging with our surroundings. We talked to strangers, observed our environment, read travel books, and relied on our resourcefulness. Just give me a folded map, some cash in my pocket, and a comfortable pair of shoes, and I'm ready to explore a new place—that's what travel means to me. I genuinely enjoy being a foreigner in other countries. This kind of travel feels different and teaches you to be acutely aware of your surroundings while trusting your instincts.

When you find yourself alone on the other side of the world, unsure of the town or village you're in, it forces you to develop new skills. I realized that information is invaluable; it helps you navigate from place to place safely and comfortably. Being able to tap into the shared wisdom of fellow travelers is crucial. Without proper guidance, you may end up lost, alone, broke, and in tears outside the wrong airport in the rain or locked out of a youth hostel in the middle of the night in an unfamiliar and unforgiving place.

I have recently lost touch with my preferred way of traveling while in Europe. A few years ago, my wife and I enjoyed a driving trip through Italy, but fell into the trap of relying solely on our smartphones for navigation and information. By the end of the day, we were excited to arrive at our last stop, Perugia, a charming and ancient hilltop city located in the central region of Umbria.

We drove our rental car through the magnificent city gates and navigated the narrow, cobbled streets until we reached the city center. Our navigation system guided us as expected, and we arrived easily at the central plaza. The GPS prompted us to continue through the plaza and toward the old church, the last point of interest on our day's drive.

The streets were narrow and serpentine, at times with only ten inches separating the car's side mirrors from the ancient stone buildings on either side, their rough walls adorned with gray-green lichen and timeworn scars of centuries past. The air was thick with history, and the faint echo of the vehicle's engine softly reverberated off the stones, as if the presence of modernity was disturbing this old-world setting.

We were close.

"It says to keep going up this street and bear right at the top of the hill, by the central plaza," Caroline said, watching the map rotate on the screen in her hand. However, it became clear that we had missed some road signs. Looking at the map on her phone, we realized we had driven into an area designated for pedestrian traffic only.

"Are you sure we're supposed to be here?" Caroline asked, growing concerned.

"I have no idea; what does it say?" I said, steering carefully through the exceptionally tight alleys.

We emerged from a narrow street and found ourselves in a vibrant, open market situated in the most picturesque pedestrian plaza in the sun-filled city center. Evidently, we didn't belong there; all eyes were on us, and people were pointing.

"We shouldn't be here," Caroline said, with growing urgency.

I nosed the car into the piazza, hoping to blend in. We were in the middle of a walking tour in front of the church we hoped to find. A crowd of tourists surrounded the car as the tour operator spoke into a microphone, pointing to the gorgeous architecture in front of us. I rolled down the windows so we could hear the guide better. The older tourists rested against the car's warm hood, listening to the guide talk about the church's history. I could only catch snippets of the presentation.

I reached out my window and touched the arm of someone in our tour group, asking, "Did you catch the year this was built?"

"What are we going to do?" Caroline asked, looking all around for a way out.

"There's nothing we can do; I'm stuck until they all move," I said, trying to lighten the mood with a playful smile, signaling I was trying to hear the guide. "Let's just enjoy the tour."

"It's not funny," she said.

A few minutes later, the crowd moved through the plaza, led by their now-annoyed guide, who glanced back to ensure we weren't following them. I carefully drove through the area, hoping to find a way out of this awkward situation. I gestured to the people dining in the plaza, using creative hand signals to ask them to move their tables to the left or right. In return, we received some rather unfriendly hand gestures. It was embarrassing. Some men began shouting in Italian, pointing angrily at signs that displayed an image of a car with a red line through it.

I was tempted to shout something in German out the window or even start singing the Canadian national anthem—anything that might deflect attention from the fact that we were silly Americans who couldn't put our damn phones down long enough to read a simple road sign. However, I didn't want to drag anyone else into our embarrassment. Instead, I offered a friendly wave and mouthed *I'm sorry* to everyone staring at us.

A kind man approached my window while we were trying to get a couple having coffee to move their table. He offered to help with directions, indicating I should follow him to the exit, which I did. I dug into my pocket, pulled out a handful of coins, and offered them to the man, who was also being yelled at.

A few weeks after returning home, I received an expensive traffic ticket in the mail, which I paid happily.

In my earlier travel experiences, I discovered the value of being able to approach people and talk to them in a way that makes them feel at ease and not perceive me as a threat. I became skilled at starting conversations with strangers on the street or in a bar. Body positioning and friendly, disarming eye contact can often achieve this. It was a survival skill for me when I was out in the world, stomping around by myself. I learned to identify someone from a distance who would most likely be open to a discussion or help me get the information I needed. Perhaps this is why I moved into corporate sales later in life.

One skill I developed as a solo traveler was the ability to walk quickly and purposefully. This gave the impression that I knew where I was going, even when I was actually lost. Standing alone in the middle of a dimly lit street in an unfamiliar part of town, fumbling with a map, can attract unwanted attention—almost like throwing a bucket of chum into shark-infested waters. This situation can draw in individuals looking to exploit your vulnerability and possibly relieve you of your valuables, which could force you to book the next available flight home.

In moments when I felt threatened or found myself in situations that could quickly escalate into danger, I made sure to stand tall, move with intention, and stay aware of my surroundings. I learned to identify the exits nearby, observe the movement of people around me, and analyze whether there was any coordination among them. I would scan the area to see who was looking in my direction, making brief but intentional eye contact to convey that I noticed them and could likely describe them if needed.

Additionally, I sought out places where other travelers were gathered, ducked into businesses, cafés, or hotel lobbies as needed, and paid attention to choke points or areas where I could get trapped.

Be aware, open your eyes, keep moving, and stay calm.

While traveling in Indonesia, I visited a temple of some significance. The temple attracted lots of travelers, so many hawkers and pickpockets circled nearby, watching for an easy mark. After wrapping my bare white legs with a sarong, I walked toward the temple. A large tour group was gathered near the entrance, fiddling with their cameras and pointing, so I searched for an alternative entrance—a side door. I walked around the temple, away from the crowd of tourists. I suddenly felt like the antelope that had wandered away from the herd and was now being watched by the lions in the tall grass.

Hearing footsteps behind me, I looked over my shoulder as I walked and saw two young local guys walking casually behind me. "Mister! Hey, mister!" one said as they closed the distance between us. "You want a special tour?" His English was well-rehearsed.

I spun around and, walking backward, said, "No, thank you." I kept moving. They closed the distance even more, now just six feet behind me. No one spoke. I was passing the point of no return as we rounded the corner behind the temple in an overgrown alley with only splintered daylight. I stopped when I saw cigarette smoke coming from around the corner just ahead of me. The guys behind me stepped closer as I stood there, evaluating the situation I'd got myself into. I knew what this was. They'd corralled me into a pinch point, out of sight, where they could have an opportunity to roll me and then scurry back into the dark, bougainvillea-covered maze of alleys and side streets.

I planted my feet, turned, and looked them right in the eyes. No one spoke. The man with the cigarette was now in view just behind me, along with another guy. The four guys circled me as we stared at each other. Luckily, I was not dealing with seasoned older criminals but rather young men looking for an easy target to grab some beer money. I pulled the second strap of my pack onto my shoulder and clipped the center harness in place. The two guys in front of me started chatting nervously about "something special for me," but I shifted my weight forward and moved hard and fast toward them with heavy steps, like a charging rhino, looking right past them. I felt this was not the time to be a polite traveler. I walked through them as if they were not even there, sending one stumbling backward against the temple's stone wall with a muffled thump. Someone grabbed my pack from behind; I turned sharply, ripping his grip from me so hard I could hear one of his fingers pop, and I shouted, "Get the fuck off me!." I kept walking.

One of the guys, and there is always one who is braver than the others, decided to follow me and throw some taunts at my back as I stormed off down the alley. "Come on, big boy!" he yelled. When I reached the corner of the temple, sunlight was again on my face, and other travelers bustled nearby. I turned, dropped my pack, and put my arms out, inviting my brave new friend to leave the safety of the shadows. He stood there with a devilish grin and lit a cigarette. A guide from a nearby tour saw my unfriendly hand gesture and came over to see what was happening. The guys slipped around the corner and down the alley. I'd got into that situation as a result of not thinking. I knew better.

CHAPTER EIGHT
A STEP CLOSER TO THE EDGE

Security is mostly a superstition. It does not exist in nature,
nor do the children of men as a whole experience it.
Avoiding danger is no safer in the long run than outright
exposure. Life is either a daring adventure or nothing.

Helen Keller

While in Indonesia, I traveled to Irian Jaya, now known as Papua. My former employer, Norman, served on the board of directors for one of the large mining companies that operated significant copper and gold mines in the mountainous region of Irian Jaya. He recommended that I visit the mines during my stay in Indonesia and arranged for someone in his office to handle all the necessary arrangements.

I was aware that the region had faced violence recently, mainly in the form of kidnappings. At that time, an ongoing conflict existed between two indigenous groups: the Asmat and the Dani tribes. The Asmat tribe was notorious for its practices of cannibalism and headhunting, which, although banned in the 1950s, were believed to have persisted well into the 1980s and even later in more remote regions.

The Asmat and the Dani are both indigenous tribes, but they have many differences. The Asmat are known for their aggressive behavior toward other tribes. One of the most well-known stories related to the Asmat's cannibalism involved an expedition to the Asmat region in what was then called Dutch New Guinea in 1961, led by Michael Rockefeller. This expedition was brief and ended on a disturbing note. Michael, the son of then-governor Nelson Rockefeller of New York, was captured by the Asmat as he swam to shore after his dugout canoe overturned. According to the tribal elders, he was ultimately killed and consumed.

The Dani are recognized for their structured ideology and organized intertribal warfare, which follows a set of rules. These skirmishes between tribes aim to alleviate tensions without escalating to full-scale warfare.

The commonality between the two tribes is their shared disdain for the Indonesian Army and the large mining companies in the region, which disrupt their way of life.

I received several warnings about traveling to this location, including from the US State Department, as it was highly unsafe for Western travelers, especially those linked to mining operations. Despite this, I decided to go because Norman's office had made all the arrangements, and I felt reassured by that support.

A few months before my arrival, twenty-six hostages, including a pregnant Dutch woman, were taken into the jungle by the Free Papua Movement. This incident prompted a strong response from the Indonesian Army, which eventually secured the release of many hostages. Unfortunately, two of the white hostages were killed by their captors, leading to the urgent travel warnings from the State Department.

I flew from Denpasar via Sulawesi to Timika, Irian Jaya. When the plane touched down at Mozes Kilangin Airport in Timika, it was clear that this place was experiencing heavy civil unrest; you could feel it in the air—the chain link fence all around the airport building bore witness to the turmoil of the place. Indo Army soldiers were everywhere, their SS1 assault rifles firmly in hands. Their uniforms were dusty and wrinkled. These guys were not there for show; they expected trouble at any moment and were prepared for it.

I grabbed my pack and walked toward the front door of the small and, at the time, run-down airport building. The exit doors were chained shut on the inside; an Indo Army soldier was standing by. He took the open padlock off and noisily pulled the length of three-eighths-inch chain from the metal doors as I approached to allow me to walk out.

"Why are there so many people out there?" I asked the soldier, but he didn't respond. I stepped out of the building, sheltered by a large metal roof, and into the agitated crowd of locals. They were upset about the arrival of employees from the Indonesian government and mining companies that day.

A few other passengers on my flight, including guests and employees of the mining company, were quickly whisked away from the burgeoning crowd by their fast-moving escorts. I was the only white person in a sea of dark faces, so there was no blending in. A few men started to circle me as I stood in the parking area in front of the building. I desperately looked around for my ride coming down the dusty road.

Nothing.

The locals circled closer, bumping into me hard enough to knock me off balance. I was being tested to see how I would respond. I kept moving through the crowd toward the road, and the mob moved with me. *Keep moving!* I reminded myself. I put my pack on to free my hands, but they started pulling on it from behind, making walking hard. Arguments erupted within the crowd, building tension and hostility. I was in a precarious situation.

Looking back at the airport doors, now about fifty feet behind me, I started to move in that direction. Suddenly, I was pulled backward. I felt a strap on my pack give way as I pressed forward, giving myself just enough space to step out of the crowd and catch a glimpse of a white Toyota minivan, with the mining company's logo, speeding up the dirt road in a large cloud of dust.

The van stopped near me, and a big white guy with a reddish beard quickly stepped out and said, "Dave Becker?" I eagerly nodded as I pulled my pack off. "Hey, I'm sorry. We have you coming in tomorrow. One of the other drivers said they saw you here alone, so we figured out the mix-up and came right over. Sorry for the hassle."

"No problem. I'm just happy to see you," I said, tossing my dirty pack on the bench seat and climbing in. He closed the door behind me, jogged around to the driver's seat and we drove off before I could sit down.

"Sorry, man, that is not a place you want to be hanging out right now," he said with a confident smile. He extended his meaty hand. "Pete. We are going over here to the Sheraton near town." He pointed down the road before us.

"You have a Sheraton here?" I asked, seeing nothing but small clusters of dust-covered roadside shacks dotting the edge of the dense jungle.

"Yep, the company built everything here: hotel, roads, schools, airport, anything our team and their families would need while working here."

I was amazed by the hotel as we rolled up to the beautifully landscaped entrance and came to a stop. It turned out to be only about a year old and far more luxurious than the budget-traveler places I had been staying at. I was tingly and excited at first, and then a wave of anxiety washed over me. *How the hell am I going to pay for this place?* I had been on the road for about a month and a half, and my cash reserves were low, bordering on paltry.

"Is this the only place I can stay?" I asked Pete as I pulled my pack up and over my shoulder.

"This is it, my friend. This is where we set up our employees and visitors, and you will be safe here." Sensing my stress as we passed the Indo Army guards by the front door, he turned and said, "Not sure who you are, my friend, but orders came down from on high that you are to be taken care of." We walked through the lobby, and Pete greeted the desk agent. "Herman, this is Mr. Becker; he is a VIP guest, and all his expenses should be sent to the office." The desk agent calmly nodded, smiled, and said it would be their pleasure to have me as a guest. It felt surreal in this shiny new lobby in the middle of the jungle, surrounded by such raw civil unrest.

Out of the corner of my eye, I noticed someone reaching for my pack, leaning against my left leg. "Whoa!" I quickly grabbed the pack.

"Excuse me, sir, can I carry this for you?" the startled bellman said. I was accustomed to watching my pack closely; pure muscle memory compelled me to prevent anyone from touching it. I apologized for my reaction.

Pete said goodbye and told me he would pick me up at 8:00 a.m. the next day to show me around. As he turned to leave, he said, "Hey, Dave, make sure to enjoy the whole hotel! Order whatever you want— it's on the house, buddy!" He flashed a big grin and pointed at me.

I followed the bellman through the window-lined hallway, where I saw more Indo Army soldiers standing in the tree line. "They are always here?" I pointed outside.

"No, just recently, sir," he said. "Don't worry. It is okay, and we are safe here. Just don't leave the hotel."

I dropped my pack in the corner of my top-floor room with a beautiful jungle view. I kicked off my dusty shoes and watched the sun slide behind the trees. I was dirty, smelly, and hungry. After the most delightful shower and shave, I dug through my pack to find my least filthy shirt and headed to the main dining room. It almost felt like I was the only guest. There was hardly anyone else there.

"Hello, Mr. Becker. Welcome," the man standing at the podium said as I approached.

"Sorry, I have been traveling," I said with some embarrassment, gesturing to my wrinkled and smelly clothes.

"That is no trouble at all, sir. Would you like to be seated for dinner?" He graciously showed me to a table. As he returned to the podium, he waved over the bellman and talked with him. After serving my wine, the host returned to my table and informed me that he had spoken with the bellman. The hotel offered to clean all my clothes if I would leave them outside my door this evening. *Wow, Norman has some pull here.*

Pete picked me up the following day and showed me what they call the lower land operations, which included administrative offices, support teams, and the like. We drove through town, where I felt so many eyes on me. "You get used to it," he said as he turned onto the road that would take us up to the mining operations. "You don't have an issue with heights, do you?" He laughed.

"Haven't yet," I said.

The road had become so steep that the vehicle struggled to hold the loose gravel and even slid backward a few times as we navigated the sharp switchbacks. The long drive took us to the main mining operation, eight thousand feet above sea level. Most of the mining employees reside at this elevation in a town called Tembagapura, located in the district of the same name within the Mimika Regency, now a part of the Indonesian province of Central Papua. This town was built to support the operations of the mining company.

I asked what it was like for those living there. Pete explained that the town provided everything needed for comfort. At that time, it had a population of over fifteen thousand residents. The new town featured a soccer pitch, coffee shops, an internet café, a grocery store, a school, basketball courts, a fire department, a police department, a movie theater, a hospital, a church, and hundreds of Western-style homes for employees and their families. We drove through a beautifully situated neighborhood with charming, red-roofed cottages nestled within lush jungle gardens with tropical walking paths, where mine managers and their families lived.

The clouds slowly crawled up the sun-warmed mountainside in the late morning, their thick formation casting soft shadows over the vibrant green vegetation. As the day progressed, a palpable humidity filled the air, heralding the cloudburst downpours that would arrive almost every afternoon. Heavy raindrops tapping against the leaves created a soothing symphony that enveloped the forest. This was my first encounter with a tropical cloud forest, an enchanting ecosystem where the interplay of light, moisture, and life painted an unforgettable picture. I remember telling myself I would happily live here for a year or two. I found this place enchanting and dripping with expat adventure.

The cabin measured thirty feet by twenty feet with two single beds, a simple kitchen, and a bathroom. I had the place to myself. My hosts advised me to stay inside that evening and assured me the cabin had everything I needed.

"Lock your door tonight, buddy. Someone will come get you around 8:00 a.m.," Pete said, giving me a comforting wave as he walked back to the truck.

Though still happily enjoying myself, I felt an undercurrent of tension. As the sun sank behind the mountaintops, casting a warm glow that gradually faded into twilight, the activity on the town's dirt roads gave way to an unsettling stillness. Shadows stretched longer, and the familiar buzz of life transformed into an eerie silence. I was acutely aware that I wasn't the only one staying indoors after dark.

The following day, another mine manager, Bob, picked me up and took me to the mine. We rode in a cable car to the elevation where most of the mining occurred, approximately fourteen thousand feet above sea level. The snowy peaks of the massive mountains loomed at just over sixteen thousand feet. During the ride, a woman geologist with us suddenly collapsed on the floor, overwhelmed by the altitude. As a result, the staff promptly dropped us off at one of the mines and took her back down the mountain to receive medical attention.

"You good?" Bob asked as he looked into my eyes to make sure I was stable and not in danger of losing consciousness as we approached the top of the ride.

"I'm doing just fine, thanks."

We quickly surveyed the mine, which was extraordinarily vast and overwhelming in scale. Bob mentioned that this particular mine is the world's largest gold mine and the third-largest copper mine. Its immense size is evident in the mile-wide open pit that can be seen from space, making it the largest man-made open excavation on the planet at that time. I stood next to the enormous Komatsu and Caterpillar dump trucks, which required climbing two flights of stairs to reach the cab. The tires, standing over twelve feet high, made me feel small in comparison.

Bob explained that they had a security issue at the mine and had seen a few vicious attacks over the years. He explained that many local tribes were unhappy about the mining companies in the area.

"We have to keep our eyes open here, Dave," he said. "These guys can come walking out of the forest anytime. We have lost good people."

Mining equipment had been damaged and fires set. Even with this information, I remained comfortable with the idea of working there for a while if the opportunity arose.

Later that day, Bob and I drove down the mountain from Tembagapura to Timika in the lowlands along those steep, slippery, gravelly switchbacks. Once we reached the bottom of the hill, I asked Bob if it would be okay if I walked through town for a little while to take photographs. He said he would be more comfortable if one of his guys were with me, so he arranged for me to be picked up at the hotel at 8:00 a.m. the following day to check out the town.

"In the meantime, Dave, make full use of your stay at the hotel," he said out the open passenger window as I pulled my pack onto my shoulder. "Everything is on the house."

"Thanks, man!"

"Don't leave the hotel tonight unless these guys are with you, okay?" he said, smiling and pointing to the Indo Army soldiers bracketing the front doors to the hotel.

As I walked by the dining room, the host asked if I wanted anything sent to my room that evening. I enjoyed being on the receiving end of excellent service for a change. I took advantage of this opportunity and looked through the menu he handed me, along with the wine list. "The 1990 Penfolds Cabernet Shiraz is very nice," he said.

"Perfect, thank you," I said, and had them add some of the pâté along with the fillet of beef with Gorgonzola and a big slice of New York cheesecake.

"I will have it brought up very soon, Mr. Becker," he said, offering a polite nod. I felt a little guilty; the wine was on the list for over one hundred dollars US, but Pete did say to take full advantage, right?

My guilty feelings quickly drifted away as I sat with my feet up by the window of my room, gazing out at the sunset over the treetops and sipping my remarkable wine. I watched the camouflaged Indo Army soldiers drift in and out of the tree line fifty yards from the hotel. This was an image I had only seen on the news of faraway conflicts, never with my own eyes. I felt the vast separation between different ways of life. I wondered what the soldiers, risking their lives, would think of me reclining in the window of this luxury hotel, drinking fine wine and eating steak and nibbling on blueberry cheesecake. Part of me wanted to open the window, lean out, and shout to them, "Hey, guys! I'm not paying for this! I can't afford it!"

The following day, Pete was waiting for me outside the hotel entrance in his white mining operations pickup truck. When we got to town, we walked down the small streets on the outskirts of town. With my camera slung around my neck, I stepped over mud puddles on the dirt road and tried not to slip. Simple wooden shacks and large sheds with peeling paint lined the streets, dirt splattered up their sides from last night's heavy rains. I felt eyes on me as we walked. I avoided some large puddles and approached a small house where a group of kids sat on the porch rail. They were following my every movement with their serious eyes. I gestured with my Nikon 35mm film camera and asked if I could take their photograph. They just watched.

"Not sure they know what your camera is, Dave," Pete said quietly.

As I turned from Pete, I stepped into the middle of a deep puddle. The warm, muddy water rose to about six inches below my right knee. "Oh, fuck me!" I said as I pulled my soaked boot out of the mud with a loud, wet sucking sound. I looked up, and the kids stared, unsure what this giant, clumsy white man was doing on their road. I looked up and just laughed. Their faces lit up, and they burst out laughing, as did Pete, which made a beautiful black-and-white photograph. Their kindness and warmth shone through despite their natural wariness.

I was dropped off at the hotel again a couple of hours later. On the ride back, Pete explained that they had arranged for me to fly out the following day. "Dave, things are heating up here, so we are going to put you back on the plane a few days earlier than we had planned," he said calmly, as he carefully steered the truck through the muddy streets.

He told me that things had become a little tense, with threats and local conflicts escalating this week, and it would be best if I cut my trip short and hit the trail. He was heading back up the hill to the mine later that morning.

The pool was a good choice for my last day in Irian Jaya, especially since the sun was still out. I changed into my board shorts and wandered down to the boulder-lined lagoon-style pool, stopping by the bar to grab a couple of ice-cold South Pacific Lagers. I spent my last afternoon sipping cold beer in a beautiful pool, the only other person in sight the bartender.

The next morning, with a pack full of clean clothes and a belly full of good food, I was leaving the Sheraton Timika for the last time. The desk agent approached me in the lobby and explained that the flight was late due to some issues at the airport. So, I waited in the lobby. Two hours later, the hotel van approached the entrance, where I was waiting just inside, and the driver hastily waved me over. Things felt different this morning. The tension was palpable. There was a heaviness in the air at the hotel that wasn't there when I arrived, and the friendly service had been replaced with a quiet prudence. I tossed my pack on the middle bench seat of the van and pulled myself into the front seat. I looked at the soldiers as we pulled away, holding their shotguns like they were guarding a bank.

The driver did not speak. I was becoming unsettled with all this and knew I would have to move quickly and get on that plane. I had a pit in my stomach. We stopped about twenty yards from the airport's front entrance. I slung my pack over my right shoulder, turned toward the entrance, and started walking. Once again, there was a crowd of men gathered outside the building. It looked like a mix of Asmat and locals from Tamika, probably close to a hundred people. They pressed into me as I walked, making it difficult to move through. They were pulling at my pack. The white hotel van was now a cloud of dust, moving quickly down the road and back to the town's safety.

The sounds of a violent fight erupted behind me. I turned to see two shirtless men attempting to kill each other just a few feet away, sending hostile vibrations through the crowd like ripples from a stone thrown into a still pond. I used this distraction to move quickly to the terminal's front entrance and pulled the door hard, but it was locked and chained from inside. The mob pressed against me as I pounded my fist on the door, my heart racing. The shouting grew louder. A soldier peeked out, quickly dropped the chains from the door, and pushed it open.

"You are not safe here," he said.

"Yeah, no shit!" I said, stepping through the airport door and past the guard.

I pulled the pack up and got both shoulders through the straps so it sat squarely on my back as I moved urgently to the counter. I was breathing heavily, my heart still pounding. Many people had gathered in the small terminal, trying to get off the island. There was a stench of stress in the place. Babies were crying. Men were pacing. I got my paper ticket from the counter, shoved it in my pocket, and waited by the door leading to the tarmac where the Garuda Indonesia turboprop plane was waiting. I leaned my pack against the chain link fence.

The agent walked over to the gate entrance and unlocked the chain, letting it fall to the ground. The distressed crowd quickly moved toward me by the gate, pressing me against the wall and disregarding the agent's instructions to stand back. I pushed toward the gate door, where the frazzled Garuda employee stood. He examined the paper tickets thrust at him as quickly as possible and moved people past, one at a time, for boarding. "Queue, please! Queue, please!" he shouted at the agitated mob. I handed him my ticket, and he waved me through the gate to the gray metal door leading to the boarding area. The space had become noisy and tense, with people shouting, pushing, and arguing.

When I reached the door leading out to the tarmac and the waiting plane, I felt a sharp tug on my pack, pulling me backward. Two men pushed me against the doorframe as they tried to get past me. Something in me snapped. With all my strength, I shoved one of the men into the opposite side of the doorframe. The side of his face hit the metal with a bony thud, and he fell back into the crowd behind him, which erupted in more shouting.

I quickly walked to the plane, climbed aboard, tossed my backpack into the broken overhead compartment above my seat, and sat down. The condition of the aircraft was unlike anything I had ever seen. My eyes followed the exposed wiring above, hanging precariously outside the overhead luggage compartments. I noticed cockroaches darting across the aisles near my feet and the lavatory door hanging askew on its hinges, unable to close completely. Typically, these issues would cause considerable concern to me and anyone accustomed to flying on more modern and well-maintained aircraft. However, today I found that I no longer cared. I just needed to get out of there.

A few minutes after I took my seat, a local man boarded the plane escorted by an armed soldier. Seeing a sidearm in the aisle of a commercial aircraft felt surreal. The shirtless, bearded man had his hands shackled and secured to a chain around his waist, which was connected to ankle chains. I could smell his musky, wild scent as he walked past me. Bits of leaves and dirt were caught in his coal-black beard, clearly indicating the struggle that must have occurred during his arrest.

When our eyes met, I saw that, despite their cold and dark appearance, there was fear behind them. They took their seats two rows behind me.

I placed my headphones over my ears, turned up the volume, and pressed play on my Sony Discman. As the plane began to taxi across the wet and broken pavement, Pink Floyd's "Shine On You Crazy Diamond" played, helping to frame this pivotal moment in my life.

Like a child, I wandered, wide-eyed and naïve, into a reality I was unprepared to experience. Humbled and thankful, I walked away a wiser man.

The turboprop aircraft gracefully climbed above the lush green canopy, revealing the intricate tapestry of rich foliage dotting the landscape below, camouflaging the unrest and tension. As we turned toward the western sky, the warm hues of the setting sun painted the horizon, prompting me to reflect on this incredible journey. Though I may not have fully appreciated the experience then, I am profoundly grateful for the opportunity to have visited such an amazing place. As we ascended to cruising altitude, the breathtaking landscape of the dark, exotic jungle world slowly faded from view, transforming into a cherished memory etched in my mind.

CHAPTER NINE
SHIFTING GEARS

There is nothing so stable as change.

Bob Dylan

After returning to Los Angeles, I spent the next couple of years designing and installing estate gardens in Bel Air and Beverly Hills for some friends of Norman, even though I had left his employment. I bought a new truck and some tools and hired a friend who had recently returned to LA after a long tour as a roadie for Ted Nugent. While this work paid well, I soon realized my heart was no longer in it. I completed the projects competently, but I strongly desired to move away from catering to such an upscale and affluent clientele.

I also grew tired of being summoned to the master bedroom by the lady of the house to examine some potted plant that required my immediate attention, followed by the awkward encounter that usually ensued. I practiced quick and graceful exits from those situations. While some guys may enjoy the notion of succumbing to such tempting scenarios, it doesn't feel good as a person to allow that into your life in that way. As a result, I always made sure to have an escape plan.

After work, I often sat on the beach near the pier in Santa Monica, where I lived with my girlfriend, Stef. She eventually became my first wife and the mother of my two amazing sons, Max and Ben. We lived about fifteen blocks from the beach, so I would make the short drive to relax with my toes in the sand and gaze at the soft, golden horizon of the Pacific Ocean. I have always found that I do my best thinking near the sea or in the mountains.

One late fall afternoon, while sitting and inhaling the salty air, I realized I was at a crossroads in my life, and the understanding that it was time to pursue other passions settled within me. I took stock of my interests then: music, wine, travel, writing, and gardening. I focused on each interest, like picking up a beautiful stone, examining it carefully, and then setting it down again.

I recalled the deep connection I felt to wine while working with Ron. After leaving my estate management job, I continued exploring my growing passion for wine by reading everything I could find on the subject. Every week, I spent hours browsing the selections at nearby wine shops and conversing with wine professionals whenever I had the chance. I was truly immersing myself in the world of wine, and it felt right. The joy it brought me and the lifestyle surrounding this remarkable beverage were incredibly inviting. My interest in working with wine captivated me more than anything else; it felt like the right fit. I wanted to enter the wine business, but now I needed to figure out how to break into this elusive industry.

My passion for wine had deepened into something more significant than just a hobby. I compare it to the enthusiasm of a baseball fan who knows every statistic about their favorite players and teams. I had researched an all-star lineup of winemakers and founders, such as

Robert Mondavi, Mike Grgich, Warren Winiarski, Heidi Barrett, Paul Draper, and many exceptional producers from France and Italy. As a result, I quickly fell in love with their craft.

I often found myself lying awake at night, creating imaginary wine lists for the fine dining restaurant I envisioned owning one day. *The left bank Bordeaux doesn't feel right*, I would think while staring at the ceiling. *I need more selections from Saint-Julien and Saint-Estèphe. And oh my goodness, imagine if I had a few vintages of Château Margaux!* I would mentally run through the best vintages, picturing how to effectively arrange the descriptions on my list to showcase my little gems. I was deeply in love with this idea, nearing the point of obsession.

A few days later, I walked into Wally's, my favorite wine shop in West Los Angeles, where I had spent hours poking around the vast wine sections looking for the next little gem to try. I caught up with one of the stewards I knew and inquired if they needed help. My steward friend treated me to an espresso and asked me to wait momentarily. He returned with the general manager, who invited me to his office for a chat.

"What are you into right now?" Chris asked as he leaned back in the chair at his desk.

"I have been diving deep into Rhône wines lately," I said.

"Yeah, sure. North or south? What producers are you drinking?"

"Just popped an awesome Côte-Rôtie a few days ago at a barbecue. Loved it."

"And the producer?" he asked.

"Guigal. Also getting into bubbles a lot."

"Champagne? What houses?" he asked, looking down at his blinking phone.

"Well, I could say Moet and Veuve, but honestly, I find Billecart-Salmon and Ruinart much more interesting."

Chris stood up from his desk and extended his hand. "Wanna work with us?" he asked with a smile.

I wrapped up the two estate projects I had been working on, broke the news to my one employee, and found myself in a completely different world a few weeks later. It was the fall of 1996, marking the beginning of a long and memorable career in the wine business.

Wally's was an impressive establishment, attracting wine enthusiasts of all types and a range of West LA celebrities with its seemingly endless selection of fine and allocated wines from around the world. Wine retailers such as this hold significant influence in the market and often have the first option to acquire the most highly sought-after wines. Over the following months, I received training in nearly every area of the business. I worked at the sales counter, assisted buyers at events, managed inventory, worked on the sales floor, and even delivered orders. I embraced it all and thoroughly enjoyed learning about this new world of retail wine.

On one of my first days working behind the counter, Mr. T walked in, high-fived a few employees he knew, and made his way to the deli counter. Having grown up watching *The A-Team*, I thought this was a big deal. "Holy cow! I am about to meet B. A. Baracus!" I said to the younger sales guy leaning on the counter beside me, who seemed less impressed.

Mr. T came up front to pay for his sandwich and could not have been nicer. "I pity the fool who tries to take my Wally's tuna fish sandwich!" he said, slapping a twenty-dollar bill on the counter in front of me with that big smile. I couldn't help but stare at those gold rings on his humongous hand. *I would hate to get hit by that.*

I quietly monitored the delivery schedule posted each day behind the counter and offer to make the deliveries if I noticed something interesting. I was fortunate to visit the private homes of incredible entertainers like Danny DeVito and Bob Newhart. That November, I delivered chilled champagne and Guinness to Pierce Brosnan's green room in Burbank as he prepared for his appearance on *The Tonight Show with Jay Leno.*

Being LA, not all our patrons were as principled as those mentioned above. Late one Saturday afternoon, I was at the front counter next to Steve, the owner, when a suspicious fellow stepped into the store wearing a hoodie, milled about awkwardly for a few seconds, and then quickly snatched a bottle of something delectable from the Bordeaux wall and darted out the door. Without thinking, I said, "I'll get him." I pushed past my associates behind the counter and started for the door after the surprisingly agile Bordeaux bandit.

Steve grabbed my arm. "No, let him go." As I returned to my post behind the counter, he pointed at me. "But I like that!" he said and gave me an appreciative wink.

Soon after, I was asked to take on a significant project for Steve. He had purchased a small warehouse adjacent to the store, intending to use it for a part of his rapidly growing business—wine futures. Most of his clientele were deeply interested in investing substantial sums of money in wine futures, particularly from Burgundy and Bordeaux.

Wine futures, also known as *en primeur*, involve purchasing wine after it has been produced and aged in barrels for a few months, before being bottled or made available for sale. Once writers and journalists review and score the wines and vintages, select wholesalers and retail buyers can purchase them. When the wines are eventually bottled, they are shipped to the buyers.

The adjacent warehouse would serve as a secure storage area for these expensive and highly sought-after wines until their new owners could retrieve them for their cellars. I worked alone. My job was to receive the wines, inspect them for breakage or any signs of damage, record them in the inventory, secure them, and update the in-house buyers on the stock. I created my storage system and carefully secured and cataloged the magnificent wines. I would marvel at the deliveries that came into our little futures warehouse, including Calon-Ségur, La Tâche, Margaux, Chateau Pavie, Mouton Rothschild, Lafite, Pétrus, and even Cheval Blanc, which was seen years later in the movie *Sideways* as the exceedingly expensive and cherished wine that Miles enjoyed out of a Styrofoam cup in that fast-food restaurant, and yes, it is a merlot.

A year or so later, we moved back to the East Coast. Stef had secured a consulting job in New York City, so we relocated. I remained passionate about wine, so we rented a small house in the mid-Hudson area, a well-respected wine-producing region, and maintained an apartment in Manhattan through Stef's work. I soon landed a job at Millbrook Winery in Dutchess County, which is known for its exceptional wines. I trained in various departments, including the tasting room, winery events, winemaking, and the bottling line. This diverse experience provided excellent training. We often traveled between our home in the wine country and the city apartment via MTA's Hudson Line.

A year passed quickly, and we found ourselves again packing for another big move, this time to the Pacific Northwest. We were expecting our first child and knew New York was not where we wanted to settle for the long haul. Stef, an architect, was offered a position at a firm in Portland, Oregon, and I was confident I could land something in the wine business; it was Oregon, for goodness' sake! So, I packed a twenty-foot moving truck and drove it out to set up our new home outside Portland.

I returned to wine retail as a steward, which I was comfortable doing. First, I worked at a high-end grocery store called Zupan's, and later, I was invited to manage the much-higher-volume wine and beer department at a new flagship Safeway store up the hill in West Linn. One thing led to the next, and I found myself overseeing all 123 wine departments for the chain in Oregon and southwest Washington in the newly created position of Field Merchandiser—Alcohol. I enjoyed working with the Safeway team and made many friends there. They are such wonderful people.

Later, I received an offer for a more prominent sales role at one of the larger wine suppliers in the industry. In this new position, I worked closely with my former team at Safeway, who had transitioned from being my employers to becoming my customers. Little did I know that this wine supplier would play a significant role in my career, taking me on a roller coaster ride I would not soon forget.

CHAPTER TEN
TRY TO SAY THAT WITHOUT USING THE WORD "ROBUST." THE CORPORATE YEARS

If you want to kill any idea in the world,
get a committee working on it.

Charles F. Kettering

"Are you back tonight, Dave?" Janice the flight attendant asked as I slid into seat 1A, as I always did on the short flight to Boise.

"Nah, I have a dinner tonight over there, so I will be on the early one tomorrow," I said as I dug around with my left hand to find my seat belt.

Taking out my printed presentation for a final review before landing in Boise, I felt a mix of comfort and loneliness about flight attendants recognizing me by name. *I have been traveling too much.* This realization led me to reflect on how many times I had taken this flight, or similar ones, over the nearly fifteen years I'd been with the company. I estimated that I'd made the hour-and-ten-minute journey from Portland to Boise on Alaska Airlines approximately 140 times, not to mention even more flights to Seattle.

I walked out of the gate area, up the escalator, and past the gift shop. I waved to the counterperson, whose name I should have known by now, before exiting through the front entrance of the airport. It took me four minutes and seven seconds from stepping off the plane to the airport's front door—not my best time, but still respectable. I swung my black bag off my shoulder and let it drop onto the frost-covered bench beside my zipped leather presentation binder while my cell phone remained pinched between my right shoulder and ear, as it usually was. I waited for my ride.

As a supplier in the corporate wine industry, I worked with several major grocery chains in the Northwest. At one point, my team and I were responsible for managing all grocery chain accounts across a five-state region, which accounted for approximately 85 percent of our division's total business. These large grocery chains were crucial to our company's success, and this responsibility came with significant pressure.

Meetings with chain buyers were a critical part of my job. A successful meeting could lead to the approval of our regional or national programming, resulting in thousands of additional cases of wine being sold within a short promotional sales period. Sales managers for larger wine companies, like the one I worked for, were expected to secure this level of programming regularly. Failure to do so could jeopardize our position with major accounts or lead to more severe consequences. That was the job.

As an example, on a given day I might make a sales call at the headquarters of one of the large chain retailers located in the Seattle area. While this chain has impressive sales volume, it isn't my largest or favorite account. The employees and store managers are friendly, hardworking, and operate well-maintained stores. However, my meeting is not in one of the stores; I am meeting with the senior buyer for my category at the company's office. This individual oversees all alcoholic beverages for hundreds of stores within the chain's sales region and is the sole decision-maker for the wine sold in those stores. He wields significant influence in the industry, especially concerning suppliers and distributors, and he is very aware of his power. He can make or break even the largest wine suppliers, including the one I represent.

The atmosphere in the buying offices at large grocery chains can sometimes be uncomfortable. Common issues include bullying, dishonesty, gift expectations, and intimidation during sales calls. I have experienced these problems at this chain and others.

Buyer meetings at headquarters typically include suppliers, buyers, and distributors, with around four to six participants, often sales managers and analysts. Buyers receive brand information from distributors, covering marketing details, pricing, trends, and promotional programs to aid decision-making. Sales managers from larger suppliers engage directly with buyers for major retailers, offering analytics, market insights, and promotional strategies, with a strong focus on the numbers in wine planning.

Buyers focus on pricing when making decisions and use past sales data to set target profit margins for ads or promotions. Discussing pricing can be tricky, as only retailers and distributors can have these conversations; suppliers cannot. Once we sell our product to the distributors, it is no longer our responsibility to manage or price it. This rule is part of the three-tier system for selling beverage alcohol in the Northwest. In this system, distributors buy from suppliers and sell to retailers, who then sell to consumers. Each party makes a profit.

Most corporate buyers are knowledgeable about this system and abide by its laws. However, some individuals may push everyone to the limit to achieve their goal: a lower cost of goods.

I would begin by reviewing the promotional activities from the past few months, utilizing data from sources like IRI or Nielsen to analyze a specific brand's performance within the retailer's business. Additionally, I would incorporate data on price analysis, profit margin improvements, and household penetration trends. All these elements would be combined to create a compelling narrative: "You ran our brand, and it generated significant profits for you, so you should consider running it again." This approach embodies straightforward, fact-based selling.

Set up the "win."

At this point in the discussion, it all comes down to numbers. The conversation flows smoothly whenever the right data points were presented. I always aim to provide honest information. Occasionally, large retailers would call me to verify the work of others. "Does this seem accurate to you, Dave?" they would ask over the phone. I would pull the current industry data, create a snapshot report, and send it back to them as a resource to help them evaluate the work of less-than-reputable sales managers. I became a trusted source of market information in my industry because I never played unfairly. I used accurate numbers, whether good, bad, or otherwise.

As one of the larger wine companies in the industry, we often held some of the largest market share in our category, which presented us with a unique set of challenges. We needed to be high performers since we represented a significant portion of a retailer's business. If we sneezed, the retailer would catch a cold, and vice versa.

Our goal was to be the best team among suppliers. We needed top-notch analysts, strong category managers, and skilled sales managers to compete effectively with other suppliers. It was essential for us to outperform the competition consistently. Unlike smaller suppliers who anxiously awaited in the lobby for brief ten-minute "meet and greet" appointments with buyers, we were focused on collaboration, building stronger relationships, and delivering measurable results.

I usually had first pick of the best meeting times and often held the longest ones. I was also given priority when big buyers had lunch or dinner times available. In some instances, my biggest buyers became friends outside of work. We frequently got together on weekends for dinner or drinks. One of these buyers even had his band perform at my birthday party in my backyard. This helped to foster a comfortable, respectful, and professional working relationship.

It was satisfying to know that my competitors had to look at the screensaver picture of me standing next to their buyer, holding a fish, while they nervously made their presentations.

Reaching this level in the industry required considerable time and effort. When I transitioned from Safeway to the supplier side of the industry, I faced a challenging adjustment. Although I was still in the same field, I now viewed it from a different perspective. I finished my work at the Safeway office on a Friday afternoon and started my new position with a large wine supplier the following Monday morning.

My new boss, a spirited woman named Veronica, invited me to join her on my first morning in my new role. We were scheduled to meet with one of the major buyers in Oregon, who happened to be a fierce competitor of the company I had just left. This was her appointment with the buyer, and I was there to observe as part of my training. The Friday before, Veronica and I had met for lunch, during which she gave me my new Blackberry phone. I hadn't fully set it up or switched it to silent mode, so, of course, it rang just as he started talking— definitely a rookie mistake.

"Give it to me," he said coldly, with a plug of chewing tobacco pinched in his lower lip as he outstretched his brick-like hand.

"Give you what?" I asked, looking over to my boss, unsure what was happening. He snapped his fingers several times at me and pointed to my pocket, which housed my new, recently silenced Blackberry. *Why is this man snapping his fingers at me?* "You want to see my phone?" I handed it across the desk. The buyer proceeded to disassemble my new phone in silence, dismantling it piece by piece and laying out the components across the desk as if field-stripping a revolver. I looked at Veronica quizzically. She giggled nervously. In the few seconds that our eyes met, I could see she was also terribly uncomfortable in this awkward situation. I later realized she did not have the strength or courage to stand up to him and say, "That's enough. That is company property." She, too, was a victim of corporate bullying.

Right there in front of my new boss, Mark delivered an absolute tongue-lashing about a supplier's phone ringing while he was talking. That was chiseled in stone directly under "Thou shalt not kill" in the Ten Commandments. I must have missed that one in my Sunday school classes.

I was a young dad with kids, a mortgage, and a big house remodel underway that, by all measures, we could not afford. It was a challenging time in my life because my first wife and I had just recently made the agonizing decision to go our separate ways and file for divorce. I was in a very vulnerable position financially and emotionally. I had no choice but to sit there and take Mark's abuse. This behavior was a part of my new job, but I was compelled to set aside a part of myself that day and carefully place it in a drawer labeled "Open When Safe." I understood that I needed to earn money to support my family, and this was the way to do it. This was the path I chose to follow, and there was no sense in dwelling on it.

That phone never worked right after that day. All because my wife called to wish me a happy first day at my new job.

This experience marked the beginning of nearly fifteen years of enduring aggression and bullying from middle management. Instead of complaining and reporting these workplace issues, I chose to work hard to excel in my role. I did this partly to shield myself from further abusive criticism. I dedicated countless hours to studying the business of my major buyers, learning what drove them, what they needed, and how they preferred to receive it. My focus on avoiding mistakes became my sole priority. However, this led to exhaustion and fatigue.

I would spend an entire day building a presentation for my big buyers and another day rehearsing, polishing, and fine-tuning the delivery until it was perfect. I would master the small nuances needed to deliver a meaningful and engaging presentation, sharply focused on overcoming any possible objection or concern, even a ringing phone. I excelled in my role.

My defensive strategy focused on achieving perfection in all aspects of my work, whether interacting with buyers, distributors, or colleagues. Unfortunately, the environment was often unfriendly. Unlike my previous jobs in hotels, my time with Norman, or my experience at Safeway—where I felt safe to express my true self and ideas without fear of criticism or attack—this situation created a deep, unsettling anxiety. I realized that I needed to protect myself in this role.

As the months passed, I became increasingly proficient in my work and refined my presentation skills. During meetings with retailers and distributors, I was sometimes compared to a news anchor, delivering information calmly, skillfully, and analytically. I presented pragmatic ideas without emotion, always building to a strong close.

I was learning how to build a fortress around myself, and that took a great deal of emotional resources and discipline but was, I felt, necessary. I was closing myself off. Looking back, I was building a new version of myself—an avatar, of sorts. In these situations, a simulacrum would replace my authentic self, which could survive in this bleak and sometimes hostile environment while my true self retreated to a safe, quiet hiding place.

I once faced a particularly challenging situation that reinforced my overly defensive attitude. One of the lead buyers I worked with at a large grocery chain in Washington was a unique form of bully. He introduced a program for his wine category that offered coupons for purchasing multiple bottles of wine. While this approach aimed to encourage sales and initially seemed reasonable, it quickly became chaotic and exceedingly costly for suppliers. As a result, many suppliers began to withdraw, leaving only the larger ones and a few smaller ones who felt too intimidated to speak directly with this dominant buyer.

Consequently, we and the other remaining suppliers were depleting our budgets on the program.

I reached a point in my business where I had to stop participating in the program because our spending had become exorbitant, and the return was decreasing. It was no longer a responsible use of my company's money, and I needed to stop it. At this point, some legal gray areas were developing in the program, which gave my team some indigestion—a line I would not cross. I needed to make a responsible decision for my company and redirect our budget dollars to other programs that would provide a more desirable result.

I sent a detailed email to Dick, the buyer in question, explaining our company's reduced participation in the program. The email included specific data and reasoning, outlining this change's rationale. I also scheduled a meeting with him in his office the following week to discuss the matter in person. Unfortunately, this meeting turned out to be the most uncomfortable experience of corporate bullying I have ever encountered, and I have dealt with my fair share of such situations.

I followed Dick out of the lobby and up to his office; he didn't say a word. We entered the "cube farm," a large room on the second floor filled with dozens of cubicles outside his office. Instead of walking across to his office, he turned and asked me to step into another room just to our right. It was the smallest meeting room I had ever seen. The room contained only two chairs, nothing else. He pointed to one of the chairs, curtly telling me to sit. He closed the door behind us in the windowless room, turned his chair around, and sat in it backward so he could lean on the backrest while facing me.

"What do you think you are doing?" he said, leaning in, with building aggression in his eyes. Assuming he spoke about the coupon program, I reiterated what I had emailed him, explaining why my company would stop our participation. The buyer then began to scold me, professionally and personally. I let him take his jabs at me, including his questioning what kind of man I was and even what kind of example I was for my kids, and then threatening to pull all my brands from his category if I didn't "play ball," as he phrased it. This was a shakedown.

As he finished his attack, I leaned toward him, looked him in the eye, and calmly said, "I am not comfortable with how you are speaking to me, so it needs to stop."

"That's too bad, Dave. Get used to it."

"I am sure you are not asking me to do anything illegal or unethical, are you?" I asked in a cold tone.

I felt I was splitting into two parts: one half remained professional and composed, while the other half was a big guy who could easily overpower the angry little man in front of me. I sat calmly and represented my company well. After he took his pound of flesh and tired himself out, we moved into his office to meet with the others. I then began my presentation, but it did not go well.

During my mostly ignored presentation, I fantasized about another way this could play out, perhaps in some other reality, soothing a darker and more damaged part of me. I envisioned the bright yellow caution tape stretched taut across the entrance to the cramped, unheated meeting room. A police radio crackled urgently in the corridor, filling the air with fragmented snippets of tense communication. The lights were out. First responders were diligently cutting the duct tape and working to extract the furious buyer, who had been unceremoniously stuffed into a large trash can, upside down, now an incongruous centerpiece in that minuscule meeting space. The kicking, squirming, and thumping were accompanied by a barrage of the most offensive profanity. A piece of copy paper was neatly taped to the side of the trash can. The note read, "A Dick in a Can," accompanied by a perfectly drawn arrow pointing upward, as if it were the title card for some offbeat art installation.

In the doorway, a cluster of office workers gathered, their faces illuminated by the glow of their smartphones as they snapped pictures, capturing the bizarre spectacle. The man's bare legs thrashed wildly in a frantic attempt to free himself from the embarrassing confines of the smelly bin, as muffled laughter mixed uneasily with gasps of disbelief. The scandalous images and videos flooded Instagram within moments, spreading the surreal scene far beyond the office walls.

"What the hell happened here, Sergeant?" the captain asked.

"Never seen anything like it before, Captain," the sergeant said, patting his forehead with a damp white handkerchief. "Some big wine guy went completely berserk and shook this old fella up pretty bad. They found part of a shoe by that gal's desk, way over there, and the rest of his personal items were stuffed into the microwave in the breakroom. We have been unable to locate the victim's trousers, but the K-9 unit is en route."

"What would cause a man to do such a thing, Sergeant?" the captain quietly asked while scanning the odd crime scene.

"Something about a coupon."

"What's wrong with you, Becker?" I heard Dick ask coarsely, with that thick Texas drawl, yanking me from my oddly pleasing daydream.

"I'm sorry. Where was I?"

"Who knows," Dick said as he turned back from checking his email.

After the meeting, I called my boss, Mike, to explain what had happened. "You should call Jim and tell him," Mike said. Jim was our general manager, overseeing our entire region. I spoke with Jim for a while, and I found him to be supportive. He even suggested that I call HR to file a complaint.

However, I didn't see anyone from our team rushing to call Dick and defend either the company or me; too much sales volume was at stake. I felt alone in this fight; it was my responsibility, and I wouldn't say I enjoyed it. I did not take Jim's advice to report it.

The weeks passed, the abusive behavior continued, and our business rapidly declined in this massive account. I would receive angry texts, calls, and emails from Dick at odd times, such as the morning of Father's Day, pressuring me to "do the right thing" and buy into the program. He would call occasionally to eviscerate me for product pricing, knowing that this was a distributor discussion, and I could not engage.

"You will have to call Chris on that one, Dick," I would remind him, between the name-calling and shaming. "His company controls the pricing of our brands in your market."

I was feeling beaten down and broken. My stress levels had become so high that I found sleeping, relaxing, or concentrating on my work challenging.

More time passed, and my boss reached his limit. Mike is a giant man with salt and decades of industry scars. Mike asked me to schedule a meeting with Dick, where he would be in attendance.

"This shit stops now," he assured me.

About a week later, we headed out to meet Dick in his office. We had invited our national account lead for this chain, a VP, to join us. He would bring national context to the discussion and give a final say on whether our company would participate. The VP was going to be the heavy. Before the meeting, we discussed ending our involvement in the coupon program and even rehearsed our lines for the discussion with Dick. We would also have strong analysts in the room who could provide fast air cover with supportive data. We were loaded for bear. We were clear on the objective, or so I thought.

We were all escorted to a large meeting room with a U-shaped setup and took our seats. We fiddled with our laptops and phones for a few minutes in anxious silence as if preparing for battle. I half expected to hear a snare drum playing quietly in the corner. Dick walked through the door quickly in a snit, sat down, and started in on me again as if he didn't notice the others in the room. He was heated and ready for a fight. Dick launched into a full-court press to explain why we would participate in his ridiculous program. Again, I started to answer the best I could, explaining our reasoning with many data points. Our VP panicked in the tense room and pitched some softballs to calm the buyer. "How about we play in the program, say, once a quarter, Dick?"

My boss saw my eyes roll as I sat back in my chair mouthing the words *For fuck's sake*.

"Listen, Dick, I think the team is trying to explain that this program doesn't make sense for us from a return-on-investment standpoint, and we are not going to participate anymore, for all the reasons Dave just outlined," Mike said.

"Who the hell are you?" Dick snapped as he turned his focus from the soft spot in the room, the now-melting VP.

Mike looked down his nose and over his reader glasses, leaned into the table, and said, "Excuse me?"

"You heard me," Dick said. He then explained that if we didn't participate, he would find a new partner and promote their brands instead. He began packing up his belongings.

We all knew why we were being strong-armed like this; if we walked away from the program, all the other suppliers would have permission to do the same. We were well respected in the industry for being a large supplier and one of the more cautious ones. If we stepped away, Dick knew there would be a mass exodus from his dying coupon program. And there were whispers that this program was tied to his bonus.

The discussion continued for a few more minutes. Unfortunately, our vice-president didn't have the stomach for it, compromised with the buyer, and approved limited involvement in the ongoing program. As a result, I found myself back in the meat grinder. I had to allocate more of my budget to this program for a few more months until it eventually died of natural causes.

It was especially uncomfortable when our VP went in for an awkward sideways "bro-hug" with Dick as we left. I did not understand this behavior. This man was holding our business hostage. I texted Mike across the bare U-shaped table as we watched the halfhearted hug be angrily swatted away.

Text to Mike: Stockholm Syndrome?

Text from Mike: LOL--That took a funny bounce!

Mike's pirate-like laugh pierced the awkward quiet of the room as we packed up to go.

I have observed this behavior frequently in the industry. Buyers can be abusive toward salespeople, and often, those same salespeople will seek to win their favor or friendship, or at least what they interpret as such. I never did that. If you intentionally harm me, my team, or my business, you will never be allowed the opportunity to do so again.

I held tightly to the cherished memories of my earlier working days, finding solace in the nostalgia that reminded me I was more than just the sum of my current circumstances. I vividly recalled the countless mornings when Anders and I would arrive simultaneously at Norman's estate, our trucks almost synchronized in their approach, or the times one of us would jump into the other's vehicle and head to the cozy little coffee shop on the corner of Main and North Water. We would enjoy warm bagel sandwiches and strong coffee while sharing laughter and stories with the girls behind the counter. The tranquil island streets would come alive as the cool morning fog gradually pulled back, like a blanket, revealing the familiar faces of old-timers shuffling into the corner store for their daily newspapers. Each one would offer us a wave as they crossed the street.

"Dave? What do you think?" someone said through the black speakerphone sitting on my desk, pulling me from my daydream drift. "What do you think the chains will do for OND?" (October, November, and December.) This was the most common question I'd be asked on internal conference calls. It baffled me and was a little precarious for me to answer. My past experiences with these managers taught me that setting overly ambitious forecasts to satisfy people in a meeting could have negative consequences later. I wanted to avoid seeing my name displayed with a big red number next to it at the end of the quarter.

"You must have an idea," the robotic corporate voice on the speakerphone would inevitably say.

I didn't have a clear answer. I'd explain that my buyers had not yet finalized their plans, so anything I mentioned would be merely a guess, and I wasn't sure how that would be helpful.

"That's okay; just take a guess," the voice on the speakerphone said.

I never understood this way of working. It was counterintuitive to what I knew from my past jobs.

"I think we will hit what we had last year, plus 2 or 3 percent." My response had no meaning whatsoever; it was purely conjecture. But to the folks in this working environment, it was the appropriate and somewhat pacifying answer they needed for the reports they were required to submit later that day to their managers.

I sat through endless circular discussions during meetings rich with business clichés and corporate platitudes. Eager midlevel managers took turns speaking, each one pontificating about the business and often repeating or rephrasing the vague statements of the previous speaker. It seemed their main goal was simply to talk and be acknowledged, with little regard for substance. I would quietly scan the meeting room, observing the nondescript figures in button-down shirts who waited uncomfortably for their turn to speak.

The salespeople were not to blame. We adjusted to the environment and acted appropriately to ensure survival in this competitive setting.

During this time, I noticed golf's increasing role in our business. I do not play golf, and honestly, I was beginning to resent everything it represented in the corporate workplace, from the attire to how players spoke and used it to measure one's value in the meeting room.

"My boy Tom over here is a hell of a stick," someone would say as we opened our laptops.

"I shot a seventy-six yesterday at Pumpkin Ridge!" the white Oxford shirt would proudly announce.

My mind immediately went to the fact that it was Wednesday, which meant these guys were playing golf and drinking beer while I was at my desk building this presentation.

I recall a comment made by my former employer while I was on the island. On a quiet Sunday morning, Norman stood with a few staff members in the kitchen of his magnificent Martha's Vineyard home. He was listening to one of the guys from the boat crew as the man talked of his plans to play nine holes that morning. He spoke with vibrant enthusiasm, highlighting the clubs he would use and the people he would be playing with—no doubt to impress the boss.

Norman's response took me aback. He turned to the group, his expression serious, and pointed his cold Macanudo cigar at us as he said, "Gentlemen, golf is a monumental waste of time. It is the sport of middle management; if that's what you aspire to be, then by all means, have at it!" After lighting his cigar, he looked up, shook his head, and left the room.

Although only one man's opinion, those words resonated with me, surfacing in my mind whenever I heard a corporate individual talking in a meeting about their golf game or the fancy course they just played—most likely at someone else's expense.

Upon closer examination of my feelings about golf, I realized that my concerns do not stem from the game itself but from its enforced integration into corporate culture. No matter how hard you work, not being on the golf course often means being left out of meaningful discussions. In many corporate environments, some individuals do not enjoy golf or cannot play due to physical or time limitations. This situation can lead to a fracture in team culture and may not always align with the company's objectives. Furthermore, this underlying clannishness can create a sense of exclusion and division, which I have frequently experienced.

If a salesperson on my team spent time discussing their golf game during a meeting, I would typically turn to them and say, "I'm glad to hear that you are seeing improvements in your swing; it must have taken a lot of hard work. How are your sales numbers? Tracking to hit plan?"

Although I am not a golfer, I appreciate the game's appeal and the opportunity it provides for social connection. I vividly remember a scene that remains etched in my memory of a cool, early autumn Sunday morning in Scotland. I was there for a friend's wedding. As I strolled through the tranquil streets of Elie, the world was still waking up, and the soft murmur of the sea met the silent embrace of the early morning fog. The air was rich with the inviting scent of buttery bacon rolls wafting from the open kitchen windows, intertwining with the subtle hint of wood smoke, crafting a peaceful and enchanting atmosphere.

As I wandered along the dew-covered cobblestone paths, I couldn't help but notice golf bags carefully lined up on the sidewalks beside the slightly ajar doors of charming gray stone cottages. The bags, each well worn yet well cared for, rested below window boxes overflowing with vibrant petunias, delicate violets, and cheerful pansies, a picturesque scene that felt quintessentially Scottish and beautiful in its simplicity.

Many of the golf bags belonged to children, who sat beside their half-sized clubs. They waited patiently for friends or family members to join them, their excitement palpable as they shared their anticipation of a morning spent on the links. The deep-rooted love for golf in Scotland is a cherished tradition, an almost sacred bond woven into the fabric of the culture. This lovely tableau, filled with innocence and joy, is an image that will forever remain with me, warmly nestled in my memories.

While in corporate, I struggled with the frequency of meetings, many of which seemed gray and meaningless to me. I developed performance anxiety around these meetings that eventually caused a great deal of stress for me personally as well as in my work. I used to think this way of working was designed for a specific person: the extrovert or external-processor type. These individuals often prefer to discuss their work out loud with others, assuming everyone will find it as helpful as they do. This way of working is distracting and inefficient for me; it slows me down. I always did my best work when given the time and space to put my projects together with careful thought.

Salespeople often find themselves confined to meeting rooms or stuck on endless video calls, which sometimes hampers their ability to complete essential account work. These restrictions make it difficult for them to connect with clients, close deals, and, ultimately, generate revenue for the company. Many salespeople work long hours, staying late after meetings and video calls to finish their account work, which can lead to burnout and high turnover. As a result, sales trends decline, leading to even more meetings and emphasizing process over goal-oriented thinking.

This way of working and the business environment it fostered came from above. Our senior leaders seemed to behave this way at the time, which instilled a deep fear culture within our company and among our distributor partners. We sometimes operated as if preparing for internal or distributor review meetings was more critical than driving sales. I found this behavior confusing: posturing and conjecture without any measurable result.

In my earlier working days, I was conditioned that the result was and should remain the primary focus—the goal—the reason for doing the work in the first place. However, in this midlevel corporate sales environment, the focus was tracking your business, building reports, recapping your colleagues, and defending your numbers. The logical outcome of managing your business that way was the slow erosion of sales volume and a strengthening of the fear culture, resulting in even more need to defend your numbers because they are down.

Everyone was down because we focused on the wrong goal—the process.

I witnessed a simple but excellent visual example of this many years ago when working as a wine steward at Safeway, a company that was very focused on customer service. The store manager called for a "service huddle" in the back room. A service huddle was a brief stand-up meeting of any available employee in the store to discuss a specific aspect of customer service as a training exercise.

The woman leading this service huddle asked the five or six of us to kneel and pack the boxes before us as fast as possible, with the grocery items next to the boxes. Being a competitive bunch, we attacked the exercise, placing the items in the boxes as quickly as we could, hoping to be the first to finish and enjoy the bragging rights. The whole time, we were focused on packing our boxes and measuring our progress compared to our associates. The woman leading the exercise walked around us, pretending to be a customer needing assistance by holding a list and looking up.

No one noticed her playacting, and she left the room after being ignored. We'd hurriedly packed our little boxes, overlooking the needs of our customer, who eventually lost interest. The lesson of this little exercise stuck with me for thirty-some years.

My company had become so focused on the process and the behind-the-scenes work that the sales results turned into an after-thought. Much of our time was spent filling out reports and forms and creating new templates for reports intended for internal meetings. These reports were often discarded and replaced with new versions shortly afterward.

Monthly business reviews transitioned into twice-monthly meetings, eventually evolving into weekly reviews. Before long, I found that more than 70 percent of my time was consumed by preparing for and attending internal or distributor meetings, many of which did not directly contribute to driving sales. It wasn't always like this.

CHAPTER ELEVEN
WINE IS SUPPOSED TO BE FUN

Wine is constant proof that God loves us and loves to see us happy.
Benjamin Franklin

I had a largely enjoyable and positive experience during my early years in the wine industry. Although we had reports to complete and meetings to attend, the atmosphere was friendly and welcoming rather than adversarial or hostile. I fondly remember our team celebrating wins and supporting each other during losses. This was the old wine business. We were passionate about what we sold and deeply connected to the wines in our portfolio, knowing them intimately. I truly enjoyed that time in my career.

In those early days, our team meetings revolved around wine. We would taste different wines; discuss them; explore the viticulture, regions, and winemakers; and analyze price points that made sense for our markets. We also discussed who the target retailers would be, how to promote the wines, shelf positioning, and what kind of planner support we would request from our retail partners. That's right—I said partners.

In the early 2000s, I found buyers to be more professional, personable, and reasonable. It was an enjoyable industry to be a part of. People from other sectors often expressed a desire to join such a relaxed and pleasurable industry. We had fun working together, and corporate mischief ran rampant. I received some helpful tips from my friends as I began this way of working. One piece of advice was to not fall asleep on flights when traveling for work. Another was never give out your hotel room number!

Not long after, I understood why. One of us would inevitably doze off during the flight to the meeting, allowing the opportunity for someone to gently place an ice cube on the sleeper's lap. As the ice cube melted, it would leave an embarrassing wet spot.

If you accidentally revealed your room number while at a bar with forty of your sales colleagues, you could find mysterious charges on your bill when checking out. This would make submitting your next expense report quite uncomfortable. I remember standing next to our new marketing director, who was also checking out of the resort where we had been staying for several days. He was trying to understand why he had a bar bill of over four thousand dollars on his account. It was a rookie mistake.

I remember when our company hired an outside trainer to work with the sales teams to enhance their presentation and negotiation skills. The trainer was a disciplined man in his sixties, with a military background, and he often shared stories about his challenging beginnings in the consumer packaged-goods industry.

Such training sessions were held off-site, often in a central location to facilitate efficient company travel. This meeting occurred in Denver, with thirty sales management team members from around the nation. We arrived the evening before and, as was our tradition, went out to dinner together. Our dinners focused on enjoying fine wine, and we worked with local teams to ensure that our company's wines and spirits were well-stocked at the hotel bar and the restaurants we visited. Much like employees of a soft drink company, we were expected to enjoy only our products.

We gathered around a large table in the restaurant, discussing the wine list and searching for the placement of our wines. Back then, budgets were a bit looser, and we were encouraged to have fun with our products while working together, as long as we delivered results. When someone spotted an interesting item from our portfolio, a hand would shoot up to catch the attention of the soon-to-be overworked servers. "Excuse me, please!" one of us would call out, urgency in our voices but always polite, as we understood and appreciated the hard work that restaurant servers and bartenders do. We also knew these dedicated professionals would bring us many delicious offerings to enhance our evening. It was truly a symbiotic relationship.

We began sharing our starter and entrée selections with the server, who appeared to be watching a tennis match from a position halfway down the large table. "So, what did we decide on?" she asked, slightly confused but enjoying the excitement surrounding the food and wine.

"All of them!" someone from our group said with a laugh.

We then chose a representative to finalize the order more seriously. "We would love three bottles of this Napa Chardonnay, two bottles of this New Zealand Sauvignon Blanc, three bottles of that old vine Zinfandel, and three bottles of this 2007 Russian River Pinot. Oh, and please include a bottle of this Alexander Valley Cabernet," he said with a smile.

We enjoyed the wines while discussing how they paired with our array of starters. "Oh my God! You have to try this 2000 Reserve Cabernet with the Wagyu bruschetta!" someone said. Almost immediately, everyone began passing around a luscious, high-elevation, dry-farmed Napa Cabernet and the bruschetta to experience this incredible pairing together.

"You need to try this!" one of us said, as we handed our server a glass along with a bite to sample. Our group had a unique way of involving our servers in our dining experience. Most of us had, at some point, worked as servers or bartenders, so we understood how challenging these roles can be. We all knew how to collaborate with a professional server to align them with our epicurean endeavors. Before long, they had become part of our group, eager to make us happy and share in our gastronomic adventure and playful banter. Once this energy was aligned, people began to let their guards down. Suddenly, half bottles of exquisite Napa and Sonoma wines were quietly taken to the back of the house, and marvelous off-menu delicacies started arriving at the table, sent by our new friends.

I recall an evening when our group visited a beautiful steakhouse in Boise, Idaho, joined by one of our larger retail buyers and his team. The venue featured dueling pianos as entertainment. The servers were attentive, the music was lively, the wine flowed, and everyone had a good time, laughing together. Even the most serious corporate types at the table began to relax and enjoy the atmosphere. I was sitting next to a VP of sales from our largest distributor, a friend of mine. He sat stiffly in his suit, scrolling through the email on his phone, clearly confused about the evening's direction and why we weren't reviewing the follow-ups from the presentation earlier that day to the buyers.

"Shouldn't we be finalizing this?" he whispered to me.

"This is more important," I said.

My good friend, Chris, an Idaho distributor partner and a true "buyer whisperer," gave me a grin and winked as he stepped away from one of the piano players, folding bills back into his pocket. "Watch this," I said, leaning over to my stiff, gray-suited friend as the music quickly changed from barroom jazz to some rousing classics by Elton John, Van Morrison, and Queen.

Suddenly, the whole table broke out in song. We were all belting out these musical memories at the tops of our voices. Nearby tables joined in, as did our new server friends. Before long, the entire restaurant erupted into a Hollywood-like scene, with everyone arm in arm, singing Billy Joel's "Captain Jack" at the tops of their lungs. My VP friend sat quietly and awkwardly, but with a few encouraging nudges from me, he loosened his tie and started singing his favorite lyrics. It was magical.

In the weeks following that incredible dinner, we secured one of the largest programs ever sold and implemented within this huge chain. Throughout the program, we increased our high-volume brands in our retailer's category by over 40 percent during the peak sales season. It was a huge success.

The wines in our portfolio then were superior to those I encountered later in my career with the company. Like many larger corporations, we acquired wineries while striving to maintain their essence and sense of place. We made a concerted effort to keep the winemaking teams intact, allowing them to continue their craft. As a result, our portfolio expanded to include exceptional brands from some of the most impressive wine regions, including Napa Valley, Sonoma, Lodi, Alexander Valley, the Russian River Valley, Tuscany, France, New Zealand, Australia, and Washington State, among others. The wines were fantastic, and we took great pride in selling them.

The day after our dinner in Denver, we entered the meeting room as our trainer, Bob, diligently practiced with the slide projector. Stories about the late-night activities at the hotel bar circulated the room, accompanied by laughter and a few blushing faces. The last ones to arrive were some guys from our Southern California team. They strolled in just as the bell rang, bringing a couple of bottles of one of our new Chardonnays, which were nicely chilled.

In his best drill-sergeant voice, the trainer called for our attention and instructed us to settle down. His tone was new to us, but that was fine. "Let's go, everyone. Find a seat," he commanded.

The bottles of Chardonnay were passed around and discussed freely. Wine descriptors floated through the room quietly as we sipped, slurped, and swirled.

"Oh yeah, okay . . . I get the toasted almonds now," someone on the far side of the table said. "Very nice."

"And coconut. How about those tropicals!" another said as he pressed his nose deeper into the glass and spit his next sip into an empty coffee mug.

"What are you doing?" our confused and now upset instructor asked impatiently.

"Oh, yeah, this is our new reserve tier Chard. You know . . . Barry's wines, man," one of the soul-patched SoCal wine guys said. He turned in his chair, pointing toward Bob. "Hey, someone get him a glass."

The instructor's face reddened, his face stiffened, and the room fell quiet. Bob was fed up. "It is 9:17 in the morning!" he said, tapping his watch. "What is wrong with you people?"

I would argue it wasn't what was wrong with us but, rather, what was *right* with us. We were a friendly, happy, knowledgeable group of skilled wine professionals who loved what we sold. That is what I loved about the wine business for many years. It was a passion-based industry that created beautiful products that enhanced the lives of so many. I was proud to be in the wine business.

We went through several training sessions with Bob over the years, and he eventually warmed to our ways and, dare I say, even came to like us in the end. He went as far as to ask me to help teach one of his classes in Chicago. Bob is a good man and a great trainer; he just needed to relax. After all, this wasn't the toilet paper business or widgets; we sold wine and damn good wine to boot! Why wouldn't we be excited about that?

I enjoyed working with many fun and exciting people in my early days in the wine business. Some of the most enjoyable colleagues were the winemakers and founders of the wineries. Although our company purchased these wineries, they worked hard to maintain each one's distinct personality, even if it sometimes caused issues and sleepless nights for the HR department.

Many of the wine production and viticulture staff came from an agricultural background rather than the corporate sales side. They were less concerned with meetings, corporate jargon, light-blue dress shirts, and spreadsheets and were more focused on the creative process and farming. Their passion made working with them a lot of fun.

In most cases, when the winery founders sold their businesses to our company, they received a substantial financial payout. However, they were often retained as creative advisors, consultants, or brand ambassadors. One example that comes to mind is my friend Barry, a man in his late sixties. He sold his large winery in Washington State to our company and was more than happy to take on the role of ambassador for his beloved wines. Barry and I often spent time visiting stores, conducting in-store tasting events for his wines, and taking buyers out to dinner. He had a memorable personality.

We often scheduled visits to major retail locations, such as Safeway and Fred Meyer, where I would bring Barry to engage with customers about his winery. It creates a pleasant experience for wine customers to have the chance to chat with the founder of a winery they enjoy, and this was where he truly excelled. My challenge was to keep him focused on the customers instead of letting him wander off into the store's aisles in search of his next big marketing idea. On one occasion, he excused himself from a small group of shoppers in the wine department and disappeared around a corner, heading down the back aisles of the store. I asked the group of shoppers to give us a moment and quickly followed my old farmer friend, who was turning onto the stationary aisle.

"Barry, what are you doing?" I asked, now out of breath.

"I can't see a fucking thing, Becker," he said as he impatiently ran his finger down the eyeglasses on the rack.

"Listen, go back to the customers, and I will get your glasses and meet you there."

"No, no, I got it," he said as he shuffled to the front of the store and set his new readers on the check stand belt along with a twenty-dollar bill. I reminded him that this was an advertised event, and he needed to talk to customers in the wine department. He turned and said, "All in good time, Becker, just relax, for goodness' sake. Jeez."

The belt moved, and I nudged him forward to finish his purchase. I looked back toward the wine department and saw the steward and a couple of customers watching us, confused. I raised my finger to indicate that we needed a minute.

I was drawn back to Barry's transaction when he began speaking loudly. "What do you mean, I need to pay you? I just did!" Barry snapped at the checker. "I set twenty bucks right there by my glasses. Someone obviously took it!" The line was building behind us, and the customers left the wine department. The store manager arrived with tools to remove the belt cover and see if he could find Barry's missing twenty-dollar bill underneath the equipment housing. "Your damn machine must have eaten it," Barry thundered as the young, red-faced manager began to turn the screws securing the metal cover at the end of the belt. Barry's hearing aids suddenly made a high-pitched whistle that could peel paint off the wall, adding to the moment's already high tension. The man standing behind me offered to pay for Barry's glasses right after I had set my debit card on the belt and nodded to the annoyed cashier.

"No, I already paid these people, Becker," Barry said, sliding my card back in front of me.

The manager could not locate the crisp twenty-dollar bill that Barry had set on the conveyor belt and was still pondering what to do about his unusual, squealing customer when Barry said, "Oh, here it is!" Laughing, he bent down to retrieve the bill from the floor, partially obscured by his well-worn brown wing-tip dress shoe. "Look at that, everyone! It was right under my damn foot!" With a deep sigh and some heavy eye-rolling, the manager quietly gathered his tools, stepped into his office, and closed the door.

Later that day, while riding in the car, Barry said, "Becker, according to my calculations, I haven't been paid in over three months."

"Well, maybe you should reach out to someone, huh?" I said with a snort.

"I have an assistant, but she has no idea—not even sure what she does, to be perfectly honest." He dug through his big brown leather case.

"Get someone from HR or payroll on the phone, Barry. I am sure they can help you," I said as I turned into the parking lot for our next scheduled customer meet-and-greet.

"Ba! They'll figure it out eventually, then I'll be rollin' in it!"

"They pay you? After they bought your winery?" I asked with a little poke.

"I'm an important man in some circles, Becker. And I don't work for free!"

As the automatic doors to the Safeway opened with a whish, Barry said, "I am willing to bet there is a halfway decent bar in this neighborhood. What do you say? We'll go and find it. Got to shake off some of this stress you are causing me." He gave a belly laugh.

"Barry, we've got to nail these events. This banner is my biggest account, and the stores report back to my buyer, so please, I'm begging you. Focus!"

"I will agree to your terms, Becker, but *then* the bar," he said, wagging his finger at me as we entered the wine department.

"Fine, and *then* the bar."

We were a group that believed in both hard work and having fun. We dedicated long hours to our tasks, achieved strong results, and enjoyed the process together. Each year, we organized several trips with our distributors to show appreciation for their hard work and help them meet their goals, which they typically did. One memorable trip took a few of our distributors to New Zealand, where they explored some of our wineries.

While these trips were luxurious, demonstrating to our distributor partners that we recognized and valued their efforts on our behalf, there was a strong focus on education. The trips were always connected to significant sales goals that needed to be achieved, but they also provided a vital opportunity for our partners to connect with our wineries in person.

My first trip to New Zealand was an exciting experience. There were about fifteen of us in total. We gathered at Portland International Airport enjoyed a few drinks at the bar. I recognized most people on the trip, but only knew some by name. My somewhat unusual corporate personality often made me uncomfortable in groups with individuals I didn't fully know within the industry.

The guys—particularly those in sales or execution roles—tended to cluster together and quickly form connections. I'm not sure how they managed it, to be honest. They discussed football, golf, and specific accounts they handled, or they would chat about some retired salespeople from years past. This type of conversation sends strong signals that they belong to the same tribe—*Come on over! You are one of us!*

Such communication is common among midlevel corporate salespeople, and it's a language I never quite learned. I excel in one-on-one interactions, as this is when I can perform my best in both business and social situations. I can quickly gauge where my conversation partner stands by visually assessing their body language. This skill enables me to engage in more in-depth and productive discussions, ultimately driving results in a business context. I'm not one for small talk or casual chitchat, so I prefer to sit quietly alone if I can't engage in a more meaningful conversation.

I remember this flight well; it was only my second trans-Pacific overnight flight. I was seated next to an All Blacks rugby player from Auckland. I enjoyed learning about his sport and the lifestyle that surrounded it. We hit our first pocket of rough turbulence in the middle of the night. I was awake, watching a movie, as was the man next to me. A few folks were up, digging through overhead bins or adjusting something by their seats when the plane made a sudden and rather severe drop. Some people standing or not buckled in flew upward and smashed against the cabin ceiling. People were screaming. The pilot made an urgent announcement, and the seatbelt signs remained on for the rest of the flight. There was something incredibly unsettling about this experience for me. We were over the Pacific Ocean in the middle of the night. Absolute darkness.

"Shit, bro!" the Kiwi man next to me said as he tightened his seat belt.

I was happy when we landed in Auckland, not because of the rough flight—I had already moved past that—but because I was delighted to be traveling again. We landed in New Zealand early in the morning and had the entire day ahead of us. These trips were highly organized and designed to be comfortable, as they were meant to reward hard work. The last thing we wanted was to stress our distributor partners with difficult international travel.

Felicity, our friendly and somewhat eccentric guide from the Auckland office, met us in the baggage claim area and quickly recognized members of our group by the telltale wet spots on the front of their trousers, which she had noticed with other of our company's groups before us. "Right this way, friends!" she said, tucking her cell phone into her bra and waving her arm toward the bus just outside.

Felicity gave us some time to settle into our rooms then gathered the group from the hotel bar around 10:30 a.m. She led us on a short walk to a nearby marina, where we boarded a retired America's Cup racing yacht for a two-hour sail through Waitematā Harbour.

Some in our group enthusiastically seized the opportunity to sail this world-class racing yacht, which shimmered under the brilliant New Zealand sun. We were soon divided into rotating teams to operate the sail winches, affectionately called "coffee grinders." The atmosphere was electric as our team quickly adapted to the rhythm of the boat.

Before long, we had taken over the responsibilities of the experienced crew on deck, who now stood off to the side.

"Most groups just want to watch," one of the crew members remarked with a laugh.

We cranked the winches with all our strength, sweat dripping from our noses as we looked up at the sails, our voices echoing across the water as we shouted for rotations with each fast tack. "Go! Go! Go!" The thrill of the wind in our hair and the spray of saltwater on our faces made every skinned knuckle and bruised thigh from the flyaway winch handles seem inconsequential. It was a small price to pay for the adrenaline rush of sailing this multimillion-dollar beauty as it sliced through the sparkling waters off Auckland at an exhilarating fourteen knots on that picture-perfect, breezy afternoon.

Once back on the dock, Felicity marched the still-grinning and sea-wobbly bunch up the stairs to a beautiful patio restaurant with a commanding view of the entire marina. Our long linen-dressed table was set right on the patio rail. Buckets of our chilled New Zealand Sauvignon Blanc were waiting for us, along with the most beautiful assortment of fresh oysters from the area. *Delightful.* The wines splashed, and the laughter started, and we had a wonderful, lazy afternoon there, doing what we loved to do.

The following morning, we met our cheerful guide in the lobby, each holding a cup of coffee. Our bus was waiting outside to take us back to the airport, where a private plane was waiting for us on the tarmac. Once everyone had boarded, we took off to visit one of our vineyards in Gisborne, followed by a trip further south to Hawke's Bay.

We explored the vineyards at each stop, observed the winemaking operations, and tasted wines alongside the winemaking teams. Each vineyard team provided us with a unique experience, setting up tasting events in the heart of the vineyard. The late afternoon sun warmed our backs as we sipped wines from the very block of vines where we stood, allowing us to feel the divine connection between the vine and the earth and the gorgeous wines in our glasses.

It was late in the day when our plane landed in Marlborough, the final stop on our winemaking tour. Felicity quickly gathered the group onto a bus waiting for us on the tarmac. The bus was well-stocked with chilled Sauvignon Blanc and ice-cold beer. After a short ride through the beautiful valley of the Wairau River, we arrived at our destination for the three-day stay.

The vineyard owners greeted us and showed us to the small collection of charming cottages nestled among vines outside Blenheim. Each supplier was paired with a distributor counterpart, with two people assigned to each cottage. My bunk buddy was a man known as "Chopper." He was a few years older than most of us on the trip and had a wealth of experience in the industry. From the name, some might have thought that Chopper was tough and not to be trifled with, but he turned out to be the kindest and most pleasant roommate anyone could hope for. We enjoyed our time together on that trip and became fast friends.

Just a few miles down the road was the charming village of Blenheim, on the northern tip of the southern island of New Zealand. We stepped off the bus and followed our upbeat guide into our dining spot for the evening. Once again, we all took our places around a giant table and began ordering food and wine as if there were no tomorrow.

It is usually met with an eye roll when I tell people that, after dining like this so frequently, you get tired of it and just want a beer and a burger.

The social extroverts in our business thrive during gatherings, which I appreciate. I enjoy these events, too, but as an introvert, I need to take breaks and unplug occasionally. I find it challenging to be in situations where I cannot pull back after spending a day or two with others. My energy drains, leaving me empty, hollow, and mentally foggy. There have been times when I reached a point where I couldn't talk anymore. Throughout my life, I have sought to understand this and strike a balance between socializing and my need for solitude. I have achieved only moderate success in this endeavor, but I must be mindful of this balance.

It's true that my need for solitude largely depends on the company I'm with. When I am at home with family and friends, I can go much longer without retreating and recharging. However, in work situations or when I need to be "on" socially or emotionally guarded, I require solitude much sooner. Some people, in particular, seem to drain my energy just by my being around them, leaving me exhausted and sometimes even feeling physically ill. I jokingly refer to them as "energy vampires." I need to be very mindful of how much time I spend with them, as it can lead to both physical and emotional distress. My wife has witnessed this happen many times.

My biggest challenge during trips like this is finding time to be alone to think and process everything quietly—to recharge my mental and emotional batteries. A few days into a unique and luxurious journey on the other side of the world, I felt overwhelmed by the energy of those around me and the constant talking. Fortunately, my roommate shared a similar personality. Although he was fierce at work, he also valued his privacy. So, when the others finished their drinks and desserts and started discussing hitting the bars in town, Chopper and I decided to head back to the cottages to take some time to recharge.

I settled into a cozy spot in the cottage's backyard, my feet propped up on a weathered wooden bench, savoring the tranquility of the fading evening light. As I sipped a Marlborough Pinot Noir, the air was imbued with the faint scent of blooming lavender and freshly cut grass. This serene moment provided me with the perfect opportunity to think deeply, breathe in the cool evening breeze, and let my worries drift away. I thought of my creaky little Adirondack chair in the woods and smiled.

The next day was educational. We visited vineyards in the Wairau Valley and walked through their adjacent "tank farms," our name for the large areas where the big steel fermentation tanks stood like shiny monoliths in the bright New Zealand sun. We spent time walking the vines, gaining an understanding of the soils and microclimates responsible for producing some of the world's finest Sauvignon Blancs. For those of us who get all wiggly and giggly with excitement over great Sauvignon Blancs and Pinot Noirs, like me, the Marlborough region of New Zealand is an extraordinary place.

The Marlborough growing region is divided into three primary wine-growing areas, each with a unique mesoclimate or microclimate: the Southern Valleys, the Wairau Valley, and the Awatere Valley. This area, comprising three growing regions, is known as "Te wāhi o te kōhao kapua" to the Māori. Loosely translated, it means "The place of the cloud-opening." This region offers more sunny days than most other areas in the country, and combined with cooler temperatures, it is ideal for growing these two delicate and finicky varietals.

We spent the morning learning about these subregions and tasting the wines grown there, often with the people who made them. It is always enjoyable to see groups of wine people like this exchange ideas with winemakers, even though it can be overwhelming for the winemaking teams to have a couple of dozen wine sales professionals shooting rapid-fire wine-nerd questions at them for an hour. We could be a bit much.

We next visited a picturesque farm in the hills above the Awatere Valley, where a beautiful lunch awaited us. We walked around the farmhouse into the backyard and enjoyed the most magnificent views of the valley and vineyards below on that crisp sunny day. One long table was in the grassy yard, dressed in fresh white linen, with a row of vases filled with colorful sprays of garden flowers down the middle.

I fondly recall the enchanting gardens that framed the yard, a breathtaking display of nature's artistry. Towering blue hydrangeas burst forth in vibrant clusters, their petals shimmering like blue jewels in the sunlight. Delicate, trellised pink fairy roses tumbled gracefully over the edges, their sweet fragrance mingling with the earthy scent of New Zealand fern trees that swayed gently in the breeze.

With their sculptural forms, stonecrops and artichoke agaves nestled beneath large, wispy red-hot pokers. These striking plants sported fiery red and orange blooms, creating a stunning contrast that brightened the garden, reminding me of fireworks.

I've always admired well-designed English gardens; there is an undeniable charm and magic about them, and I can confidently say that these gardens were truly among the finest I have ever encountered.

Another fantastic meal in a beautiful setting. It was not lost on us, though; we marveled at the idyllic charm of the place and enjoyed every bite and sip of our lunch. While strolling around our massive table, Felicity told us about our scheduled group activity, a look at how a working New Zealand sheep station operates. "Follow me, friends!"

We all downed our last few sips of Reserve Sauvignon Blanc and waddled behind our guide down the hill and around a gnarly stand of oak trees to a small barn. There we watched three middle-aged men, their skin a deep, tanned brown resembling weathered leather, skillfully and silently shear sheep with a speed that felt almost magical, as if we had stepped back in time. Loose sheets and clumps of gray-white wool cascaded to the barn floor, creating a soft, mottled carpet beneath their feet. As the men worked with rhythmic precision, a young boy darted around, eagerly gathering the precious merino wool into an old wicker basket.

The late-day sun sifted through the slats of the barn wall, creating dust-swirled shadow lines on the floor reminiscent of bars in a jail, which made me think of the sheep. I had prepared myself for a scene of chaos and high emotion, expecting the sheep to be frightened, their bleats echoing loudly in the old barn as they tried to escape. Instead, a serene calm enveloped the old building. It was as if an ancient, symbiotic bond or agreement existed between the men and the animals; the sheep stood still and tranquil, resembling woolly statues awaiting their yearly transformation. Once sheared, each sheep received a gentle pat on their bare, pink bottom, prompting them to trot out the door with quiet dignity. They gracefully ascended the grassy hill to the south, their freshly shorn bodies glistening in the afternoon sunlight. It was beautiful.

As my hand grazed the sleeve of my Icebreaker wool half-zip pullover, I felt a renewed appreciation for this amazing fabric.

The following day, we loaded back onto our bus and were taken to a marina, where we boarded a boat for a day of exploration. We spent the day slowly cruising through the Queen Charlotte Sound on our private charter. As we sipped on Marlborough wines, we enjoyed the magnificent scenery of forested hillsides and stony meadows dotted with sheep drifting by from the aft deck loungers. The crew pulled up crop ropes filled with green-lipped mussels, allowing us to see where our late afternoon lunch was sourced.

It didn't take long before the first tipsy guest in our group decided to do a swan dive off the aft deck, splashing into the chilly waters of the sound accompanied by a loud "whoo-hoo!" Once the first person took the plunge, most of us quickly followed suit, regardless of whether we wore proper swim attire.

"Hell no!" the red-faced captain bellowed as he swung down from the flybridge. After being reminded firmly of the boat's rules, we all agreed it would be wiser to stay inside in the warmth and play board games for the rest of the cruise.

Later that day, we were back in one of our cottages, where our colleagues from the New Zealand office gathered us for a trip recap and education session. We reviewed and discussed some of the things we'd learned on the journey as best as a group of sloshy wine sales folks could. After crushing our hour-long review and quiz session, we returned to our late-day boozy antics.

At one point in the early evening, we had difficulty adjusting the temperature in the cottage as the sun began to set and the vineyards cooled off. It was getting chilly! Assistance came from the property manager, who seemed to find our group less than enjoyable. Once he had corrected the temperature on the thermostat, he turned to those of us who had somehow remained upright through this Sauvi marathon of a day and explained the proper way to change the temperature. As he spoke, he noticed a small, concerning arrangement of red drips on the new white carpet near where he stood. "What happened here?" he asked in his most professional voice. The wobbly group of intoxicated sales managers quickly filled the awkward space with soft, helpful answers to this question.

"Oh, yeah, I think that was there when we arrived," one said casually.

"You know, that should come right out with a little baking soda and water," another said.

"I know what will work—white wine!" yet another said, as she spun around with a half bottle of room-temperature Sauvignon Blanc.

"No!" the manager snapped, raising his hand to us. His eyes urgently found more drops. And more. He followed the trail of red drips and splashes through the cottage, as if tracking a wounded deer, until he found the source of the offensive stains. Jonathan, a street-hardened fortysomething sales manager from Idaho, who seemed to enjoy the Pinot Noir Reserve, was face down behind one of the sofas, with only his feet visible to the rest of us. Upon further investigation, he was discovered to be snoring peacefully in a large circle of red on the new snow-white carpet, an empty bottle of the gorgeous Pinot Noir lying askew beside him. It reminded me of a low-budget murder scene from a high school play.

Professor Plum did it! In the study with the candlestick—or wine bottle, in this case.

CHAPTER TWELVE
ODD MAN OUT

I am not concerned with your liking or disliking me.
All I ask is that you respect me as a human being.

Jackie Robinson

In 2014, I decided to step away from the wine business. Caroline and I saw this as an excellent opportunity to explore something new. Feeling more financially stable, we believed it was a good time to pursue a different path for a while. We had always been intrigued by the idea of owning a business—though I was perhaps more interested than Caroline, it was a concept that appealed to both of us. After months of researching various business models, franchise opportunities, and other options, we opened a gym. The business model made sense to us, and we found several promising franchise options that we liked. So, we dove headfirst into building, owning, and running a gym.

We built a beautiful fitness center that operated 24/7, and I managed the business for three years. The first year was a success; we had many members and achieved high rankings within the franchise organization. Everything was going well. However, halfway through our second year, a competitor opened a massive facility just a mile away. At well over five times our size, they offered an extensive range of equipment, classes, and services at a monthly price we could simply not match. As a result, running the business became a significant struggle, and we scrambled to attract enough members to remain profitable.

After three challenging years, we ultimately faced defeat. The relentless stress, long hours worked, and ongoing financial turmoil wore us down, weighing heavily on our spirits. We were desperately shoveling cash into the business to keep the lights on at that point. It became clear that it was time to part ways with our struggling venture before it took us to the bottom. We found a buyer—a driven entrepreneur who owned several gyms along the West Coast—and negotiated a price that felt right, though the sale was bittersweet.

As we transitioned from this chapter of our lives, we carried with us the remnants of our crushed hopes and the echoes of broken dreams. It was a difficult lesson, but we gained valuable insights along the way. When challenges arose and the business began to struggle, we realized that our connection to the fitness industry was superficial; we were primarily interested in making money from it, which ultimately left us unfulfilled. One key lesson we learned was the importance of following our hearts and pursuing our passions rather than merely chasing after money.

Fortunately, we found our footing, shook off the dust, and closed this chapter of our lives. Even though an entire book could be written about this experience, some of the memories are still too painful to revisit--perhaps someday I will have the courage to do so.

I felt a strong urge to move forward, once again stepping into the familiar currents of my life's journey to see where it would lead me.

The CEO of the healthcare facility in Vancouver, Washington, where Caroline was employed approached me with an opportunity to assist with various projects on campus for a few months. Since I had no other commitments and was about to finalize the sale of our business, I gladly agreed to help. The work paid well, and I genuinely enjoy project management.

The property was set to undergo extensive renovations to transform an outdated nursing care unit into a modern, state-of-the-art acute care facility. My focus would be on organizing and executing overdue projects at the assisted living facility on campus, as well as helping to reorganize various systems and departments. As a project manager, I was hired as a temporary employee, reporting directly to the CEO with a dotted line on the org chart to the facility administrator. A makeshift office was set up in an unoccupied resident unit in the main building, located down the hall from the team I would work with most closely, Building Services. I worked quickly to identify and define the scope of the projects; build spreadsheets, schedules, and trackers; and get the teams working toward the goals. I met with the building services director, Karen, each morning in her office to discuss the projects and ensure her teams had everything they needed to succeed. Easy enough.

The morning I arrived on the property, I saw a small, older man alternately pushing and dragging a rickety old aluminum service cart through the two inches of crunchy snow and ice in the parking lot. I watched him for a few minutes while I finished a call in my truck as he wrestled with his little cart of food intended for the residents in the nursing home on the other side of the frozen parking lot. I ended my call and stepped out to offer some help. He waved me off impatiently and continued in his struggle. I knew right then that this place was stuck in a time warp.

After settling in, I asked the building services director about the method an employee was using to transport hot food to the other facility. She told me about a connector tunnel situated beneath the parking lot, linking the two sides of the facility. However, over time, this tunnel had become impractical, as it was filled with outdated equipment and furniture, resulting in its current use as a storage area. This situation provided an initial insight into the management challenges I would soon observe within the organization.

I found my way to the tunnel later that day, and what I encountered was straight out of a horror movie. After a few tries, I managed to get the automatic doors to shudder open, revealing a sight that chilled me to the core. I stepped into the tunnel, a vast, corrugated metal tube with a grimy concrete floor, and was immediately confronted by the eeriness of the scene before me—dozens of broken and rusted wheelchairs, abandoned IV stands wrapped in tangled cords, decrepit hospital beds leaning at unnatural angles, battered medical carts, and dented bedpans were scattered like forgotten relics.

Most of the fluorescent lights flickered intermittently, casting a sickly green-gray glow that barely illuminated the grotesque remnants once used in a place of healing. As I clicked on my Maglite, the beam sliced through the dusty shadows, revealing a landscape of medical debris stretching endlessly before me. I waded deeper, stepping carefully over discarded equipment, until I reached a barrier of old, moldy mattresses piled high, their surfaces stained and sagging, a grim testament to facility neglect.

The air was thick with a heavy, dark energy that hung like a shroud, oppressive and suffocating. It was an abysmal place that felt like the end of life itself. The smell of ancient, urine-stained mattresses—musty and pungent—lingered in my nostrils.

I returned to find Karen, the director of building services, in her office. I suggested that the tunnel should now be the top priority. After sprinkling the room with well-worn excuses on why the tunnel looked like that and why they hadn't taken on this project sooner. "Let's slam this out," I said. "It will show great progress. And it will be fun!" The idea was met with many words, most of which were supporting reasons why it couldn't be done, but she finally agreed.

At this time, I saw firsthand that this property had a "thought stagnation" issue. Most of the employees I had met thus far had been working there for over fifteen years, with several having worked there for over twenty years or longer. They had the same jobs, the same desks, the same parking spots, the same teams, and the same odd little cat posters on their walls.

Nothing had changed here. This place was anachronistic.

I marched back to my office, closed the door, sat at my laptop, inserted my earbuds, and turned up Toad the Wet Sprocket. I hammered out a plan. I built a timeline, a list of resources and materials, and schedules for contractors. I also built a team, assigned a team leader, and arranged for large dumpsters to be placed at the back of the property. I loved this work!

Over the next week, we removed the ghastly pile of hospital debris from the tunnel. We sold some of it, donated some, and disposed of the rest. Karen would stand at the end of the tunnel, wringing her hands and commenting to me about her discomfort with the project.

"Sir . . . I don't know about this," she would say as I stood there with my clipboard and phone to my ear. "Some nurses over there will be mad that we are touching their stuff."

"Karen, most of the stuff is broken and hasn't been touched in years. It's time to take the tunnel back." I assured her I had communicated our intentions for this space to the entire property. I invited all department heads to explore the tunnel and retrieve any items they deemed valuable to their work. "It's okay," I said.

"They are going to kill me; just you wait, sir!" she said as she padded down the hall away from the tunnel entrance.

"If anyone has an issue, Karen, they are welcome to see me," I said.

I called the in-house electrician to fix the awful lights once the tunnel was cleared. I first asked him to remove the motion sensors at each end of the tunnel. As you stepped into the tunnel, the sensors were meant activate the two working lights. Still, the sensors often malfunctioned and could randomly turn off the lights when you were about halfway through the tunnel, leaving you stranded in the middle of a cold steel pipe underground in complete darkness.

The tunnel was empty, clean, and had proper, always-on lighting. *Progress!* I scheduled our painter to give the tunnel a fresh coat of paint from top to bottom and end to end. I wanted it to look as if it were new.

"If we are going to do this, we do it right!" I said to the team.

About ten days after the project began, we were finished. The tunnel looked brand new and was done on time and within budget.

With his squeaky little food cart, my new friend Ray could now cross to the other side of the campus without braving the snow, rain, and ice. That went squarely in the win column.

Karen stood at the end of the tunnel, squirming nervously.

Don't get me wrong. Karen was pleasant to work with. She cared deeply for this place; no one was better at working with the facility's residents. Having been there for over twenty years, Karen had become ingrained in the day-to-day operation of the place. However, she was in a rut, riding on rails. Any project outside the ordinary course of work would cause her great stress. She often became a fearful victim when we began exploring new projects, budgets, staffing, and expectations. She usually referred to her past experiences with managers who were no longer at the company and the disastrous outcomes when they attempted to exceed average expectations and step outside their comfort zone. Karen would likely receive a low adversity quotient if she were scored.

It was clear this was how I could bring value. I was not as interested in the cautionary tales from years past, when old so-and-so tried something like this and was fired. *Blah, blah.* I knew I was there only briefly and did not carry the weight of those who came before me. I didn't care about that. I cared about getting stuff done.

The CEO at the time agreed with my assessment of this department and asked me to get more involved. "Get into it, Dave," he said, with a pat on the back as we walked down the hallway.

My next project involved updating the lobby and constructing a bar in an adjacent room for residents and their families to enjoy together. I collaborated with the designer, Gary, to develop a plan for giving the outdated lobby a much-needed facelift. Once we finalized the plan, I organized my teams and created a simple Gantt chart to help schedule the contractors efficiently.

After consulting with an engineer, we cut through the floor to install outlets in optimal locations for the new furniture layout. The existing flooring was removed, and the large room was cleaned and prepared for painting. We set up a temporary lobby and office in a nearby space to ensure that the front-office teams could continue their work during the construction.

Six days later, we moved the new furniture into the remodeled lobby. Gary stood in the center of the cavernous space, waving his arms and directing the movers as if he were joyfully conducting an orchestra. We completed the project two days ahead of schedule and stayed within budget, thanks mainly to the fantastic teams of contractors and Building Services employees. I thoroughly enjoyed this project.

"We made this better for them," I said proudly to my team as we stood in the lobby, ready to welcome our residents back into the beautiful new space.

Karen had an unconventional approach to her work, but consistently delivered results. Her technical skills had not kept pace with the evolving business environment, and she relied on manual processes to manage her tasks. Karen did not use Excel, Word, Outlook Calendar, or any other Microsoft Office tools that could help streamline her work. Instead, she preferred to communicate verbally and always in person. As a result, there were often several members of her team, a contractor, and sometimes a resident standing outside her office door, patiently waiting to ask her questions. She typically avoided email communication and always carried a handheld radio, ready to respond to queries and resolve problems.

Although I offered suggestions to improve her efficiency, she would not change. She worked one way, and it became clear that she would keep her process the same. I pointed out that it is not only a poor use of her time to sit in a room and have people lined up to ask her questions, but also a waste of *their* time. I would see, for instance, a painter standing outside her office for fifteen minutes, waiting to ask a question about a project he was working on. Behind him were a maintenance employee and a housekeeper.

I encouraged her to "dollarize" the process by taking the hourly wage for each employee and contractor waiting outside her door, dividing that hourly wage by sixty minutes, and then multiplying that number by the number of minutes they spent waiting for her each day, week, month, and year. By not adopting a more efficient management model, she was costing the organization a substantial amount of time and money.

I coached her on how to delegate tasks and empower her department leaders. I encouraged all teams and employees to direct their questions or issues to their department heads instead of going directly to Karen. She had become the go-to person for the facility and seemed to enjoy that role. It was as if she insulated herself with constant busyness, creating an image of being invaluable and irreplaceable. Judging by appearances, she was either scared or relished creating a facade of being overwhelmed. She seemed to thrive in chaotic situations.

I was trying to help Karen. I was not her supervisor or in charge of her department, but I enjoyed efficiency and wanted to share what I had learned in my professional experience. In my first meeting with the facility administrator, Karen's actual boss, I was informed that she was at risk of being let go. It seemed that her working methods and communication style had become irritating to senior management. As I recall from that conversation, her writing skills had been questioned. In short, the management wasn't sure she could write with any degree of proficiency—such an odd accusation to hear in a professional environment and somewhat alarming.

I asked the administrator, "Do you honestly feel that one of your directors cannot perform basic written communication, like email?" Although this was strange to hear in my new workplace, I realized I had never received a complete written message from Karen since I had been there. All my communication with her had been verbal, either on the phone or in person. I felt uneasy even thinking this way, but it was interesting that someone could become a director and supposedly not know how to write clearly.

This organization was insular in its business practices, particularly in developing managers, training, hiring, and promoting. Many midlevel managers were placed in their roles years ago simply because the position was open, leadership generally liked them, and they were available. Much of the decision-making in these cases was driven by relationships, not necessarily the qualifications of the person applying for the position.

After two months of crunching out projects like the tunnel, I was asked to take on more responsibility at the facility. The CEO asked if I would sit in on some meetings with the construction management team and help bridge the gap between the organization and the team. The construction management team struggled with how the facility's leadership team worked with them. The property staff and management submitted numerous change orders, resulting in issues with the construction timeline and budget. These change requests occurred almost daily and became very expensive for the project.

Many of the changes were related to surfaces, furniture, and fixtures in the property's management offices, not the residents' areas, which struck me as odd for a not-for-profit organization that cared for seniors. This was just the beginning of the strange behavior I was to witness on the property.

I watched staff and managers physically cringe every time the construction trailer was mentioned. I was in Karen's office one afternoon when the construction development manager, Shawn, called with a question related to her department. Karen almost froze with fear when she saw the caller ID. I encouraged her to grab the call and told her I could wait.

"He is going to scream at me!" she said.

"Just see what he wants," I said. I watched her hands shake as she listened to Shawn on the other end of the phone. When she ended the call, she explained that the construction managers were harsh and mean, especially Shawn, who was in charge of the entire project. This news made me slightly anxious because I was now expected to attend their weekly meetings and report back to the CEO.

"Are these people that bad?" I asked.

"Sir, you have *no* idea."

Karen and I walked across the main parking lot and up the hill to the dreaded construction management trailer that following Tuesday morning. We stepped in and through the project superintendent's office, turned right, and passed the stained coffee pot and the well-used bathroom, entering an open space in the middle of the trailer with a large boardroom table. Around the table sat about half a dozen men.

"Who the hell are you?" a vested man sitting in the center of the far side of the table blurted out. Karen nervously introduced me to Shawn and explained what I was doing there.

"You guys got a revolving door of idiots over there," he said as he poured himself a fresh cup. I sat, listened, and took notes. Toward the end, I had some clarifying questions for the construction team, and then we were back out the door and walking down the hill.

I did this for a couple of weeks, providing the CEO and the rest of the executive team with detailed recaps of the meetings in the construction trailer. Updates on timelines, change orders, budgets, safety notices, traffic detours, inspections, etc. Clear, bullet-pointed, and concise. The executive team appreciated these recaps because they did not feel comfortable attending these meetings for obvious reasons. Many had been asked not to return to the trailer, so having all the pertinent information delivered this way was a significant relief.

Everyone was now reading from the same sheet of music. *Progress!*

It didn't take long before I took a more active role in the construction meetings in the trailer. I understood more of what was being discussed and had ideas to share. My recaps became more detailed and valuable as my understanding of the project expanded. A few weeks into this new process, Shawn asked the CEO if he would appoint me as the sole liaison between the organization and the construction team.

Request granted.

Shawn and I felt this was an excellent way to streamline information and reduce the number of change requests submitted. If anyone from the property had a question or request regarding construction, they were sent directly to me. I would gather and filter the requests and questions for Shawn's team and cover them in the following week's construction meeting.

The CEO tasked me with personally reviewing each request to ensure that the proposed changes were truly necessary. This approach allowed me to present only the most relevant concerns and questions to the group for discussion, which significantly improved communication and reduced frustration within the project.

For each suggested change related to construction, I would assess the validity of the request. If the requests were justified and pertained to security, patient or resident care, or safety, I would prepare a change request, review it with the CEO, and then present it to the construction leadership.

I also developed a shared Excel document with the construction managers that ranked all requests by priority or importance. For example, if a program coordinator requested a larger office, different paint colors, more expensive furniture, or a better view, these types of requests would no longer be included on the list.

Shawn and I worked closely together and kept each other on speed dial, speaking several times throughout the day. I spent a few hours each day in the construction office with the team and enjoyed it. I felt very connected to the project and could comfortably discuss it with the executive team or board members if needed. The project was getting back on track, significantly reducing the tension. Passersby could even hear hearty laughter coming from the trailer from time to time. Overall, things were going well.

Around this time, I was asked to join the executive management team as the senior operations director for at least one year or for the duration of the construction project. The position had much more responsibility and a large team. I was tasked with overseeing three primary areas of the organization: the Building Services department, the Culinary and Food Services department, and, of course, construction. I managed a team of nearly one hundred personnel and a multimillion-dollar budget.

After spending time in my new departments, I quickly found several common themes among the teams. The strengths included excellent property knowledge, an expert-level understanding of procedures and protocols, a wealth of history and experience to draw from, intimate knowledge of the team and how they work, and the ability to repair or solve equipment issues at minimal expense.

The weaknesses included limited professional development, a lack of skill evolution, and an adherence to traditional methods, which resulted in a constricted thought process and hindered creative problem-solving.

This organization struggled with terrible "in the box" thinking. I found myself constantly challenging their everyday practices. "I understand that is how it has always been done, and I see the value there, but is that the only way it can be done?" I would frequently ask.

One of the issues I observed daily in this organization was the overvaluation of employees' opinions and preferences. My org chart suggestions would often be met with an objection from Karen. "But Herman will never do that because he likes painting more than the rest of the maintenance work, and he doesn't like the hours he would have to work."

"But in the org chart, he is listed as a Maintenance Level 2, FT," I said.

"Yeah, but he will never do that; he just wants to paint with his brother-in-law, Peter, because they want to drive in together," she said as she turned for the door. "Trust me, sir!"

"Karen, I am sure that has been the case in the past, and you have explained why, but the bottom line is, we need Herman to perform the duties for the role he is currently in. If he wants another job within the organization, he can apply for one, but for now, he needs to do what the position requires of him."

"Well, sir . . . good luck with that!" She flashed a big, fake smile.

The management style I observed across all areas I was responsible for was quite evident. Employees often dictated their schedules and the tasks they were willing to perform to their managers. As a result, mistakes occurred, quality diminished, and, ultimately, the organization suffered.

During my first few months at the property, I observed the organization's tendency to hold frequent meetings. Midlevel managers and directors often gathered to discuss various matters. Each day began with a morning "stand-up," the term suggesting a brief meeting format. However, these meetings quickly transformed into hour-long casual discussions held in the administrator's office.

I remember attending my first morning stand-up meeting and listening to concerns about not having enough chairs for everyone. I quietly remarked, "Does anyone see the irony here?" They did not.

They would all squeeze into the office and go around the room, taking turns talking about what was going on that day, often inviting others to join their meetings and asking to join others' meetings. There was never an agenda; it was a meeting about meetings. It was one of the unhealthiest workplace meeting cultures I had ever seen.

I stopped attending these meetings and asked my department heads to limit their time in these morning stand-up meetings to ten minutes. I provided them with a simple template outlining the items they should share with the office group: staffing or coverage/scheduling issues, operations or equipment concerns, safety and security concerns, menus for the kitchen team, and large-scale maintenance projects or contractors on site. I asked them to stay for a moment to field any questions from the administrator or other department heads, then excuse themselves.

I collaborated with my team leaders to address meeting challenges that affected productivity and work quality. Many were spending excessive time in unnecessary meetings, hindering our progress.

Other leaders in the organization were a little put off by the new guidelines my team was operating by. This efficiency-focused work style clashed with the organization's decades-long fossilized operating style. Tensions mounted, and the sideways looks in the hallway increased, but we stayed true to the course and got the work done.

Clem, the executive chef, embraced this new way of working and used the extra time in his day to focus on his department. We talked frequently about ways to improve the kitchen and food service. We planned how to expand the food service to the new facility currently under construction. I would occasionally bring Clem into the construction trailer meetings so the team could hear what was needed directly from the chef.

Progress improved.

Karen was less enthusiastic about the changes and slowly returned to her old way of working. I saw her sitting in the morning stand-up meetings with her friend, the administrator, for a good chunk of the morning, talking about their meeting schedules for the day. She had a lineup outside her office again and refused to respond to email communication. She could not evolve her work methods or chose not to, so the coldness between us grew. Instead of joining the rest of the team in the new way we were working together, she quietly aligned with the other managers in the organization who had been there for a long time and who also did not welcome change. Things became political, divided, and unfriendly.

The turnover at the top of the organization was astonishing. During my tenure of just over one year, I reported to three different CEOs, each eager to make their mark on the organization and each bringing their own challenges. This frequent change created significant disruption in the organization's culture. When senior leadership changes frequently, middle management often feels unsettled, insecure, and somewhat anxious. If this situation persists too long, it can foster a culture of fear and infighting among middle management. This organization had an unstable senior leadership team for a considerable period. Shawn's harsh assessment on that first day in the trailer—that it resembled a revolving door of idiots—seemed more accurate than I had initially wanted to believe.

During the management meetings, I observed that we were not promoting our strongest players, which led to noticeable issues within the organization, especially with our second CEO. This was his second time as CEO of this organization. He was a charismatic man who exuded a grandfatherly work persona and found great value in being revered by the old guard in the middle level of the organization. He was somewhat old-fashioned in his work approach, frequently choosing to hold in-person meetings that often dragged on without much to show for them. He did not like using email, Excel, or any standard business tools to streamline information flow. I often emailed my boss updates and a question or two, but I rarely got a response. Instead, shortly after, I would find him leaning in the door of my office with a cup of coffee, ready to answer my question. This was becoming an all-too-familiar pattern.

A few months later, our new CEO, Stanley, joined the organization and began steering it in a different direction. Stanley was a nervous man who seemed to have trust issues. We worked closely over the next few months and found a comfortable rhythm. However, Stanley often struggled with anxiety and frequently second-guessed himself when communicating with those in positions of power. This created some turbulence within the organization.

Passive-aggressive behavior in a professional environment can be toxic, at least for me. Gossip, dirty looks, whispering, and cliques are indications of an unhealthy workplace culture. The atmosphere at this property was among the worst I had ever experienced. Honestly, it got into my head. I often returned to the construction trailer and set up my laptop there for a few hours to escape the schoolyard bullying and backbiting, primarily from senior managers. The trailer became a space where men spoke like men. It wasn't mean or aggressive; it was direct and to the point, with absolutely no drama.

I don't fear the enemy I can see; it's the one I can't that scares me.

I knew my work was appreciated, but how I worked made some people very uncomfortable.

"You see what we mean?" Shawn said with that snarky grin from across the conference table in the construction trailer. "They are an *odd* bunch."

Shawn, the project manager, Rich, and I spent time walking the construction site together every day. During these walks, we discussed timelines, schedules, and any issues or delays related to the large project. As we approached the final 120 days before completion, my focus shifted toward ordering equipment and furnishings. I dedicated countless hours in meeting rooms alongside Shawn, our vendors, and the new facilities administrator, creating lists of everything necessary to equip the acute care facility and the new senior living center.

We outlined the equipment and furnishings for each room in the new buildings, including hospital beds, chairs, medical equipment, mirrors, televisions, lobby furnishings, lamps, and artwork, among other items. We carefully examined each space, room by room. It was truly a monumental task.

I reviewed the list with my CEO and received his approval to proceed with the project. Once we finalized the list of furnishings, fixtures, and equipment needed for the new buildings, I met with Philip, the new chief financial officer.

Philip spent most of his time sequestered in his large office behind a closed door. Almost immediately after his arrival, he began to pull only a few senior management team members close to him. The rest of us were treated like peasants in his kingdom. I found myself in that latter group, which quickly became problematic, as I managed one of the largest teams and oversaw one of the most significant budgets in the organization.

Strangely, Philip would not allow me to enter his office without an appointment, while others would casually pop in to ask questions or engage in small talk. If I dared to stick my head through the door to ask a question, he would hold up his hand like a traffic cop to signal me to stop talking, then gesture toward our executive assistant.

"Philip, I just need a few minutes to discuss the FF&E order I sent you yesterday for the new buildings. It's finished and within budget; we need your approval." I stepped into his cologne-drenched office, but he continued to gesture toward the executive assistant's desk just outside.

I leaned out his door and said, "Erika, does Philip have five minutes?"

"He sure does, Dave," she said with a wink.

"I don't have time for you; I am doing something for the board, so you must make an appointment," Philip said with a sneer.

"No problem. I will just pop in and have Stanley sign off on it," I said, stepping back toward our boss's office.

"Wait," he said, turning away from me to look out the window while pointing to the corner of his desk. "Leave it here, and I will look at it later."

"Don't wait too long, Philip. As I mentioned in my email, they need it submitted by the end of business so we can get the orders processed and stay on schedule." I closed his door.

As the construction of the new facility approached completion, the atmosphere began to change rapidly. During this time, I experienced two contrasting impressions. On one hand, the staff seemed genuinely excited about the project's completion and the imminent opening of the new facility. On the other hand, I sensed something darker and almost sinister. The behavior of the senior management team was peculiar and unsettling. I had the distinct feeling that something was lurking in the shadows of this place, and I was about to walk right into it.

The general staff was an excellent team; they were friendly and hardworking, and most seemed happy in their roles, with only a few exceptions. The majority of the residents and patients were also pleasant. I truly enjoyed my conversations with the staff in the hallways and got to know many of them as kind and wonderful people. I was deeply moved by the way they cared for the residents. It was heartwarming to see how the staff and residents interacted, treating one another as family.

The senior management team was becoming increasingly isolated from the cultural core of the organization, and their working methods were becoming more troubling. Although I was a member of this group, I never felt a close connection to them. I felt more at ease with the staff, residents, contractors, and construction teams.

It was becoming clear that the this management team and the board had lost sight of what truly mattered: the residents, patients, and families who relied on us to create a safe, comfortable, and enjoyable environment for healing after difficult surgeries and for the care of their elderly loved ones. During my time there, the focus shifted almost entirely to the needs of senior managers and certain board members, rather than on supporting the residents and patients. This situation deeply saddened me.

My job had become quite busy, and I enjoyed the challenge of managing major projects along with two large departments that required much of my attention. With less than three months remaining before we opened the new facilities and became fully operational, my primary task was to assist in completing the construction project . Next, I needed to ensure that the nearly finished buildings were furnished correctly, equipped, and staffed to meet the tight deadline for the grand opening. Finally, I had to relocate all the offices scattered across the campus into one central location within one of the new buildings, which was no simple task.

I was responsible for managing office assignments and overseeing the property's furniture. Each day, I received requests for larger offices with better views and upgraded mechanical sit/stand desk systems. Additionally, the board requested new, comfortable high-end chairs for their monthly meetings, each priced at nearly one thousand dollars.

I found this behavior shameful and difficult to accept, especially knowing that our main kitchen had ovens over twenty years old that barely maintained the required temperature. Additionally, the resident

HVAC systems were failing almost daily. Yet, despite these pressing issues, the expectation was that Philip should have an even bigger office with a more elaborate chair on which to set his plump bottom.

It was apparent to me that the little piggies were lining up at the trough, so I began to resist and even decline the requests from the management of this reputable nonprofit care facility. Shawn and I would sit in the trailer, reviewing each request.

"That's a no," I said as I flipped the paper over and picked up the next.

"Here is one from Karen, Dave. She needs an L-shaped electric desk system and chair for about $2,100. Thoughts?" Shawn said with a raised eyebrow.

"It's a no," I said, with some embarrassment.

He took the request, crumpled it, and tossed it in a high arc into the trash can by the door. "Three points!"

I spent weeks creating a master move plan for nearly forty offices. I collaborated with human resources, department heads, administrators, and employees to find suitable work areas for everyone. I put in my earbuds, closed the door to my office, and drafted a detailed schedule. I met with my maintenance leads and appointed them as move captains. Each captain was assigned three helpers, including a housekeeper and an IT support technician.

A week before the move, I provided each team captain with their moving schedule and instructed them to contact the individuals they would assist. They needed to review the plan and help each person prepare his or her office, bringing moving boxes and packing supplies to everyone scheduled to move and assisting them in their preparation.

I hired a moving company to provide six professional movers and equipment to assist the move captains. "Three days, everyone. Three days," I said to my moving team as we gathered at 6:30 a.m. on a foggy Wednesday, the first day of the move. "By Friday evening, I want us to be completely moved in, with every office space fully operational. Monday morning, we are business as usual."

It was a thing of beauty. I watched as my team of competent captains and movers pushed their dollies, carts, and roller bins down the hallways and through the tunnel, carrying desks, chairs, computers, lamps, file cabinets, and boxes containing coffee mugs and cat posters. Each team focused on one office move at a time, from start to finish. The captains would stay in touch with everyone on their list for that day and keep them apprised of timing and logistics.

The staff member scheduled for the next move would watch as a team of six entered their office and began to work. The IT technician carefully disconnected their computer, monitors, phone, and printer, packing them neatly into boxes. Meanwhile, the other five team members swiftly wrapped file cabinets and desks in shrink wrap and moving blankets, loading them onto dollies and transporting them down the hall.

The boxes were loaded onto six-wheeled hand trucks and were quickly pushed through the tunnel and across campus to the new building. The team moved efficiently and with care. The captains worked in front of their crews, waiting in the new office space to ensure it was ready for setup.

Upon arriving at the new office space, the moving teams quickly reassembled the office. The IT technicians took this opportunity to run system updates on each computer workstation as they set them up. The captains called their designated housekeepers to inform them they were ready for cleaning. The housekeepers came in to vacuum, dust, wipe down desks and furniture, and clean the windows. Each cross-campus office move took approximately forty-five minutes from start to finish, achieving perfection before moving on to the next.

As I walked around the campus observing the teams at work, I was accompanied by a contractor for the telephone systems and the IT director. Shawn was always on speed dial. Meanwhile, the chef and his crew prepared box lunches for the staff and moving crews. They placed the labeled boxes on a reserved table in the employee dining area, ensuring the relocating employees or those moving them did not have to worry about lunch.

By 3:30 p.m. on Friday, all offices had been successfully relocated, and all thirty-eight employees had settled at their new desks, ready to work. Ninety minutes ahead of schedule—not bad.

The weeks passed, and the construction of the new buildings was nearly complete. All the teams had been working long hours for many months and were feeling fatigued. As the shriek of the table saws stopped and the nail guns were packed away, the property began to feel different.

I often walked through the halls of the new buildings after work in the evenings, donning my hard hat and enjoying the quiet in these fresh, new spaces. I reflected on the many stressful meetings, the rush to meet phase deadlines, and the numerous state inspections. I thought about the staff who would soon fill these rooms and hallways, diligently caring for new patients, the first of whom were scheduled to arrive in less than two weeks.

A flutter of apprehension stirred as I contemplated the tight timeline for the new buildings to open their doors. The final inspections loomed ahead, and once completed, Shawn would ceremonially hand over the keys, marking a significant milestone in our project. From that moment, the responsibility would rest squarely on our shoulders to orchestrate the move-in and meticulously arrange everything before the grand opening.

As I surveyed the tasks before us, the immensity of what lay ahead was daunting yet invigorating. I found comfort in the fact that I couldn't have asked for a better team to navigate this challenge. The office move project had served as a perfect crucible for my team. I was continually impressed by how they had rallied together, blending their strengths and talents to deliver exceptional work.

The following week would be the grand finale. Plans were complete and approved. Furniture, fixtures, and equipment had been ordered and were expected to arrive soon. Punch lists were nearly finished. We were ready.

Walking through the quiet, freshly painted hallways, I reflected on how much I enjoyed this type of work. I found it immensely challenging, yet incredibly interesting and gratifying. Although it might seem like a small detail, I appreciate the opportunity to get up and move while I work. This starkly contrasted with my previous experience in the wine business, where I often sat at my desk for ten hours or more daily with minimal movement. I worked on a thirty-acre campus that employed hundreds of people, multiple buildings, commercial kitchens, dining rooms, service areas, parking lots, outdoor gathering spaces, and extensive landscaped areas, all of which I explored daily. I believe I think best when I'm able to move.

As I moved along the empty hallways, I thought about the off-gassing from the new carpet and paint. I considered texting Shawn to ask if some fans could be set up, but I decided to wait until morning since it was getting late.

I sat in a brown folding chair at the end of a long corridor, which gave me a clear view of all three patient-room hallways that fanned out like three fingers from the nurse's station directly behind me. Sitting in this quiet, angular space, I reflected on my year of working here. My thoughts drifted back to my first significant project on campus: the tunnel. I considered it a major success, acting like bypass surgery, as it restored vital "blood flow" to the campus by opening this central artery.

I rested my elbows on my knees and leaned forward, shaking my head as I recalled the tough times I faced with some senior managers. The hurt feelings, backbiting, and childish and selfish behavior were all too vivid in my memory. I pictured Karen standing in my office doorway each morning, wringing her hands, and I couldn't help but laugh as I remembered how she always called me "sir" whenever she was upset, which happened quite often.

Then, I thought about the laughter and camaraderie I enjoyed in the construction trailer, the many "Shawn-isms" I had collected over the months, and his witty, punchy humor, which provided much relief during stressful and sometimes bizarre meetings.

A wave of satisfaction washed over me. *We did good work here*. I played a key role in turning around challenging projects and departments, benefiting an organization serving many people. My mind began to open to the possibility that my work here could continue, which felt good. I considered refocusing on the departments I managed, identifying areas for improvement and envisioning what they might look like in a few months.

On Monday morning, we had tractor-trailers lined up, waiting for their turn to back up to the main doors and begin unloading hospital beds, chairs, sofas, dressers, mirrors, coffee tables, armoires, and commercial washing machines and dryers. My team once again executed the work seamlessly.

I noticed a change in Stanley around this time. He was becoming distant and less friendly toward me. I felt like the odd man out in the senior management team meetings. Was it because I wouldn't approve their lavish furniture and office requests? I would hope not.

My wife says something about me that drives insecure corporate people crazy: "It's your quiet confidence. It makes them feel very uneasy. They want it but don't have it." That would explain why they seemed to always travel in packs around the property, like a little executive street gang. In hindsight, we should have ordered matching jackets and Segways instead of fancy new desks. They could buzz by my office in a bunch, snapping their fingers in unison, saying, "We want our big offices and expensive chairs! Or else!"

In my fifty-six years, I have only been abruptly released from one job. It wasn't a dramatic scene like in *Jerry Maguire*, with shouting, arm-waving, and a frantic scramble to collect my belongings while being wrestled out by security as I yelled, "Who is coming with me?"

Instead, it was a dull experience, oddly structured and somewhat awkwardly managed.

The morning after the completion of the 34-million-dollar construction project that I helped bring to a successful finish, the state inspectors conducted their final sign-offs, and we opened the doors.

I knew I would be out celebrating with the construction managers that night, so I blocked off the following morning in my schedule. Nevertheless, an event appeared on my calendar for the next day at 8:00 a.m.: "Catch up with Stanley." Stanley, the CEO and my boss, wanted to schedule a conversation, which wasn't unusual.

I walked into the executive boardroom a few minutes before 8:00 a.m. the next day and sat, waiting for Stanley to join me, as I had done many times before. The door opened, and Becky, our HR manager, entered and sat down.

"Good morning. Do you have something scheduled in here?" I asked as she opened her laptop on the table and searched for a plug. "If you do, I can meet him in his office; it's no big deal."

"No, that's okay, this is fine," she said sheepishly. "I will wait with you."

We sat in a strange silence for a few minutes before Stanley came charging in through the door from the executive suite.

"Sorry, I'm late," he said as he sat down a few seats to my right and across the table from HR. I found the choice of seating as odd as our uninvited guest in our catch-up chat.

After a few minutes of small talk, Stanley said, "Dave, we are eliminating your position." He told me they had to cut back as a not-for-profit organization. Still trying to pull myself from the red-wine fog from the night before, I asked him to repeat himself. "Your position has been slated to be eliminated for some time, and we cannot wait any longer; the board just won't approve the budget."

I looked up at Becky. "Really? The morning after we opened the new buildings?" I asked in disbelief.

"Yes, you did an amazing job helping that happen, and we really appreciate it," Stanley said, squirming in his chair. Becky nodded, her face red, as she looked down at the table in front of her. After they reviewed the payout details, Stanley stood up and reached for my hand. I didn't shake his hand.

"A little notice would have been great, Stanley," I said, as he turned back to the door from which he had entered less than seven minutes before, according to the clock on my laptop.

"Becky will run through the rest of the plan with you, Dave. Again, I apologize for being so abrupt; I had promised the board. Dave, I had no choice." He glanced back as he walked out of the room, and I could see he felt bad.

The fog started to lift, and panic began to set in. "I have four kids at home, Stanley. A little notice would have been nice," I said again to his back.

"This was never a permanent position, Dave," Becky said.

She was right; this role was never intended to be permanent. What started as a one-year project had evolved into a more significant position. However, I had expected a reasonable separation plan to be arranged either at the end of the fiscal year or the end of the quarter, which would have made sense from a budgetary perspective. I certainly wasn't anticipating a sudden dismissal on that gloomy February morning.

Instead, I would advocate for a more collaborative strategy, engaging with the outgoing manager to identify the best time to create an "off-ramp." This would ensure that all work is completed and facilitate a smooth transition. Such an approach allows the organization and the outgoing manager time to prepare for the change, preserve dignity, and conclude the professional relationship respectfully. Unfortunately, a swift and abrupt termination was chosen for my situation instead.

Becky and I sat stiffly in the half-lit and chilly boardroom before I stood up to leave. "I can follow you to your office and help you if you want."

"Help me do what, Becky?"

"Pack your things, Dave."

"You need me to leave right now?" I asked, with growing confusion. I was now feeling oddly sleepy.

"Stanley promised the board that your position would be eliminated by today; I'm so sorry, Dave," she said from genuine discomfort.

"Well, okay, I will leave today then," I said as I stepped out the door and turned toward my office. I noticed that Becky was following me, but her office was not this way.

"Are you walking with me?" I asked with a half turn.

"Yes. Is that okay, Dave? I am supposed to help you prepare and ensure you have everything you need."

I stepped into my office, turned to her, and said as politely as possible, "Becky, I don't need help. You are welcome to stand in the hallway if you would like, but I don't need help." She apologized, said it was weird for her, too, and agreed there was no need for this unfriendly exit.

"I think someone on the board asked Stanley to do this," Becky said quietly, as I scanned my office for personal items.

She leaned farther into my office and said, "Take as long as you need, Dave. Go say goodbye to your teams if you want; it's no problem." She quietly walked out, and I sat at my desk.

As I set some personal items into a box, my phone rang. I stared at it.

"Hey, where have you been, boss? You coming up to meet that landscape guy?" I turned to see our maintenance manager, Alvin, leaning in my door with his coffee-stained mug.

"No, man, I am not," I said as I stood up. My desk phone rang again. I explained the situation and told him I enjoyed working with him.

"I bet she did this," he said, pointing to the office beside me.

"Karen didn't do this, the board did. It's okay, Alvin. The board never approved this position; we knew it wouldn't last forever."

"Clem knows?"

"No, no one knows yet," I said, lifting the box off my desk.

"You are leaving right now?" he asked with mounting frustration in his voice.

"Yeah, man. I'm just going to slide out quietly before it turns into a thing, ya know?" My laughter seemed oddly loud and out of place at that moment. "I will call you guys later," I said. As we walked out, he raised his middle finger to the closed office door next to mine. Becky's pink, round face peeked from behind us as we walked toward the doors to ensure I had left the building.

"*Easy,*" I quietly said to my friend as we turned the corner. "You have to walk back in the door, brother; I don't."

I started the walk of shame across that damp, cold parking lot in Vancouver, a walk many had before me. The rain was coming down now as I climbed into my truck. My wipers pushed water and small pieces of frozen rain from the cold windshield. I watched them momentarily, amazed by how close they were to the tempo of the song playing on the radio, which reminded me of the old Eddie Rabbitt track, "Drivin' My Life Away." I was in shock. I saw a couple of pale faces in the doorway, pressed against the glass, looking in my direction. I slowly pulled around the corner and started the thirty-minute, rainy drive home.

My head was spinning. Why did that just happen? My phone was ringing; it was Shawn. "I'm standing in your office. What the *fuck* is going on?" he yelled into my ear. I explained what happened and thanked him for being such a great partner on the project.

I ended the call and found myself in the throes of a building panic attack. My emotions were splintering as my mind toggled back and forth between the loss of money and the idea of having to find another job. My thoughts raced. Why didn't they give me any notice? I was a senior manager, and this was not performance related. "I crushed it—did a great job. So why did this happen?" I asked the defrosting windshield.

As I pulled the truck into my neighborhood, I braked hard because someone had pulled out of an alley and didn't see me coming. I started to drive past the man in the blue Honda Accord and turned enough to see his middle finger pop up on his steering wheel. This was Portland, where such things were not unusual. But not today—not in *my* neighborhood! I looked over again, and he now had both middle fingers extended in my direction. I jammed the truck into park and got out. He got out.

"Can I help you!?" I asked as I stepped toward him. The situation quickly escalated to the two of us standing toe-to-toe in the middle of the street, blocking traffic. People stepped out of stores and restaurants to see what all the yelling was about. "This is *my* neighborhood, mother fucker!" I yelled with my finger in his face. As the insults were being lobbed back and forth at high volume, I pulled things together, stepped back, and asked myself, *Do I want to add jail to this already horrible day?* I returned to my truck and drove around the corner to my house.

I walked through the house and into the backyard, where the office and studio were located. I sat there for an hour to regain my bearings. My phone was ringing nonstop. I yelled and paced, but mostly, I tried to formulate a plan for what I would do next.

The last few years had been challenging for us. We sold our

struggling business, which left us in a difficult position, both financially and emotionally. Our debt was piling up while we had four
hungry boys in high school, two of whom would soon be heading off
to college. On top of that, we were living in a 130-year-old home that
required significant repairs, and we had a sizable mortgage. Our cars
also needed maintenance, and our grocery bills were astronomical. To
make matters worse, we had just lost about 50 percent of our income.
This hit us hard, especially during such a tough time.

Stanley, Philip, and most of the other senior managers were relieved
of their positions shortly after I departed from the organization and
were replaced by an entirely new management team. Several members
of the board also left, signaling a welcome shift in the organization's
direction. I wish the new team the best and hope they remain focused
on supporting this facility's residents, patients, families, and staff.

I miss the caregivers, department leaders, and staff I got to know at
this place; they are such kind, hardworking people. I miss my mornings
in the construction trailer with Shawn and the team—all great guys
and incredible project managers, from whom I learned much. I remain
very proud of the work we did there.

CHAPTER THIRTEEN
BACK IN THE SADDLE

Right now, I am having amnesia and déjà vu at the same time.
I think I have forgotten this before.

Steven Wright

Sudden job loss can hit hard, like a gut punch that leaves you reeling, especially for men in my age group. While I recognize that unemployment is a challenge for anyone, it strikes at the very core of our identities as men and fathers. Growing up, my generation absorbed the belief that hard work and the ability to provide for our families were not just important but fundamental to our self-worth, just as it was for our fathers and their fathers before them. When we lose the means to support our loved ones, we often feel a profound sense of disconnection from our roles in the world. The gratification and self-esteem that come from fulfilling this responsibility can vanish, leaving us grappling with uncertainty and questioning our value in a society that places a high premium on the traditional male provider.

In short, our self-worth is often closely linked to our ability to earn a living. When we find ourselves unable to provide, it can lead to a crippling downward spiral of panic, self-doubt, shame, and destructive thoughts. I began to experience this myself. I couldn't help but wonder: *Who am I if I can't provide for my family?*

In these moments, our true selves can be revealed, as we often feel exposed and vulnerable for everyone to see—or at least, it can feel that way. I had a strong desire to be alone, to remain unnoticed, and to blend into the dull background of my life—to hide away. Like a wounded animal, I just wanted to crouch in a quiet corner of my studio office in the backyard, avoiding contact with others and hoping to escape being seen in this state—broken, weak, and powerless.

A couple of weeks passed, and I finally stepped outside to feel the sunlight on my face again. It was time to reenter the world and take a more proactive approach to my life. During that time, I had immersed myself in home projects, desperately trying to cultivate a sense of purpose. I did my best to avoid friends, neighbors, social gatherings, and family because I didn't want to explain why I was not working. I felt embarrassed and hurt.

I wondered what had motivated my firing. Was it guilt, selfishness, an attempt to mollify the board of directors? Or was it simply the result of a few insecure senior managers who wanted to vote me off the island?

My sudden termination—or elimination of my position—was unrelated to performance issues or anything that would justify such an abrupt and damaging removal. One moment, I was thriving, having completed major projects that significantly contributed to the organization's business and goals. The next moment, I found myself unemployed, driving away in the cold rain with a hastily packed box containing a few framed pictures, some books, a vase, a coffee mug, and a stash of snacks from Trader Joe's.

This lack of insight was hindering my ability to process the event effectively. The sensation reminded me of the odd feeling experienced after unexpectedly being bitten by a friend's dog—shock, confusion, embarrassment, denial, betrayal, and, finally, pain.

I felt humiliated when I drove across the river to Oregon City to apply for unemployment benefits. I parked my truck around the back of the rain-stained brick building to avoid being recognized. While waiting in the lobby of the worn-down single-story government structure, I nervously held my hat in my hands and read the employee rights posters on the wall. I would have preferred to be anywhere else, but the harsh reality was that we needed the money.

I listened carefully as the government employee inquired about the résumés I had submitted and the number of interviews I had attended since becoming unemployed. I watched her examine my résumé, trying to understand it and quickly categorize my professional background. It felt as though she needed to fit me into a small box labeled "sales director," "multi-outlet retail manager," "estate manager," "operations director," "wine guy," or "entrepreneur."

Our eyes met when she asked, "Which of these is your professional focus?"

"Well, all of them," I said. I decided not to mention that I could also design and install an award-winning English garden, prepare a stunning grilled lobster served over saffron and lemon risotto, and split a cord of maple for a small wood stove in under ninety minutes. I was certain there wouldn't be enough space on her form for that.

"This will be easier if you just choose one career path," she said. "It can be confusing otherwise."

"Confusing for whom?" I asked. "I have done, and can do, all of those things." *Doesn't that make someone like me more valuable, not less?*

She was growing impatient with me. She turned her screen toward me and pointed to the blinking cursor in the left corner of a small cell on the benefits form she was completing while we talked. "I can only put one thing, Mr. Becker. What would you like me to enter?" she asked, looking over my shoulder to the crowded waiting area.

A baby was crying in the lobby.

"Just choose the option you believe will best meet the requirements," I said, feeling like a strange beast in this room full of timeworn gray cubicles. My finger traced slowly across the dingy fabric covering of the cubicle divider beside me. Examining my now gray-stained fingertip, I wondered what it was made of. *Is this even fabric?* At that moment, I felt like I was being pulled in two directions. One part of me wanted to explain to this person the advantages of having a diverse work history—the deep knowledge and broad skill set it provides, along with the value it can bring to various organizations. To use a sports analogy, I saw myself as a utility player who could adapt to fill multiple roles within an organization and perform well, often providing a strategic advantage to the team. *Do you need a third baseman, shortstop, pitcher, referee, or team manager for today's game? I can step into any of those positions reasonably well.*

However, the other part of me recognized that the only way to navigate this bureaucratic entanglement would be to surrender to their process and help move things forward as required, thus maximizing my chances of a quick payout, which was the ultimate goal.

Condensing my diverse and colorful work history into a small gray box on this woman's form proved challenging. Each experience felt significant, worthy of its own box. Yet, I was left with the daunting task of summarizing decades of experience, growth, and learning into just two words on a county form that would most likely not even be seen by human eyes.

I reflected on my friends who had committed to a single career path since high school: a doctor, a lawyer, a teacher, and an architect. In that moment, the streamlined nature of their professional lives felt incredibly appealing. I appreciated the simplicity of it. They were "one-cell" people, fitting neatly into the forms on the flickering government computer screens. In that sticky little bureaucratic moment, being able to say, "I am a ___" seemed almost luxurious. But alas, that was not me.

It felt as though I was asking for a handout, which made me feel like I was begging and filled me with shame. This was a dark moment in my life. As I scanned the room, I noticed the other unemployment applicants; some were younger, some older, but they all shared troubled expressions—worry, stress, frustration, embarrassment, and, some like me, a sense of shame. I never wanted to go through this again. This experience did not support the version of myself I was working so hard to create and put into the world.

A month passed as I occupied myself with various home projects and job searches. As my wounds began to heal, I gradually regained my confidence. I reconnected with former colleagues from the wine industry. It was terrific to catch up with each other. I told them I was looking to return to the wine business.

Not long after, I received a call from a vice-president at my former wine company, who had heard that I was seeking new opportunities. We discussed the industry and the experiences I had gained while away from the wine business. He offered me a position on his team similar to my previous role. Although I was brought in as a regional manager instead of the national sales position I had held before, the compensation was the same as when I left. I was pleased with this arrangement because the regional role meant less travel for me. Therefore, I happily accepted the offer and returned to a familiar environment. I was genuinely grateful for the opportunity to rejoin the team.

Within a few weeks, I was reassigned to my old accounts and got back to work. Although most buyers had changed since I'd left in 2014, many systems remained unchanged. Upon my return, I noticed that the company had a different atmosphere. The culture had become more severe and less friendly during my four-year hiatus. It felt like a big, angry machine that seemed to harbor some disdain for its employees, particularly the sales teams.

Shortly after my return, layoffs began, and the leadership team quickly distanced itself from the rest of us. They used phrases like "right-sizing our organization" and "streamlining our structure to better position ourselves in an increasingly competitive market." Initially, this seemed reasonable, but as more of my colleagues were quietly escorted out—without announcements, well-wishes, or farewell celebrations—I became increasingly troubled. It felt like a quiet corporate bloodletting behind closed doors, and witnessing so many people vanish without a trace was concerning.

I worked tirelessly to ensure that my accounts performed optimally, and I consistently met my goals. I pushed my chain accounts hard and drove strong results. This dedication helped me survive multiple rounds of layoffs. Unfortunately, the company culture deteriorated into a dark and fearful atmosphere. Most conversations among the sales team were about the fear of being laid off rather than discussing accounts, quarterly objectives, cases sold, or business strategy.

"Did you hear they let Bob from the national team go yesterday? Yeah, they just disabled his email, and while he was on the phone with IT trying to resolve the issue, someone from HR called to inform him it was his last day."

"Wait, my email has been messed up today!" someone else would say with rising anxiety.

We rode on our squeaky little merry-go-round of fear, suspicion, rumors, and self-doubt for years, exhausting ourselves and each other. Our company's new prime directive was to promote women and create a more diverse work environment. Don't get me wrong; this, in itself, is wonderful. I firmly believe it is time for more women leaders and a more diverse workplace; this is beneficial when done thoughtfully.

However, our company's approach felt harsh and reactive; it almost seemed they were hastily responding to an imminent legal threat. The weekly mandatory training webinars on harassment in the workplace hinted at this. I pictured the scene from the movie *The Hunt for Red October* where Alec Baldwin's submarine is pursued and fired upon by an aggressive enemy determined to destroy it. Radical evasive maneuvers had to be taken quickly.

This situation felt like a corporate "Crazy Ivan!"

A new director role on our team has opened up, similar to my previous position at the company. It was quickly filled by a woman from another group, which was a positive development. However, it soon became clear that Cindy had limited leadership experience and struggled to build professional relationships, especially with her male colleagues. I felt a sense of unease as I was the only male on her team.

I had known Cindy for about fifteen years. We came up in the industry together. She came from the distributor community and was relatively new to the supplier side. I came up through the retail and supplier side of the business. She had a reputation for being a skilled and knowledgeable salesperson, but was often uncomfortable around people. In our first phone conversation, I was sensitive to the new dynamic and reiterated my intention to support her and the team in any way possible. I was comfortable with this work and drove strong results, as many team members did.

She seemed to appreciate the discussion, but tension between us began to develop soon after this. As the months passed, the situation between Cindy and me became increasingly complicated. She would often call me at the end of the day, seeming agitated and aggressive. Occasionally, she made threats and accusations against me, which caused a great deal of stress because I cared deeply about my job, my reputation, and the rest of the team. I vividly remember one particular call. It was on my fifty-first birthday. My wife and friends were waiting in the kitchen to take me to see Ziggy Marley at the Edgefield Amphitheater to celebrate.

My wife stood at my office door, wondering why I was still at my desk. She listened as the woman on the speakerphone berated me, going so far as to call me names and question my parenting abilities, along with other hurtful personal attacks.

"Who is that?" my wife demanded as she reached for the mute button on the phone.

"It's my boss," I said as I redirected her hand from the phone. I put up my finger, asking for one more moment. That conversation left me feeling hurt and upset.

We left for the show shortly after. "Dave's company is a real shit show!" my wife said as we piled into the car.

CHAPTER FOURTEEN
THE THING

The fear of death follows from the fear of life.
A man who lives fully is prepared to die anytime.

Mark Twain

In the summer of 2017, during a challenging period in the wine business, I was on vacation with my family at Lake Pend Oreille in Idaho. The northern part of the state, not far from Sandpoint, is lovely. Toward the end of our trip, I started to feel unwell. The symptoms hit me suddenly: I was coughing and felt exhausted and feverish—it seemed like I was coming down with a cold. I didn't usually get sick and attributed it to bad timing.

A few days after returning home, I began to feel even worse. I went to see the doctor and was diagnosed with pneumonia, which was unexpected for someone my age and in otherwise good health during the summer. Fortunately, the pneumonia was treated successfully, and I recovered quickly. However, about a month later, I started feeling sick again, this time with more difficulty breathing. I struggled through my usual morning workout, which consisted of a mile-long swim in an outdoor saltwater pool—my slice of heaven!

I was again diagnosed with pneumonia in an area of my lower right lung, not far from the previous infection but, to be sure, a different infection. This pneumonia was more aggressive. I was on more potent antibiotics and inhalers. It wiped me out. A hard rattle developed when I breathed, and I was more fatigued than ever, but I recovered. Another month passed, and while we were taking down our Halloween decorations, once again, I felt unwell. I had trouble breathing, along with debilitating fatigue, fever, sluggishness, sweating, chest pain, and dizziness. Walking up the stairs felt like I was running a marathon. Something was wrong.

Pneumonia number three in as many months. My doctor was baffled. She explained that this was highly unusual for someone not in their eighties. She sent me to the hospital for a CT scan. The report she received from the radiologist a few days later was a little surprising: Nothing. Clear.

She agreed that something was wrong and sent me to a pulmonologist for some tests. Most pulmonologists were very busy in November, so I grabbed the first available appointment in Salem, Oregon, about an hour away. The weekend before my appointment, I decided to run over to the hospital and grab a copy of my CT on a disk to avoid delays.

I worked in my home office that Sunday morning, the day before my appointment. I pulled the disk containing the CT images and report from my computer bag, slid it out of its white paper sleeve, and inserted it into the drive. I scrolled through the images, rolling the view around as I sipped my tea. "Huh, that's strange," I said as I looked at a white blob in my chest. The ghostly shape expanded and contracted as I rolled my cursor. I knew nothing about reading a CT scan, but found it fascinating. I Googled "How to read a CT Scan" and continued to toggle between the websites, medical journals, and images.

That's odd.

I'd found an image of a chest scan of a healthy fifty-year-old male online, now displayed on my second monitor. I could quickly identify the prominent anatomical landmarks, including the liver, lungs, heart, and diaphragm. I was getting the hang of it. I adjusted the position of my CT scan images to match as closely as possible that of the healthy person's image on the other screen. My eyes darted back and forth between the two scans. They were not the same.

The following day, I entered the pulmonologist's examination room, where his physician assistant spent a few minutes discussing my issues and symptoms with me. She pulled up the CT report they had received from the hospital and immediately went to the section from the radiologist, informing me that everything looked fine; it was all clear. She suggested that I take Advil or Tylenol for any chest pain and recommended taking a break from swimming for a couple of weeks.

As she stood up and offered me the customary "thanks for coming" wave, I asked if I could have a moment, as I had some additional questions. She kindly agreed and pulled up the images from my CT scan on a monitor. She maneuvered her cursor quickly, adjusting the view of the images in much the same way I had done in my office the day before.

"It looks normal to me," she said.

"There!" I said. "Please rotate it to the left a little more. Right there! On the bottom part of the right lung." I pointed to her screen. "What is that?"

She turned the image again and again, rolling it back and forth. She reread the radiologist's report and went back to the image.

"I am fairly certain that I don't have three lungs," I said with a hint of sarcasm, bending toward rudeness. "Can you please run this by someone?" I wondered why I was contentious at that moment, but I realized that I was feeling an urgent need to be heard, coupled with the deep understanding that something was, in fact, wrong. She adjusted the zoom and pulled the image view out further. She stared at the screen for what felt like an eternity, though I'm sure it was only a moment. She got up and left the room without saying anything.

I waited for about ten minutes before I started packing up my things and sent a quick text to Caroline saying that I was heading home. She asked how the appointment went. I told her it was strange, and the PA left without saying anything. "She just left"? Caroline asked.

"Yep. It's okay, I need to get back anyway."

As I pushed send on that last text, the door to the examination room opened again; this time, it was the pulmonologist. He came bustling through the door, his white lab coat flapping behind him like a sad little cape, the PA close in tow. He sat on the stool before me while I put on my jacket.

"Mr. Becker, please have a seat." I sat. "Mr. Becker, you have a growth," the doctor said, with very little emotion. He spun around in his chair and pulled up the CT file, rotating the image with noticeable speed and skill. "This is the growth." The tip of his index finger touched the screen in the middle of that whitish blob I looked at in my office. I watched his finger press so hard on the screen that it turned a hazy gray and purple where he had touched. "I called OHSU in Portland and spoke with a specialist I know there." He spun his chair around. "He is a cardiothoracic surgeon. This situation is above my pay grade, Mr. Becker. I'm passing you along to someone who can help you take the next step, okay?" He told me that not many surgeons accept cases like this one.

He explained that the mass was huge. It had folded over the bottom part of my lung, the apparent cause of the recurring pneumonia, shortness of breath, and chest pain. It pressed against my heart, shifting it out of place and moving it further to the left. He turned to his PA and said curtly, "Go call that radiologist up there and make sure he is aware of his mistake. Tell him to correct the report immediately."

I asked how this could have been missed, given that there had been four chest X-rays and a CT scan in the last 120 days. "I don't know, Dave," he said, shaking his head in frustration. He told me the surgeon he consulted in Portland would call me later that day. That was it. He said goodbye and left the room.

Struggling to digest this news, I walked out.

I was in shock. What the hell just happened? I put my company car into gear and drove out of the damp parking lot. Counting Crows' "Mr. Jones" played softly through the speakers as my thoughts dashed about, trying to combine the puzzle pieces of that conversation in a way that made sense.

At a stop sign, I texted Caroline quickly, "I talked to the doc, and it's not great news. Call when you are free." In my hurried daze, I texted the wrong person. A friend from work returned my cryptic and somewhat alarming message with "????"

The cardiothoracic surgeon from OHSU called that evening and discussed the next steps. He needed me to come up to the hospital in Portland for testing, the sooner, the better. The surgeon explained that since they were unsure what this was, he wanted to get it out as quickly as possible. He did not intend to biopsy the mass while it was inside me. "I want this thing out of you next week, Mr. Becker; how is Wednesday? But I need you up here tomorrow for some tests, okay?" My head was spinning.

Unfortunately, this was not the best time for me. The holiday season makes November and December incredibly busy in the wine business; we often experienced 40 percent of our annual sales volume within just those two months.

I informed Cindy that I would need to take a day off for medical reasons. In response, she impatiently asked, "So, you won't be able to participate in the market survey?" I explained that it was a pressing medical issue that required immediate testing. "Okay, just join us when you're done. I was hoping you could lead a team to survey a route tomorrow for the second half of the day since Phil, our senior vice-president, is coming into town. After that, we have dinner." I had to inform her that this would likely take all day. I would try to join, but they shouldn't count on me. "But Phil is coming!"

The call did not go well, and Cindy was disappointed.

The day of testing at the teaching hospital was intense. I had never seen anything like it, having been a pretty healthy guy my whole life.

"Well, my team has been running every kind of test known to man on you today, Dave," the surgeon said, reading a printout, "and we can't find anything wrong other than this *thing* inside you. That said, we have no reason to wait. Let's just get this out, okay?" He gave me a confident grin.

"Yes, please."

I struggled to process everything as I buttoned my shirt. Facing something like this for the first time, my mind didn't quite know how to react. Thoughts darted around, often focused on trivial, even downright silly things. My first question to the surgeon was whether I could continue swimming before the surgery. *Really, Dave?*

Grabbing the door handle, he turned back to me. "You feel like exercising with this thing inside you?"

"Sure, yeah, I guess I do."

He laughed. "Okay, fine. Why not? Just don't swim alone. You are working with a partially collapsed lung here, okay?"

"Got it, okay," I said, feeling like a dumbass.

He asked his assistant to step in and rattled off a few days on the calendar. She responded with what he had scheduled for those times. "How about Wednesday?" he asked.

"You have two on the books that day, doctor," she said.

"Clear the morning, please." He turned to me. "Okay then, Dave, we have a date! See you then, buddy."

It was Thanksgiving week, so he scheduled the surgery for the following week. He called me every evening around seven o'clock over the holiday weekend, even on Thanksgiving. He assessed my condition, mental state, and symptoms. His tone was casual and friendly, as if he were talking to a friend.

"Tell me about your breathing," he said.

"It's okay; I feel a little winded, I suppose, but that's it."

"Any fever? Bad cough? Dizziness."

"Not that I have noticed, no."

"Do you have a metallic taste in your mouth? Are you coughing up any blood, Dave?"

"No, don't think so."

It was misty as Caroline and I set out on that Wednesday morning, driving to OHSU. The world outside felt surreal, like we were gliding through a dream. During the half-hour journey through the winding streets of Southwest Portland, everything seemed to move slowly.

Upon arrival, a nurse welcomed me reassuringly and guided me into the surgical prep area. She was gentle yet efficient as she took my vital signs and assisted me in removing all my personal items in preparation for the surgery. When she lightly tapped my wedding ring, a gesture filled with meaning, she said, "I'm sorry, this too, Dave." I glanced over at Caroline, whose eyes were welling with tears. In that moment, the gravity of the day settled over us both, serving as a poignant reminder of what we were about to face.

After a thorough prep session, I was pushed into the surgical theater. The surgeon was there with his team. He pointed around the room and quickly introduced the four or five other doctors and PAs to me as the surgical nurse set up an IV next to me.

"Dave, these people are the best at what they do. I want you to know that," he said.

The IV needle pinched a little when it was inserted. Something stirred in me.

"Wait . . . just wait . . ." I said. I looked to my left; the doctors and PAs were busily working at a table with their backs to me. I noticed the big lights over the table. The people in the room looked warm, almost unearthly, like blurred angels backlit with a blue-white light as the anesthesia flowed into my arm.

I opened my eyes in a hospital bed. I couldn't see anything. Was I awake?

A nurse's voice whispered from my left. She explained that my eyes were covered. "I'm going to pull the eye cover off slowly." As she did, my eyes struggled to focus. I saw the ghostly white shapes of blurred lab coats and nurses bustling around the room faster than my tired eyes could process the information.

The kindest, calmest nurse leaned in beside me and explained that she was a cardiac ICU nurse and would stay with me for a while. "Is that okay?" she asked. I nodded and tried to speak, but it came out as a croak and a gurgle. "You don't have to say anything, Dave. I got you."

My arm felt cold. I slipped away again.

I woke up to the most intense pain I have ever experienced. My eyes opened wide in panic. I gasped for air and grabbed the nurse's arm. "Okay, what's going on? Are you feeling pain?" she said as she shone a light in my eyes. I couldn't breathe or speak. I was slipping into shock, drowning in pain.

She urgently gave instructions to the others in the room. I could hear several people darting about my huge hospital room, moving things, talking. Eyes now shut and teeth clenched, I winced in pain. Someone else was speaking to me now. It was a doctor. "Mr. Becker, we need to put you under again for a minute, okay?" People were touching my body all over and pulling, poking, pushing, lifting, pressing.

Someone was counting backward.

I heard plastic connectors and caps disconnecting and cords falling to the floor. Beeping—there was so much beeping.

"Breathe for me, Dave," the nurse said calmly. "Just breathe."

A pinch, and then everything went quiet.

I awoke in what seemed to be only a few minutes later, foggy. "Hey there, sleepy guy," my wonderful ICU nurse said, as she worked on something beside my bed. "How are you feeling? If you were to rate the pain you feel right now, what would it be, one to ten?"

"I don't know," I croaked.

"We had a little pain issue there, huh?" she said.

"I guess, yeah. What is that?" I asked, squirming in increasing discomfort. "In my side and back, what is that?" I reached around to feel it.

"Well, we have an epidural in your back. Do you know what that is?" she asked. "On your side, well, a lot is going on over there, so just stay as still as you can, okay?" I looked down and saw multiple tubes coming out of my right side; one the size of a garden hose had been surgically inserted between two ribs under my right arm. Reddish liquid flowed through it, making a ghastly sucking sound every few seconds that was disturbing beyond description.

"Jesus! What is that?" I said with a gasp.

"That's a chest tube."

My feet were tied down tightly. "What's happening? What time is it? Why am I tied down?" I felt a growing panic. My heart was racing. I reached for my bed rail to try to pull myself up.

"Easy there, Dave. You need to stay still," the nurse said firmly. "You have a lot of stitches in you."

"Why am I tied down?" I asked again, a little louder this time.

"You are a big guy. We didn't want you kicking anyone while we were working on you," she said with a smile. "We took the hand restraints off after the procedure last night." I tried again to reach my feet. "It's Friday morning. Hey, your wife has been waiting to come in since Wednesday, but your pain levels were too high. Is it okay if she comes in to see you now?"

"Yes, of course. Friday? So, I have been out since Wednesday morning?"

"Well, you were awake for a little while yesterday, but let's not count that," she said with that warm smile. She turned as she was leaving my room. "Oh, Dave, your boss called yesterday. She wanted to know about your condition and when you would be out of the hospital." Her face showed annoyance, and her brow furrowed sharply, indicating that she sensed the call was unwelcome, given my current situation. "I told her I would never disclose patient information over the phone—'Goodbye.'" She grinned. "I got you!"

It should have struck me odd then that any human being would prioritize routine corporate work over a life-threatening medical event, but it did not. I almost expected it.

Caroline was walking in as my nurse explained my boss's phone call. She seemed irritated by the information but waved it off as she sat beside me and held my hand.

"You have been waiting so long to see me," I croaked.

It's okay. The doctors called me to tell me what was happening," she said. "I was just worried about you!"

"I was sound asleep through most of it."

"Regardless, it sounded just awful."

"They told me you have some nerve damage, and that's why the pain flared up so bad."

"I have no idea. I just want to go home." I grabbed her hand. "But I am literally tied down," I said with a gurgled giggle, motioning to my leg straps.

"Oh my God! What did you do?" she said, laughing.

After catching up for a few minutes, Caroline stepped into the bathroom and made a call. I couldn't hear much, but I distinctly remember her saying, "She *cannot* do that! Tell her she cannot do that!" I could sense the anger in her voice through the bathroom door.

When she returned and sat on the edge of my bed, I asked who she had been talking to. "I called your HR director and told her to warn that boss of yours to stay away from you," she said, a tear sliding down her cheek. I could see in her eyes that she was ready for a fight. We had been through so much together, and the stress had taken a toll on her. Being a senior executive well-versed in human resources, labor law, and employee rights, she was determined not to let my boss cross this line. In fact, she almost hoped to receive another message from her.

Caroline is one of the kindest people I know, but if anyone messes with her family, she will tear them to pieces. I felt so lucky to have her watching over me while my enervated body lay in that hospital bed. I felt safe. It was going to be okay.

That night, I woke up in a daze caused by the medication. I felt cold. My room was dimly lit, and I could hear the faint beeping of equipment somewhere in the cavernous room. Otherwise, it was perfectly quiet, and I was alone. Usually, nurses checked on me every few minutes.

Where is everyone?

I dreamed I could see my breath. A chill enveloped me, wrapping around my body like a cold, damp blanket. The room shimmered with a wet, bluish haze that wavered in the dim light, giving everything an otherworldly quality. An unsettling feeling washed over me; at that moment, I was convinced that I had died.

The next few days went by rather quickly. I felt better now, with less discomfort, and the pain was finally retreating like a slow outgoing tide. I became familiar with the schedules and routines of the fantastic staff that cared for me. I marveled at the number of doctors who entered my room, seemingly to have a gander at the guy who had the "thing" taken out.

My nurse would often comment on that. "I've worked in this unit for six years and haven't seen half of these doctors before," she told me. Some were in scrubs, some in white coats, some in business suits. They would come into my room, step over to my bed, say hello, and ask how I was doing. Most were very friendly. Some were not. I noticed the doctors who came in wearing suits would often not even look at me. They would talk to my nurse, ask questions, look at my chart, and then leave. She would look back at me and say something about their status or high-level position at the teaching hospital. "Oh my God! Do you know who that was?" I was less impressed. I was not enjoying my stay, nor the visitors stopping by to gawk at me, and I was ready to go.

I was feeling better.

My surgeon stopped by with another doctor from his team. They were kind and incredibly talented doctors. One sat, the other stood at the end of my bed. We chatted for a while about my current condition. "You are quite the celebrity around here," the cardiothoracic surgeon said as he sat on the stool next to me, checking the multiple hoses poking out of the side of my torso.

"Why are there so many people in here all the time?" I asked.

"We talked about it a few days ago, but you were still pretty out of it," he said.

It seems the tumor they removed from my chest cavity was very unusual, not only in type but also in size. Because the surgeon did not biopsy the "thing" before removing it, they had no idea what it was until it was, as he said, "in the bucket."

He explained the tumor was a very rare type of giant AB thymoma in an advanced Masaoka growth stage. "We have seen this kind of thymoma here, but they are rare and normally about the size of a grape or smaller, like a green pea," the lead surgeon said. Mine was unusually large. He rattled off dimensions in centimeters as if he were ordering a latte.

The other doctor laughed and explained that my tumor was not the size of a grape or a pea but rather the size of a Nerf football or a small loaf of bread. "*Extremely* rare," said the surgeon. He said that my tumor was the largest of its kind ever successfully removed, explaining that, due to its age, the tumor had developed an extensive vascular system in the thoracic cavity, with large and complex blood vessels supplying the massive growth. This made it very difficult to remove. It had become a part of me, like a large, ineffectual organ. The surgery led to substantial bleeding and nerve damage, as evidenced by the blood-filled chest tube gurgling from my rib cage.

"So that is why you are so popular here," the cardiothoracic surgeon said, laughing. "Everyone wants to see the guy with the 'thing.'"

This information shook me, and the other doctor noticed as he worked on me. "Don't worry, Dave, it's in the bucket and gone," he said with a smile. "Two surgeons were working inside you for over five hours; it wasn't easy." He patted my leg and stood up. I tried to process the image of a Nerf football tangled in blood vessels and veins being cut out of my chest cavity and pulled through my cracked, spread-open ribs.

"You made us work for our money on this one, Mr. Becker," the lead surgeon said as he walked toward the door, looking at his phone.

His colleague stayed for a minute and talked through the postsurgical issues and what they had to do to get the pain under control. "We did a lot of cutting, Dave, a lot. We had to cut through a great deal of nerve tissue to get in there and get that thing out. There is nerve damage, for sure, which we expected. The pain level spiking so high— that we did not expect. We have you on a cocktail of pretty strong stuff right now. It's working." He grasped the hose connection taped to my right side and asked me to take a deep breath.

"Why, what are we doing?" I asked, holding my hand up and signaling him to stop.

Looking up and making eye contact with my nurse, he began to count quietly. "Five, four, three, two, and . . ." Quickly and smoothly, he pulled the thick hose from my chest cavity. I was shocked at how much was coiled in my chest—a couple of feet, by the looks of it. It felt like a snake slithering around inside me. I dry heaved when I saw the length.

"You did great, Dave," he said as he dropped the blood-covered hose into a white bin on the side of my bed. It was out, and he was pressing something against my side firmly. "You made it! You are through the hard part; now we need to get you up and around again." He stepped toward the door, giving me a wave.

My nurse took over seamlessly, cleaned up the area, and got me patched up.

I left the hospital later that day with a beach pail full of oxycodone and supplies to change my dressing and clean the surgical sites. Although I felt shaky and a little dizzy, I was happy to be going home. As I glanced back at the bloodstained bed where I had spent the last six days, it felt as if I had lived a lifetime there on that mattress. My body had been under constant care through the pain, the fear, the stillness, the beeping, and the long, cold nights. Honestly, there were moments when I thought I might not make it out of that room, and I suspect I wasn't the only one feeling that way.

I stood near the door with my back to the corner of the room, listening to the pharmacy technician explaining the medication protocols and schedules. I couldn't shake the thought that I had never seen the room from this perspective before, or at least I couldn't remember it. *Is it the same room?*

While I stood looking at the bed, the pharmacy tech continued with the instructions, turning to my wife, knowing that I was not listening to him. An unusual feeling washed over me while I stared at that bed with its rumpled sheets, wires, and blood spots from the hose being removed.

An urgency came over me. *I need to go home. I need to go right now.*

I started walking out of the room. My wife said, cutting the tech off, "Well, I guess we are leaving now."

Every bump in the road, every little turn of the steering wheel, and every brake touch sent me into spasms of intense pain. I walked straight up the stairs, dropping my things onto the bed. I stood there for a few minutes, not moving—embracing the silence, stillness, and warmth. Something stirred within me. I walked to the bathroom in the hallway next to our bedroom, locked the door, sat on the edge of the tub, turned off the light, and cried deeply, feeling like a wounded animal.

I had never experienced this feeling after surgery or a medical procedure. Perhaps it was due to people working on my body twenty-four hours a day for the better part of a week as if it belonged to them. And the pain. My God, the pain. Not to mention the countless needle pokes or the automatic blood pressure machine puffing up with that dull hum every fifteen minutes, constricting around my left arm. Maybe it was the fear of dying, the utter discomfort, or complete loss of control. Whatever it was, it broke me.

I dragged my fingers across the painful place where I had the IV needle in for so long in the crook of my left elbow, feeling the tenderness and the sticky residue left by the adhesive tape.

My heart raced as if I had just finished a tough run—pounding as a rush of heat coursed through me. I checked the door lock repeatedly and sat on the closed toilet lid, pulling my head down with my hands. Thoughts racing. Sobbing. I prayed no one would try to come into this small room and touch me. I desperately needed to control this space. It was mine. "Please, please don't come in here," I muttered. I listened to my family walking around downstairs. I was shaking and sweating.

My dark hiding place was suddenly filled with flashes of light and the jarring sounds of a busy hospital. I could smell the antiseptic. I could hear the nurses whispering urgently in my darkened room, along with the beeping and clicking of the equipment. Someone cried out, "Doctor, it's time—it's coming!" I shuddered as I pictured a nightmarish, pale, blood-covered baby pig-thing squeezing out through my ribcage. Blood curdling screams echoed through the dark, empty corridors as it wriggled wildly and dropped to the floor with a wet *splat*, sliding across the cold white tile in a long red smear. Heart pounding. Pain.

Crying quietly. *God, please . . . please! Please don't let anyone touch me!*

Don't fucking touch me!

I would wake with night terrors, feeling as if someone's hand was in my chest cavity, savagely pulling, tearing at my insides as giant waves of pain crashed over me. The imagined sounds of ribs cracking and wet organs squishing inside me. "Stop! Get the fuck off me!" I would scream, jumping up from the bed and swatting at my side. I would stand with my back to the wall in the dark bedroom, drenched in sweat, heart pounding. Terrified.

I was experiencing what is referred to as severe postsurgical traumatic stress syndrome. A specific form of PTSD that would continue to be an issue for me in the years following.

I focused on resting and letting my body heal for the next few weeks. I was taking a lot of oxy, as prescribed. I had read about the dangers of this drug and other opioids, but quite frankly, it was the only thing that knocked the pain down enough for me to remain reasonably comfortable.

Dressed in old gray sweatpants and a worn Pink Floyd T-shirt, I watched every episode of every season of *Below Deck* on Bravo. The show required little focus, especially as I was drifting in a haze from the medication. The reality TV stories about the crews living aboard mega yachts brought back warm memories of my years working for Norman, making it the only type of program I could fully appreciate at the time. It was the perfect choice for my foggy state of mind.

As I transitioned back to everyday life, I realized I needed to stop using oxycodone and find a safer alternative for my body and mind. However, this turned out to be more challenging than I had anticipated. It wasn't that I was becoming addicted to oxycodone; I was on a reasonably low-dose regimen. The main issue was that nothing else seemed to alleviate my pain, which remained a significant concern.

I often felt like I was being stabbed between the ribs under my right arm. I would frequently have my breath taken away by the phantom stabs. My wife became accustomed to me bending over, grasping my right side, and groaning. "Bad one, huh?" she would say.

I'd nod. "Yeah."

In addition, a large area across my midsection, from the surgical site to about the midpoint in my abdomen, was utterly numb—pins and needles and cold to the touch, like a corpse. At first, I thought the cause may have been the massive epidural I had been given to shut down those nerve systems after the intense pain episode I experienced in the hospital. But in a video call follow-up discussion with the neurologist consulting on my case, I was told that my symptoms would most likely be ongoing due to severe nerve damage, and the pain would likely become chronic. Various medications were prescribed to help combat nerve issues and pain. Of these, the medicines most commonly discussed as the best options were relatively high doses of Lyrica and tramadol.

To this day, years later, the skin in this area of my midsection is numb and still cool to the touch.

I never filled the prescriptions for nerve pain medication; instead, I returned the remaining oxycodone to the hospital pharmacy. During this time, I rediscovered my old friend, cannabis, which had recently become legal to purchase in Oregon. Over the following months, I dedicated myself to learning about the plant, focusing on how it interacts with the body at a molecular level and which strains would most effectively manage my pain and sleep issues. Cannabis provided me with quick relief and helped me feel more like myself again. The knowledge and experiences I gained during this journey with cannabis could fill an entire book on their own.

I wanted desperately to feel my body again without any prescription medication coursing through my traumatized veins, fiddling with my brain chemistry.

I wanted my body back.

I was confident that this abnormal mass in my chest was a result of swallowing my stress for so many years. It simply had to go somewhere.

CHAPTER FIFTEEN
LIMITS AND A NEW HORIZON

There is no time for regrets. You've just got to keep moving forward.
Mike McCready

Shortly after returning to work, I was repeatedly targeted by late-day phone calls from Cindy. Still, I never received an email about specific issues, and no witnesses were present. I was reporting to a corporate bully. The calls always come in at 5:00 p.m. I believed there were two reasons for this timing: first, she wanted to check if I was still at my desk, and second, she wanted me to leave work each day feeling bad about myself.

During one of our conversations, she clarified that she wanted me to leave the company, not just her team. I asked her why she felt that way, and the discussion quickly escalated. Her voice was filled with emotion as she said, "I have your old job, and that sucks for me! Everyone liked you when you were in this role. How can I be successful in this role when you are around?"

The conversation derailed quickly, and I felt threatened; my job seemed at risk because my manager was insecure in her position. She explicitly stated that she believed I was a direct threat to her.

"We are on the same team!" I said.

"You need to go."

"Well, that's not going to happen, Cindy," I said, rubbing my painful side. I ended the call.

"How long are you going to continue this?" Caroline asked as we made dinner together. "It's unhealthy. Look at what just happened to you."

"As long as we need to," I said as I mashed the potatoes. The truth was that we were still recovering, both financially and emotionally, from some hard hits over the past few years. We needed more time with two paychecks coming in.

I would lie awake at night, worrying about losing my job while we were still in a vulnerable position. I didn't want to be bullied out of another job; it just wasn't fair.

The following day, I called our vice-president, with whom I had worked for many years and to whom my new manager reported. I was aware of the risk involved in this phone call. Although I had a friendly relationship with him, he was the one who hired her, and he took pride in that decision.

I emailed him to outline the topics I wanted to discuss and asked for some time with him that day. About twenty minutes later, he called me. He carefully listened as I went through my notes.

"Are you kidding me, Dave?" he said, as I listed some of the issues I had been facing.

"No, Mike, I am not. I just need this to stop." I asked for his help in restoring a comfortable work environment.

"Have you called HR?"

"Yep, but it didn't go anywhere."

"Okay, man. Give me a day to figure this out."

"Mike, is this an attempt to push me out? There are better ways to do it."

"Dave, no way, man. I have no idea what's happening here, but I will find out."

As weeks passed, I still hadn't heard back from my VP friend. I soon learned that he had left the company to pursue new opportunities. I was alone in this.

As time went by, Cindy became even more aggressive with me. She mistreated me in meetings and made me drive to out-of-state meetings when others flew or skipped them due to COVID. She did everything within her power to drive me out. I scheduled another call with our HR manager, who sounded distracted and disengaged during our conversation. After I explained the situation, she said: "Just talk to your manager about it."

So, I wrote down every harsh word from every phone call and added the time and date it was said. A half-inch-thick stack of detailed notes had accumulated on the corner of my desk, with a blue sticky note on which was written the name "Cindy."

I was taken aback after receiving the worst evaluation in my working years. Until then, I had always received strong or "exceeds expectations" performance evaluations from a wide range of managers in my almost fifteen years at this company. The review contained low marks, some supported by fictitious grounds or none at all. I immediately raised my concerns and requested a senior manager review the report. However, she insisted she was a senior manager and curtly told me to sign the evaluation. I stood my ground and pointed out that she was a director, not a senior manager, and requested a review by a VP or higher who was more familiar with my work during my tenure at the company.

"I would like Mike or Phil to review this," I said.

"That's not necessary," she said.

I stated my view that the evaluation did not accurately represent my performance, as I had worked diligently to deliver strong, measurable results for the company. I pointed out that some examples used to support the low marks were incorrect and asked if there had been a mistake. Cindy's dismissive response made me feel vulnerable, undervalued, and isolated, as I realized she was attempting to undermine my efforts and even jeopardize my hard-earned income for my family.

"Do you have my evaluation confused with someone else's from the team?" I said.

"So, you are saying I am confused? Interesting. I guess it is your word against mine, huh?" she said while she checked her email during our video call.

Our late-day phone calls often escalated into unpleasant arguments.

I didn't like how these discussions made me feel or how I behaved during them; it felt as though I was being provoked. I had been battered too many times by the bullies in this industry, and admittedly, I was ready for a fight. As I grew older, I became less inclined to sit back and remain silent in such situations. I was skilled, experienced, and knowledgeable in my role, but I understood her intentions and recognized the challenge that lay ahead. The situation would not improve on its own, so I would soon need to decide: fight for my job or choose to leave the company again.

Some deeper reflection made me realize that I was working for this company solely for the money and nothing else. That didn't feel good, and it was becoming unhealthy for me. It was unfair to myself, my team, my family, and my employer. I knew that something had to change. Caroline and I discussed a suitable time to leave my job that would align with our financial plans, family projects, and calendar commitments.

Trying to hold on and remain in that fight would have only caused more discomfort, sadness, and stress for everyone involved. Looking back on my earlier years, I realized that, sometimes, the mighty river of our experiences carries us where we need to go even when it doesn't make sense at the time. So, I stepped back into the current, let go of the rope, and allowed it to guide me to the next part of my journey, as it had done many times before.

The gravity of this decision was often challenging to manage. There were nights when I couldn't sleep. My heart would pound, and I felt queasy as I sat in the living room, hoping to find some clarity in my process. I allowed my anxious thoughts to swirl for hours, with the words of my friend Dan, a category analyst, echoing in my head:

"If you leave, they won't take you back. They are getting rid of us old guys." I knew he was right; if I stepped away from this industry and company again, the door would close and lock behind me.

In the weeks leading up to my planned departure, I grappled with constant "what if" questions and thoughts of *What the hell am I doing?* These worries invaded my mind at the most inconvenient moments, leaving me in a hazy state of anxious confusion. I had grown to dislike my working environment, yet I was terrified of life beyond it—especially the prospect of trying to reintegrate into the workforce as a white man in his fifties. *What if I can't get another job when I need one? What if I have to take a lesser position with lower pay? What if . . .*

Who will I be without my title and paycheck? I asked myself while pacing the living room at 2:43 a.m. on a rainy Tuesday. "Shit! What have I done?"

I left in July 2021, just over three years after rejoining the team. I shipped my computer, phone, and office equipment back to IT, and the company car was picked up soon after. I was done.

My wife and I were preparing to move out of the state where we had lived for over twenty years. In the following weeks, I became busy with various home projects. This distraction proved helpful as it allowed me to cope with leaving a career that spanned two decades in the wine industry.

I spent two weeks packing our house and preparing for our relocation. It felt great to be actively engaged in my work instead of sitting at a desk all day. We completed the construction projects needed to prepare the house for the market and removed most of our furniture and personal items. Things were happening quickly. The house was for sale, and packing continued at a frenetic pace. Caroline was busy with her job, and our two youngest boys, Ben and Oscar, were preparing to leave home.

In addition to the logistics of the move, we also processed the emotional history tied to our home. Ben was preparing for college, while Oscar was moving to Central Oregon. Our family was experiencing significant changes on multiple fronts simultaneously, but overall, it felt good.

Things were moving quickly. We found ourselves in a challenging position, having to move most of our belongings out while still living in the house in order to prepare it for sale. Oscar and Ben stayed with friends and family for a few weeks. This was sometimes difficult for the boys, as the home they had grown up in was being sold. Soon, it would be gone, leaving only the memories they had gathered there. There were moments when we could feel that they just wanted to return home, jump into their beds, and resume a sense of normalcy. But that wasn't possible.

A few weeks after listing the house, it sold on a day when Portland recorded a temperature of 116 degrees—a challenging feat, especially since our nearly 130-year-old Victorian home had adequate air conditioning only on the ground floor. We raced around the house, moving fans and strategically opening and closing doors to maximize airflow and reduce the oven-like atmosphere. Our efforts paid off, and we sold the old place just in time.

We had lived in this house for over seventeen years. As I ran the math in my head while loading my Tundra with more boxes for storage,

I turned to Ben. I said, "I have made breakfast about six thousand times in that kitchen."

The boys hovered between excitement and feeling displaced, as we did. Recently, I asked Ben how he felt during the transition from that home in Oregon. He said, "Honestly, I was experiencing such big changes when I moved to San Diego for school, so it felt easier to say goodbye to that place. We had so many great memories there, but I knew both of you would be happier—and closer to me—in Arizona, so it was a positive change. The house and neighborhood were a perfect place to grow up, but I feel we all outgrew it at some point. I didn't have a hard time parting with the Oregon winters."

With most of our furniture and boxes temporarily housed in storage units a mile down Willamette Falls Drive, eventually, I found myself standing alone in the dusty old house, its empty rooms filled with echoes of our memories. The air was thick with dust and the remnants of forgotten times, making every breath feel heavy with nostalgia. Our home turned into just a house—like when a hermit crab vacates its abode, leaving behind only a discarded shell. By that time, everyone else had already left. I had finished my packing and storage work for the day and felt utterly exhausted, and a profound fatigue began to settle in. I had been working extremely hard for several days, possibly pushing myself too far.

I sat on a bare mattress on the cold living room floor and felt unwell. Leaning against the wall in the dim, empty room, I glanced at my phone; it was just after 11:00 p.m. My heart was racing, I was sweating, and I had chest pain as waves of heavy anxiety washed over me. Something felt wrong. The sensation intensified as I sat alone in the house's dark, echoey shell.

To ensure it was nothing serious, I headed to the urgent care down the street and explained my symptoms. They connected me to an EKG machine in the intake office, confirmed my heart rhythms were normal, and sent me on my way.

While driving home, I began to feel sick and dizzy. My stomach hurt, I experienced chest pain, I was sweating heavily, and my heart was pounding. I decided to drop into an emergency room near where I lived—something was wrong. They brought me back to a room and started the testing process. My usually low blood pressure was alarmingly high, with a systolic figure over 170, and my shirt was completely soaked. The test results were concerning, and they kept me there all night, running dozens of tests.

The doctor came in around 3:00 a.m. to discuss my test results. She explained that I was experiencing a serious stress event, which could be a severe panic attack, along with nerve flare-ups from my surgery. This combination was causing deep chest pain. She mentioned that these events can become dangerous at my age if not managed appropriately. Fortunately, they got everything under control, and I was discharged just before 6:00 a.m.

I was exhausted but resumed packing after stopping at Willamette Coffee House for a strong cup of coffee and a bagel.

Caroline stayed in a hotel near her company's Dallas headquarters to avoid being disrupted by the packing and moving process. I walked through the empty rooms with a cold beer at the end of each day, reminiscing about our time there and the countless memories we had created. I noticed the faded squares on the walls where family pictures had hung for so many years, and a long, black Sharpie line that Ben had drawn on the paint as he walked up the stairs one day after school.

I stood by the hooks where the boys used to hang their raincoats and backpacks after school, next to the old pencil sharpener mounted just inside the basement door that had been difficult for them to reach when they were younger. I dragged my finger across the patch in the drywall where Max had punched a hole one night during his freshman year of high school, and saw the stain on the built-in kitchen desk left by Finn's 3-D printer, which had leaked something and left a permanent mark.

I noticed the faded stain on the carpet outside our bedroom, where Ben had a terrible nosebleed in the middle of the night when he was little. I opened the front door that Oscar had broken when he was mad at the other boys for locking him out, and I stood on the front patio, where I proposed to Caroline so many years ago.

I found myself standing in my old office in the backyard studio. I had worked there nearly every day for over a decade. As I prepared to leave this place, I was overwhelmed by a flood of memories: joyful moments, satisfying hard work, big wins, painful losses, cherished friendships, and emotional conversations. I felt gratitude for the place rising within me as I took a last sip of my now-warm Corona, knowing I was ready to move on. I expressed my gratitude to the old place for caring for our family throughout the years.

"I am done here," I said as I turned out the light and closed the door for the last time.

We chose Arizona as our next home, even though we had been

there only a few times. We were ready to welcome significant changes into our lives. Arizona would satisfy multiple needs, but the dry, sunny weather was the most obvious consideration. After twenty-two years of rain and clouds in Portland, we were desperate to feel the sun on our faces again. So, we knocked the mud off our shoes, dropped our winter clothing off at the closest Goodwill, and prepared to move south.

Our plan was straightforward: bring only what we needed and leave the rest behind. We sold or donated most of our old furniture and hired a moving company to pack a twenty-foot truck I had rented. This approach saved us a significant amount on moving costs and allowed me to make the long drive myself, which was essential for my transition to the next phase of life. I had a lot of thinking to do, and the slow roll of three days of highway driving provided the time I needed. Caroline had returned to Portland the day before to stay with the dog while I moved us in. I would fly back in a few days, and then we would drive back to Arizona together in our car.

I pulled down the rolling door of the truck and locked it just before 6:00 p.m. and stood in front of the old house one more time. *Click.* I took one last photo. I climbed behind the wheel, made some adjustments, checked my mirrors, and pressed "Play" on the blue JBL speaker duct-taped to the dashboard, just like Anders used to do. The cab filled with the sound of an old Yes album as I merged onto southbound I-205. With the window down and the fresh evening breeze brushing my face, the small speaker crackled to life as the iconic electric sitar intro of "It Can Happen" belted from the little blue box. I was smiling.

I merged onto I-5 South, allowing memories from the past twenty-two years to wash over me. As I prepared to leave Oregon behind, I reflected on my experiences in this place, remembering my time as a wine steward at Zupan's Market in West Linn, my first job in Oregon, well over twenty years ago, when the boys were so little. Thoughts of my days at Safeway surfaced, and I remembered the wonderful friends I made there, many of whom I still keep in touch with today. I also recalled my lengthy stint as a corporate wine supplier, marked by its share of ups and downs. I felt incredibly grateful for my early days in the wine business, when we worked hard and had so much fun together.

Driving past the exit for the lap pool where I swam almost daily, I thought of the enjoyable times I spent in that outdoor saltwater pool—the sun's warmth on my back during summer swims and the winter days when the sun had been replaced with stinging sleet and freezing rain as I splashed through my mile.

I allowed the less beautiful feelings and experiences to flow through my mind as I pulled the truck into the Best Western in Grants Pass for the night. It was late, but I sat in the cab for a moment in that dark parking lot, exploring the feelings that were coming up as I recounted those difficult days in my corporate job, with the bullying, the fear, and the meanness. The wounds were still tender, so I felt some anger swell in my belly. Though I knew it would pass, these cuts were deeper and would need time to heal.

After tossing and turning in the hotel bed for a few hours, I got up, splashed some water on my face, and hopped back into the truck. As the engine warmed up, my mind began to settle, and by the time I arrived at the Dutch Bros coffee shack down the street in the early morning darkness, I sensed a change within me. Something was shifting, evolving, and finally becoming unstuck. I could feel my life transforming.

As I sipped my remarkably good coffee, I looked out at the golden hills to the east. The sun was beginning to light the grassy slopes and warmed the left side of my face. Behind me, the lingering clouds hung like a heavy curtain over Oregon, seemingly tethered to the familiar past, as if they lacked permission to follow me. It felt like I was escaping the shadows of my old life, shedding the weight of two challenging decades, and steering toward a bright new horizon.

A burst of joy erupted within me as I let out a loud, sharp laugh while pressing down on the accelerator. The truck surged forward, and I tapped my fingers against the steering wheel, keeping pace with the energetic rhythm of Tom Petty's album *Damn the Torpedoes*, each note resonating against the windshield. New adventures beckoned ahead, filling me with an intoxicating sense of new beginnings.

Things were going to be okay.

CHAPTER SIXTEEN
WALKING AROUND THE HOUSE WITH A SCREWDRIVER

In the social jungle of human existence,
there is no feeling of being alive without a sense of identity.

Erik Erikson

We decided to rent an apartment for our first year in South Scottsdale. Since Arizona felt entirely unfamiliar to us, we believed that living in an apartment would help us better understand the area and determine which part of Phoenix would suit us best. Although apartment living was new, we agreed this was the most sensible way to transition to a new environment. The apartment complex was magnificent but expensive, so we understood this would only be a one-year arrangement.

I met the movers at 8:00 a.m. on Monday, having arrived in town the previous evening filled with anticipation. As I stood waiting in the sun-drenched driveway of our new apartment building, I leaned against the truck, a steaming cup of coffee in my hands. The breath-taking view of Camelback Mountain loomed just a quarter of a mile to the northwest, its majestic peak bathed in the golden glow of the desert morning. The scene was mesmerizing.

The air here was alive with vibrant new scents—notes of blooming cacti and earthy sagebrush wafted around me, starkly contrasting the damp, musty aroma of Portland's rain-soaked streets. I noticed the birds flitting about, and their songs felt refreshing compared to the familiar cacophony of squawking crows I had left behind. As I took another sip of my coffee, a thought emerged with clarity, resonating deep within me: *This is what we need.* Embracing this new chapter, away from the dull shades of gray and persistent rain, felt not just right—it felt like a promise of brighter days ahead.

I noticed the heat was quickly building. *This is new.* I closed the door again and returned to the apartment's coolness. It was August in Scottsdale, so by 9:00 that morning, the temperature had already reached one hundred degrees.

I worked diligently to get our new home ready, and by the end of the second day, it was fully prepared for us to move in—beds made, flowers on the table, and food in the fridge. I felt satisfied as I closed the door and left for the airport the following morning.

The drive back down was enjoyable. It was just the three of us: Caroline, me, and our hilarious English bulldog, Otis. Before moving from Portland, we sold our cars. We decided to buy a "fun" car to share while living in the apartment, fully embracing the vibrant South Scottsdale experience. After that year, we planned to sell the vehicle and replace it with something more suitable for our lifestyle.

The snow-white Porsche Cayenne GTS glided effortlessly along the vast expanse of empty desert highways, cutting through the

RESUME OF A RESTLESS SOUL

shimmering mirage of the Mojave Desert. The engine purred softly, the gentle hum juxtaposed with the arid landscape's silence. I watched the speedometer, the needle climbing steadily on those long, straight stretches of hot asphalt—124, 125, 136. It felt like the car was gliding along on invisible tracks, requiring barely any energy as we swept over the sunbaked pavement that rippled under the relentless heat.

Knowing that this machine could easily surge past 175 mph, I couldn't shake the sensation that it was mirroring my excitement, a metallic spirit urging me forward, almost asking, with a playful confidence, *Is that it? Is that all you want?* The thrill of the open road and the car's raw power created an undeniably intoxicating moment of pure exhilaration.

Otis was snoring loudly in the back.

Eventually, the novelty of luxury apartment living began to wane. We quickly grew tired of sharing common areas and outdoor spaces with much younger residents and their loud cell phones. We felt old there. It was clear that it was time to buy a home. After getting to know the area reasonably well, we felt confident about which part of the city to move to. We traded in our Porsche for a more practical SUV and bought a house.

Our new home was in Phoenix's beautiful Desert Ridge area, part of a large master-planned community. The first few months were filled with the busyness of moving in and setting up the big house. I spent weeks painting, making dump runs, rewiring all of the outdoor lights, and removing and replacing sinks and toilets, including those in the bathroom where I would later experience my first heart attack.

Since leaving the corporate world, I had been helping our four sons as they moved into new apartments across the country. Our boys relocated to different states during the same summer to pursue their educational and career aspirations. Oscar moved to Bend, Oregon; Max relocated to the St. Louis area for work; Ben went to school in San Diego; and Finn moved to a new apartment in Savannah. It required three moving trucks, car trailers, and thousands of miles of driving, but in the end, everyone was settled into their new homes, ready to take the next steps in their lives—just as we were in ours.

I found comfort in my hectic busyness. My mind was wholly absorbed in logistical projects, home renovations, and ensuring that our entire family was comfortably settled across the country, which allowed Caroline to focus solely on her work. However, once the dust from the renovations settled and the boys found their footing in their new homes, time seemed to slow down, and the void in my life began to expand. The sense of being valuable gradually faded, replaced by something else. Worry and a lack of purpose began to swell and flood my mind like a cold, unwelcome tide.

It didn't take long for me to start questioning myself harshly and doubting my decision to leave the corporate world. *Who am I?* I asked myself. I felt exposed without my title or comfortable salary. The question "What do you do?" became a source of real anxiety for me. I was surprised by how frequently I was asked this innocent question. Despite being a reasonably intelligent and well-traveled person, I found it challenging to respond without sounding like an absolute dumbass.

Whenever someone posed that question at a neighbor's barbecue, while walking my dog, getting the mail, or chatting with a new friend at the grocery store, my mind would spiral out of control. My heart would race, and my face would flush. The truth was, I didn't know how to answer. I often fumbled through a vague response about what I used to do or filled the awkward space with a list of recent projects, desperately trying to prove my worth.

It is a fundamental desire for a man to be recognized as someone who can "bring fish back to the village" or risk being deemed useless to the community and sent away. It feels primal.

I no longer knew who I was or how I fit into the world. My self-esteem was gone. For a couple of years, I struggled to find an acceptable response to share at cocktail parties or in conversations with neighbors. Stress, anxiety, shame, and a fragile sense of self quickly took hold, leading me to avoid the question at all costs.

Every morning, I found myself searching online for a job. My motivation wasn't just about needing extra income; it also came from my desire to have a sense of purpose in life. At fifty-three, I wanted to contribute meaningfully again. I craved a title and wanted to feel valued.

Although I was busy managing our new home, remodeling, caring for our old dog, helping the boys, and attending to various domestic projects, I felt I needed more. Part of me longed to feel valuable and recognized. So, while enjoying my coffee each morning, I searched the job listings on LinkedIn, Indeed, and other job search platforms, submitting dozens of applications.

Nothing.

It felt as though my carefully crafted cover letters and thoughtful applications were disappearing into a void, never seen by human eyes. I completed numerous LinkedIn courses and added new certifications to my already strong resume. I diligently researched resume building, reformatting mine multiple times, and fine-tuned it to what I believed was its best version, only to cast dozens more into the void.

Nothing.

In the three years I have been in Arizona, I have submitted, to the best of my count, just over 490 applications online through the job platforms I mentioned above. I submitted each one carefully and thoughtfully, targeting only the jobs for which I was qualified. I applied for jobs almost identical to my most recent position in the same industry, where I had decades of experience, a solid reputation, and a strong track record. I was still not called for a single interview. I completed countless employer assessments and tests and sent out hundreds of well-written cover letters.

Nothing.

It was clear to me that the system wasn't working.

Generally speaking, we were financially secure, so searching for a job didn't carry the same pressures as it can for many others. I feel fortunate in that regard. I often think about how incredibly stressful this situation can be for people who desperately need a job to support themselves and their families. As I read more about this, I learned that many applicants face similar challenges when applying online. Often, the application requirements and questions are established by the vendors selling employers the recruitment software package. This may explain why some required answers feel awkward or why specific questions on employer assessments seem unrelated or even absurd for the advertised position.

If we looked inside your car, what would we see? My son was asked this question in an online application for a restaurant server job in San Diego.

If lemons cost $3.00 per pound, how many lemons can you buy with 80 cents?

Another gem of an employer assessment question came across my screen recently: *You have been given an elephant, and you cannot give the elephant away. What would you do with the elephant?*

Well, let's see, I would probably walk the elephant down to their HR department and tie it to someone's desk while they were at lunch, where it would proceed to take a big ol' dump. On the desk, a basket of fresh lemons that I picked from my neighbor's yard, on which they would find a note that read: *Folks . . . Stop toying with us—this is no game. Please take your work more seriously. PS. You are paying way too much for lemons.*

As the months dragged on, I was stuck in a seemingly endless cycle of frustration in my job search. Each day that passed without a single response eroded my confidence further. The silence weighed heavily on my mind, casting a shadow over my once hopeful outlook. I began questioning my self-worth and place in the world, grappling with a growing sense of insignificance. Each morning, I awoke to a suffocating blanket of despair, and with each passing day, the waves of depression, self-doubt, and anxiety crashed over me.

I felt like a ghost—ignored, unseen, and utterly undervalued. Haunting nightmares assaulted my sleep, painting vivid scenes of being unwanted. I dreamed of standing alone in a cold rain while everyone I knew reveled indoors at vibrant gatherings, laughing and sharing joyful moments. They danced without a care, utterly oblivious to my existence as I stood there, drenched and shivering, feeling as though I had vanished from their lives. In those dark hours, the weight of my despair convinced me that I no longer mattered.

After many months of searching, Caroline and I concluded that my efforts were in vain. We realized we were chasing something we neither needed nor wanted; it was merely a habit we had formed, leading to stress and discomfort. I had been scrambling to return to a way of working I had intentionally chosen to leave behind, and that didn't feel right. As a result, we decided to shift our focus from "getting more" to "giving more."

We discussed it at length and agreed to end my fruitless quest for a corporate job and concentrate on something more rewarding: giving back. Once we committed to this new direction, things began to happen quickly. It was the right path.

CHAPTER SEVENTEEN
I SEE YOU—THE
MENTORING YEARS

When I was a boy and saw scary things in the news,
my mother would say to me,
"Look for the helpers. You will always find people who are helping."
Fred Rogers

We'd been fortunate these past several years. It was time to give back. We always had a strong desire to help others, not just through financial contributions but also by providing direct support to those in need. Over the years, we have supported our favorite charities by sending them checks to assist with their efforts, and it felt rewarding to know that we might have helped someone in need. We wanted to make a meaningful impact on someone's life and bring about positive change, even in a small way. Now that I was no longer working a corporate job and had more time to take on new projects, we agreed that I should find an organization to assist individuals in immediate need directly. Meanwhile, we continued to support our favorite charities.

I began researching nonprofit organizations that support individuals and families, quickly focusing on those that offer mentoring services. During my search, I discovered several excellent organizations in Arizona that provide volunteer opportunities to work directly with young people in need of support. Ultimately, I chose to get involved with a Phoenix-based organization that significantly aids at-risk inner-city teens.

This organization offers a one-on-one mentorship program, in which each mentor is paired with a single youth for an extended period. Most matches begin early in high school and continue through college. Over time, this relationship can develop into a valuable partnership that provides the youth with the support and guidance needed while allowing mentors to fulfill their desire to help young people achieve their goals. I completed several interviews and background checks, including an FBI background check, and was accepted into the mentorship program.

I initially believed the experience would be straightforward. I assumed I would be working with a young man who might occasionally need help with homework or navigating the complex social landscape of high school. However, I was mistaken; the experience was much more challenging than anticipated.

The mentor training program consisted of weekly sessions held over several months in a classroom located in downtown Phoenix. This training provided a comprehensive understanding of generational poverty and its effects on families and young people. The curriculum covered topics from psychology and sociology in depth. I realized that some of the young people we would be paired with were facing challenges related to extreme poverty, an experience that most of the mentors were not familiar with at all.

We learned about the socioeconomic landscape that some of our new matches and their families had endured for generations. We explored the daily challenges some of these families face, such as dropping out of high school because the need for money outweighs the need for education. Many of these families live in a state of constant crisis. We learned how the survival decisions they are forced to make can quickly trap them in a complex cycle of poverty with no clear path out.

Our training aimed to equip us to help break the gravitational pull of generational poverty by motivating these young people to give themselves a chance at success outside of this problematic way of living.

I learned that only around 30 percent of young people living in poverty-stricken communities in Arizona pursue education beyond high school. However, 95 percent of the youth in this particular program managed to graduate high school, and an impressive 85 percent of those who remained in the program continued their education at the college level and successfully found career paths, which was precisely the positive impact I was hoping to be a part of.

While the mentors were in training classes, the youth accepted into the program were also preparing for the journey in their own training sessions. One aspect I appreciated about this program was that the youth had to apply for it independently. They had to want to be there. They had to undergo lengthy interviews to be accepted, although there were some exceptions. One of the reasons this program achieved such high success was that both the mentors and the youth had a strong desire to participate. No one was dragged into the program, or at least, that was the goal.

After two months of mentor training, we began cohort training, in which the new mentors and youth would meet and attend classes together. The structure of these first training sessions was as intentional as it was intense. Attendance was mandatory for the four-day training. If either a mentor or a youth did not attend the entire four-day cohort "launch" session, they could not continue with the program and would have to start over and try again. The sessions began at 7:00 a.m. and continued until 9:00 p.m. for four consecutive days, with only a few breaks. The meeting room was cold and brightly lit to help keep us awake and alert.

It became clear that these sessions were designed to break down barriers and bust through walls that the youth and mentors may have in place. The facilitators would not allow cell phones in the room. We were all required to place cell phones, keys, hats, and any other personal items into large brown envelopes as we walked in the front door of the building each morning. No outside food or drinks of any kind were allowed in. They provided clear water bottles as we stepped into the room. No hoodies, sunglasses, or hats were allowed and, of course, no weapons. They were intentionally removing anything that someone could potentially hide behind. We all felt exposed, vulnerable, and uncomfortable; that was the plan.

We were told where to sit and were asked to remain facing forward until the session began. From the moment we walked into the room, we were being evaluated. The room was set up in a classroom style, with chairs facing the facilitators in the front. In the back of the room was a long table where a panel of social workers and psychologists sat, watching the group and taking copious notes. Everything we did or said was written down.

The mentors were brought into the room first, and we received our last private instructions before the youth were brought in. It was suggested that we not touch the youth, even if they became emotional. We were encouraged to "sit in the space" with them as we worked together. It was becoming increasingly evident that we were about to undertake some very challenging work. A few nervous glances were exchanged between the mentors as we took our assigned seats in the room.

The staff escorted the twenty-four teens into the room and seated them in their assigned places between mentors. No one spoke for several minutes. The facilitators in the front of the room sat quietly and watched us, as did the panel of social workers and psychologists in the back of the room. The teens became fidgety and uncomfortable; some became aggravated and loud, while others sank in their seats. Some tried to leave but were asked to return to their seats. The mentors grew stiff and anxious, and I wished I had my phone to shield me from the growing awkwardness. We sat quietly, looking at each other for at least ten minutes. Not a word was said.

"Good morning," the lead facilitator finally said, breaking the unbearable tension.

Much of the day was spent in that room listening to the facilitators. There were few breaks, and when we had them, they were brief. We sat and listened. Day two was precisely the same. Sitting in a classroom for over twelve hours daily and listening to someone speak is exhausting. I soon realized this was the point.

They intentionally wore us down, creating severe fatigue, forcing the "walls" to drop and putting us all in the same boat. They were building a community.

Day three was different. We engaged in more group activities and team-building exercises and were even paired off with the youth in small-group workshops. One behavior that I couldn't help but notice was the jockeying for position by some of the mentors and youth. On their own accord, they would pair up with someone they believed would be a good match for them and work hard to sit next to them during breaks, lunch, and in small-team exercises. Other people in the group of about fifty saw this and, in turn, began to urgently try to find a match before it was too late. It was like some bizarre game of musical chairs, where youth and mentors hurried to pair up with someone they felt would be fun to work with. The facilitators warned against this trend, but it continued. Later in the day, it was explained that matching is much more complicated than picking someone based on their appearance and outward behavior. The quiet panel of professionals in the back of the room and the facilitators carefully watched the behavior of the young people and the mentors—taking into account the backgrounds of each participant, the range of personal and educational experiences, their family experiences, domestic violence screening, and the youth's Adverse Childhood Experience, or ACE, score.

By the middle of the third day, an atmosphere of fellowship was developing. Although we did not enjoy the training sessions, we got to know each other as we shared this somewhat uncomfortable experience. We were all uncomfortable *together.* Toward the end of the third excruciatingly long day, the relatively routine conversational problem-solving of the small-group sessions gave way to much more challenging whole-group work.

One such activity involved the entire group standing in a circle in a large, dimly lit room. Emotional music played over the sound system as the evaluators watched quietly from the shadows. We stood for a while, instructed not to speak. We listened to "Everybody Hurts" by R.E.M. play over the conference room speakers.

The instructions for the exercise were then read over the PA system, explaining that we should listen to the statements that followed, and if we had experienced that situation, we were asked to step forward into the circle. If we had not had a similar experience, we were asked to stand quietly and not move.

The first few questions were relatively easy and didn't push us too far into our well-guarded inner selves. "Step into the circle if you have ever been bullied" was one of the first questions. I recalled many times when I had been bullied, going back to middle school, then high school, and then to my corporate years. However, I did not step into the middle. I am not sure why I didn't. Perhaps male pride and the desire to create the appearance of being a strong person or to avoid drawing attention to myself overshadowed the desire to follow the instructions in what was shaping up to be an exercise in vulnerability. Most of the fifty participants stepped into the middle and stood quietly without speaking.

"Step into the middle of the circle if you have heard gunshots in your neighborhood in the last two weeks," a facilitator asked. I watched as two-thirds of the youth and some mentors stepped into the circle and stood quietly. We were asked not to speak, not one word.

"Step into the middle of the circle if you have experienced physical or emotional abuse in your home," the facilitator said while "I Will Remember You" by Sarah McLachlan played over the sound system loudly. Again, most of the youth and many of the mentors stepped into the circle. Part of the exercise now involved allowing each participant standing in the middle to speak aloud about their experiences in that situation. If they stood in the middle, they were handed a microphone and asked to briefly describe their experience, as much as they were comfortable doing so. I was so impressed by the courage of these young people. Most of them would bravely announce to the group, sometimes with trembling voices, what happened to them and how it felt.

This exercise effectively illustrated that many participants shared similar experiences. I watched in awe as numerous individuals in the middle remained there, responding to question after question.

"Step into the middle of the circle if you have lost a family member as a result of gun violence," the facilitator calmly read. Again, most youth stepped in or stayed in the circle's center as "Tears in Heaven" by Eric Clapton played.

"Step into the middle if someone in your immediate family is currently incarcerated," was asked next.

"Step into the middle if *you* have been incarcerated." It was heartbreaking to see young people standing in the center, quietly, with their heads down, one having been incarcerated for attempted murder at fifteen years old.

The notetakers quietly worked in the shadows.

"Step into the center of the circle if you have been abused sexually." Many of the youth and several mentors stepped forward. I watched as a couple of dozen teens and mentors in the center silently looked around at one another for what seemed like an eternity while listening to the tear-jerking ballads. Their eyes cautiously met, and the intended message landed with a heart-pounding realization with the youth in the exercise—they were not alone. The tears began to flow, and I watched these amazingly resilient teenagers fall to their knees, sobbing deeply and hugging each other. It remains one of the most potent emotional experiences I have ever been a part of.

I watched one mentor step away, quietly gather her belongings, and walk out the door, never to return. We learned later that she texted a staff member from the parking lot, writing, "I'm sorry, this is too hard."

As mentors, we were asked to help create a safe space for the youth to explore these feelings and respond in whatever way they needed to. Sometimes, that response was anger or rage; sometimes, it was through tears; and occasionally, it was expressed through nervous laughter. The exercise continued, and the questions were read. We watched as people stepped inside and back out of the big circle, the evaluators quietly observing.

I was amazed by how openly these young people shared with each other and us during this training stage. The facilitators successfully broke down barriers and fostered a safe community, allowing everyone to express their feelings freely.

Later that day, we were brought into a smaller dimly lit room. The youth were asked to sit in a circle facing each other in the middle of the room. The mentors were asked to stand quietly behind the young people. The youth could not see who was standing behind them, which I learned later was another layer of trust-building. Again, we were asked to refrain from speaking. The music began to play again, this time "My Heart Will Go On" by Celine Dion.

"Mentors, please place one hand on the shoulder of someone you enjoyed connecting with during this training." We did. This was the first time in four days that we were encouraged to contact the youth physically; until then, it had been strongly discouraged. The instructions continued. "Mentors, please place one hand on the shoulder of someone you respect." The mentors quietly moved around outside the circle, placing a hand on the shoulder of one of the young people, who still could not see who belonged to the hand touching them.

"Mentors, please place your hand on the shoulder of a youth who inspired you this week," the facilitator read. The mentors moved quietly, each standing behind a young person and touching their shoulders.

"Angel" by Sarah McLachlan began to play in the otherwise quiet room. The facilitator said, "Mentors, without speaking, please place your hand on the shoulder of someone you *believe in.*" We quietly shuffled our positions behind the young people sitting in the middle, ensuring each one had a hand firmly on their shoulder. At this point in the exercise, I felt something change in the room. A relatively quiet, stoic young man whose shoulder I touched during this question started to tremble, dropped his head, and cried quietly. It may have been that many of the youth had never known what it was like to have someone *believe* in them, and this feeling, accompanied by a supportive human touch, was overwhelming. Tears welled up in the eyes of many in the room, both youth and mentors alike. It was an incredibly moving experience.

The facilitator asked the youth to stand in place and turn to face the mentors who had been moving around a couple of feet behind them. We were asked to be silent. The sad songs continued to play. Teens and mentors stood facing one another as we waited for the next set of instructions.

The Pretenders' "I'll Stand by You" began to play over the speakers. "Mentors and youth, please hold eye contact with the person standing before you for two minutes. Do not look away, do not touch each other, don't move your body, and do not speak. After two minutes, we will ask you to rotate to your right." This seemingly simple exercise brought the most unexpected result. The first few seconds were easy enough, some giggling and fidgeting, but then it changed. Something happened to many of the teens. Even the most street-hardened, unsentimental young people began to break down. After a few seconds of uninterrupted eye contact with an adult mentor, they started crying, sometimes sobbing uncontrollably, falling to their knees, and covering their faces.

Many teens did not break eye contact, even after experiencing such powerful and uncomfortable emotions in front of strangers.

I found myself in front of a high school sophomore, a young man who started to cry after holding eye contact with me for a moment. He began to sob deeply but wouldn't break eye contact, not for one second. I remember *feeling* his unspoken *Help me!* as our eyes locked for those two unnaturally long minutes in one of the most powerful human experiences I have participated in. Later, I learned of the history of physical and emotional abuse in his home. I noticed the scar on his wrist.

After the exercise, I asked one of the young men what it felt like for him. "I felt like people could *see* me . . . I felt *seen*," he said as he wiped away the tears.

Another mentor quietly packed up, left the room, and did not return.

Two of the adult mentors in the group had to leave the program due to emotional difficulties caused by the depth of the work and the level of commitment required. However, despite this, none of the teens left the program, not one.

Many of these teens had experienced not only severe poverty but, in many cases, unspeakable trauma, loss, hardship, racism, hate, homelessness, abuse, rejection, addiction, and sadness in their lives. I was struck by their strength, honesty, courage, and depth of character. I felt honored to participate in the training with them and will carry that experience with me for the rest of my life.

At the end of the four days, the facilitators hosted a matching ceremony, during which each mentor was matched to one of the program's youth. I was matched with a preteen, a twelve-year-old boy named Carlos. Carlos was the youngest in the group and had great difficulty speaking to adults. He sat silently for much of the training. It was explained that Carlos was matched to me partly because I had raised four boys. Many other male mentors were not parents or lacked experience with younger kids who struggled in school and socially, which was squarely in my wheelhouse. We walked to the front of the room and were announced as a match in front of the room full of families and participants.

I had worked with Carlos for about four months when I received a call from the mentoring organization. A very unusual situation had surfaced, and they asked me to consider taking on another young man, which was beyond the normal expectations of the program. They explained that Darius, a seventeen-year-old boy who had gone through the training and matching process after my group, was now without a mentor. After the first one-on-one meeting with Darius, his new mentor decided he could not continue. The mentor wrote a letter to the organization, explaining that he was "in over his head" and did not feel he could continue working with a teenager with such deep issues. He left without saying goodbye to Darius, which was a crushing blow. I learned that his father had left when he was very young, and Darius had no other positive male role models. He had been suspended from multiple schools, and more than one mentor had quit on him.

"Every man in his life leaves," the social worker told me.

A few days before the Christmas holiday, a quick call was set up for Darius and me to meet. His mother joined the call, and we spoke for some time. Darius jumped on the call briefly before leaving, which made complete sense to me. Why would he feel comfortable extending himself again? He had been hurt many times, so he protected himself by making only a token effort to engage.

I immediately agreed to work with Darius if he was interested in continuing the program. His mother, a woman in her forties, accepted on his behalf. She requested that I be patient and give Darius time and space to process everything. He would step back into the program when he felt ready. A few weeks passed before Darius responded to my texts, but he did rejoin the program.

As I approach the two-year mark in the mentoring program, I reflect on my journey with mostly warm memories. It hasn't been easy by any measure, and I don't expect that to change anytime soon. Building the trust required to work effectively with these two young men has taken time, but we have made significant progress. We continue to attend training sessions once or twice a month and enjoy many one-on-one outings in between.

Carlos is now fourteen years old and is very proud to be passing every class at school for the first time. He has gained the ability to confidently engage in conversations with adults and has stopped fighting at school. His focus has shifted to basketball and girls, though not necessarily in that order. Recently, Carlos made the basketball team at his high school, where he enjoys being one of the top scorers on the junior varsity team.

Much has changed since our first outings, mostly quiet car rides and lunches. Carlos is now downright chatty, and we share more openly about things going on in our lives. Being a teenage boy, Carlos has a monstrous appetite, so most of our outings involve food to some degree. Each week, we choose a different restaurant around the Phoenix/Scottsdale area to try while catching up on what's happening. Conversations usually revolve around school, friends, girls, sports, food, and family.

"Bro, I told them in the training that if I didn't get you, I would quit," Carlos told me as he took another bite of his enormous cheeseburger.

"Seriously? I said with a laugh.

"Yeah, man. I was freakin' out in that training because I didn't want to get stuck with someone boring. Weren't you freaked out?"

"Yeah, I was feeling a little anxious about it, for sure," I said. "I am happy we were matched, brother." We touched our paper cups.

Carlos invited Caroline and me to join his family in community celebrations, which has been a privilege. One notable event we attended was a family friend's quinceañera, a significant occasion in Latin American culture. This traditional social and religious event celebrates a girl's fifteenth birthday, marking her transition to womanhood.

When Caroline and I entered the community hall for the event, we quickly realized that we were the only white attendees among nearly three hundred guests. We felt honored to be part of such an important community celebration and had a wonderful time. We experienced a strong sense of welcome and comfort from the moment we stepped into the building. We were genuinely impressed by the warmth and closeness of this community.

At nineteen, Darius has faced numerous challenges on his journey. Initially, we made good progress together and enjoyed collaborating on his goals of finding a job and getting accepted into college. However, due to significant issues in his personal life, Darius began to regress and make choices that did not support his goals. As a result, our progress and communication suffered, leading to a growing distance between us. Additionally, access to a cell phone has become an ongoing issue, further complicating our communication.

I remain ready to reengage, but only when he feels ready. Right now, he seems to be navigating a cold, lonely, and frightening part of his journey as he flirts with homelessness. I look forward to the next cryptic message or call, hoping to reconnect and resume working with this remarkable and bright young man.

The more challenging aspects of this form of mentoring are the emotions, the anxiety, and the uncertainty that come with it. Occasionally, mentors receive notifications that one of the young individuals in the program has passed away. The impact of these announcements is profoundly overwhelming, leaving us breathless with sorrow.

Through this program, I have grown both as a mentor and a person. In addition to my ongoing work with Carlos, I have had the privilege of working with many young people in the program. These teenagers have taught me a great deal during our time together. I have witnessed firsthand the incredible challenges they often face daily. I have learned that even when life becomes difficult, love and joy can still be found, even in the darkest times. I have been inspired by how they value their families, friends, and communities far more than material possessions.

I am truly grateful to these young people for welcoming me into their lives and helping me understand how others in our communities live. Rather than labeling my new friends as "less fortunate," I would describe them as rich in kindness and tolerance, magnificent examples of the enduring human spirit.

Thank you. It has indeed been a privilege to know you all.

CHAPTER EIGHTEEN
A PINCH OF GRACE AND LESSONS LEARNED

Life can only be understood backward, but
is meant to be lived forward.

Søren Kierkegaard

As I take a moment to reflect on the tapestry of my life, two poignant thoughts emerge with clarity. First and foremost, I hold dear the rich mosaic of experiences that've shaped me—the vibrant souls I've encountered, each leaving an indelible imprint on my heart, and the breathtaking places I've explored, from bustling cities to serene landscapes, all of which have woven unforgettable memories into my journey. At the same time, I reflect on how my life's narrative might have unfolded differently if I'd had the wisdom and insight I possess today three decades ago. I believe this feeling resonates deeply with many others who are at a similar stage in life.

I am deeply grateful for the opportunity to be part of such a unique blended family. The journey of discovering ourselves and each other within this dynamic family unit is profoundly special and enriching. For me, embracing the roles of a dad and a stepdad extends beyond merely providing shelter, food, and the other basic necessities. It is a heartfelt journey of self-discovery and growth. When I look at my kids, I often see a reflection of my hopes, fears, dreams, and experiences in their individual stories alongside the unique and beautiful life story we are creating together.

Blended families often emerge from the remains of previous relationships, making them especially fragile. I remember reading about the success rates of blended families when we first began exploring the idea. At that time, I learned that approximately 70 percent of blended families do not succeed. I feel so proud that our funny little tribe has made it through the challenges and become stronger. I know there were moments when we all wanted to give up, but I am so glad we didn't.

Early in my journey as a parent, I discovered that striving for perfection, whether as a dad or a stepdad, is an unrealistic goal. I've made my share of mistakes and sometimes stumbled over my words, causing misunderstandings or hurt feelings. However, each of these experiences has been a valuable lesson, shaping me into a better parent over the years. The most crucial thing I can do for my kids is to be genuinely present in their lives—showing up for them during the joyful moments and the challenging times, ensuring they always feel supported and loved. It took me many years to understand that the pressure I felt to achieve perfection as a parent was largely self-imposed. In reality, no one expected me to be flawless, and the notion of an ideal parent may be a myth many chase in vain. Instead, I realized that the essence of being a good parent—or even just a good person—lies in showing up wholeheartedly, doing my best with the resources I have, and embracing my authentic self.

Life is full of challenges and difficult times, but if we can sprinkle a few laughs and moments of joy along the journey, it makes the experience all the more fulfilling. It's about progress, not perfection, and the memories we create together along the way are what truly matter. The people who walk beside us on our journeys are more valuable than the milestones or the destination.

Our boys' growth and development throughout the years has been a joy to watch, as they have transformed into truly outstanding young men right before our eyes. My chest swells with pride as I watch them confidently step into the world, embodying strength, courage, and kindness. I watch them eagerly click into their skis, ready to carve their unique paths down life's majestic mountain, fueled by adventure and purpose.

We have aimed to teach them that falling down is inevitable; however, the accurate measure of a person lies in their desire and ability to get back up and try again. They have seen us take some hard falls over the years, including complete wipeouts. They have watched us get back up; gather our skis, poles, and gloves; dust ourselves off; and try again. The only real shame in falling down is not getting up and making the effort to try once more.

A friend once told me, "If you never fall, you are not trying hard enough."

Reflecting on my travels during my younger years, I realize how valuable those experiences were for my development as an independent thinker and problem solver. Traveling alone taught me to trust myself and my instincts. I learned that there is a vast difference between loneliness and being alone. I appreciated the freedom and control as I explored the world on my own terms. These experiences improved my resourcefulness and ability to navigate challenging situations without relying on the safety net of family, friends, or significant financial resources.

While traveling, I learned to live on a cash budget and effectively manage my finances. I also developed self-preservation skills that help me stay safe in challenging environments far from home. Additionally, I improved my communication skills, enabling me to interact with strangers and quickly overcome language barriers and social awkwardness. When you're out in the world alone, handling situations yourself is essential, as no one else will do it for you.

One key takeaway from my years of corporate experience is the value of nonconformity. I've learned that it's perfectly acceptable to be different, stand apart from the crowd, challenge existing ideas while developing new ones, and push the status quo while maintaining professional decorum. Nonconformists often operate at the forefront of thought leadership and growth, driving large organizations toward their next evolutionary step.

Reflecting on my corporate career, I should have trusted my instincts more and acted less out of fear. I often had ideas for improving workflow and systems, but when I faced pushback, I retreated to the established working methods instead of pushing for change. I feared risking my income by challenging a resistant system. In hindsight, I should have confronted the bullies and stood my ground rather than allowing them to diminish my voice and power.

Early in my career, I learned there is no "easy button." If you want something, you need to be ready to stand up and work hard to get it. I used to tell our boys when they were younger that there are essentially two kinds of people in the world: those who sit down and "want" and those who stand up and "do"—strive to be the latter.

Talk is, in fact, cheap.

"Does a soul ever cease to exist?" I asked the shaman, sitting quietly before me.

"I have never been asked that question," she said with a warm smile as her mind wrapped around the idea. "I suppose it doesn't—it just changes form energetically."

"I ask because you often hear the terms 'new soul' and 'old soul,' which leads one to believe new energies are coming into this space that were not here before," I said. "So what happens to the old ones? Wouldn't it go against the laws of the universe, as we know them, to have something new added or created without the equal and opposite energetic response? According to this approach, it would be a one-in-and-one-out system, no?"

She leaned back in her chair, raised her eyebrow, and smiled thoughtfully.

As I journey through the years, moving further from the relentless pace and pressures of corporate life, I yearn for richer, more profound conversations like these. This transition inspires me to expand my perspective from the minute details to the broader, overarching themes that shape our world. Now and then, as I set my gaze upon the night sky, I catch fleeting glimpses behind the boundless curtain of our universe, igniting a deeper thirst for knowledge and understanding about the complexities that lie beyond the surface.

As we face struggles navigating the slippery paths of life, are we meant to do so in hopes of gaining wisdom and deepening our spiritual insight? Is there a predetermined journey of spiritual growth laid out for us, or are we simply fragile beings stumbling through the complexities of life, trying to avoid suffering, illness, and the possibility of losing jobs and facing financial hardship?

If the goal is to navigate a series of challenges and complex tasks, sometimes painful, to gain knowledge and evolve, what is the *ultimate* purpose? What is the point of it all? Is there a finish line? Do we receive a ribbon at the end and a hearty pat on the back, with someone saying, "Congratulations! You made it through to the next round"?

The answers to these questions are deeply personal. In the quiet moments of the night, when conversation ceases and sleep eludes me, I reflect on the idea that we are all creators of our existence.

In short, I believe the answer to the question, "What is the point of all this?" is precisely whatever you want it to be.

Some believe perceiving your life as stressful, unpleasant, frightening, or even awful calls these very experiences to you, and they will likely stay with you. If so, the opposite should be true. If you focus on goodness, joy, love, fulfillment, and happiness, you may attract more of these things.

Is the universe simply providing what we ask for, consciously or unconsciously?

This past year, I have made a greater effort to focus on the positive aspects of my life, and there are many. I am training myself to consciously choose happiness over unhappiness, love over fear, health over sickness, and acceptance over judgment. I have a lot of work to do, but this has led to positive changes in my life, and I am grateful for them.

Reflecting on the years that have gathered behind me on this journey like a pile of well-worn shoes reminds me of the missed opportunities to have lived differently. I have spent so many years worrying about having my job and money taken away, someone not liking me, or, worse, someone trying to harm me or the people I care about. Like many people, I approached my life from a place of fear, which resulted, at times, in a tumultuous existence filled with resentment, suspicion, mistrust, and unease, not to mention the occasional rare tumor. This lifestyle may ultimately lead to mental and physical health issues, and I have certainly faced my share.

What if that *gets taken away from me? What if* those *people hate me? What if* that *person leaves me? What if I run out of money or get sick?*

What if . . . what if . . .

Making the conscious decision to shift from fear-based to love-based thinking requires discipline, energy, and desire. It involves changing primary thoughts from *I want* to *I have*, from *I am scared* to *I am grateful*, and from *I hate* . . . to *I love* . . . I can only imagine the positive things that will be returned to us by expressing this message of thankfulness and joy to the universe.

It sounds easy, but it's not. I must constantly remind myself to let go of negative thoughts, look at the horizon, smile, and breathe.

As I embark on this transformative chapter of my life, I am fully committed to an introspective journey to unravel the complexities of my actions and choices within the intricate tapestry of my existence—striving to better understand my place in the world. Each day, I will work to carve out a moment or two of stillness—a quiet sanctuary amid the chaos—to pose critical questions that delve deep into my soul:

What positive contributions did I make today?

What creativity did I bring forward, or how did I help someone else's creativity come forward?

Did I take the time to pause, to fully inhabit the present and appreciate the exquisite beauty around me—from the delicate patterns etched on the leaves of the garden to the breathtaking, fiery hues of an Arizona sunset melting into the horizon?

In what ways did I extend my hand to support others, offering a warm embrace or a compassionate listening ear to someone navigating their own struggles?

By embracing these daily reflective inquiries, I aspire to cultivate a life rich in texture, woven with threads of meaning and purpose, ensuring that each moment resonates with significance.

What experiences am I calling forth for myself?

What am I asking the universe to bring me?

I do not view myself as a "victim" of corporate bullying. I do not believe it was "unfair" that I faced a few unusual and severe medical issues, nor do I think the world misunderstood or mistreated me. I may have attracted those specific experiences into my life to understand them better. I feel grateful for the experiences and those who helped bring them to me. Rather than assigning blame, holding bitterness, or adopting an acrimonious mindset about my rough experiences, I choose to leave them in the past. The trick for me is not to hold on to unpleasant experiences for too long but to learn to release them back into the universe after I have gathered the knowledge and wisdom I need, creating space for new, more joyful experiences. Some experiences cannot easily be cast back into the universe; instead, they require more attention because there is more to understand about them. I am trying to be patient with myself in this process.

Whenever I reflect on my experiences, I sometimes feel a slightly anxious, fluttery sensation, like sticky little butterflies in my chest (not to be confused with a coronary widow-maker). This feeling suggests I should examine the issue or experience more closely, as I may have overlooked something. Hold on to it a bit longer and look more thoughtfully.

As I reflect on my life, a wave of joy washes over me, reminding me of the incredible adventures I have been fortunate enough to experience. The remarkable individuals whose paths crossed mine each left a lasting impression, while the surreal moments felt almost dreamlike. Every encounter has been a treasure. The breathtaking landscapes I explored remain vivid in my memories, with their gorgeous colors and magnificent vistas. Each experience, rich with emotion and beauty, holds a special place in my heart.

Of course, there were tough times, and like most people, I walked off the field with a few bruises and scars at halftime. However, I wouldn't trade any of my experiences; they have shaped me into who I am today—good, bad, and otherwise.

Looking back, I wish I could have seen past the stress, pain, fear, and confusion that often clouded my perspective, making the simpler, more joyful aspects of my life hard to see. I wouldn't have been so hard on my body or so judgmental of it, realizing that it is just a body—and a pretty good one, at that. I have shifted my focus from how others perceive my appearance to prioritizing my well-being and health. Now, I evaluate my physical self not based on how I look, but on how I feel.

I have learned that time is the most valuable currency we have, and I try to spend it wisely.

If I could turn back time and do a few things differently, I would embrace life with a lighter heart, not taking myself, my work, or the daily pressures so seriously as I careened through this chaotic bumper-car existence. I would have trusted that everything would be okay rather than letting fear dictate my choices. I would have sought out laughter more often, welcomed joy with open arms, expressed my love with abandon, and accepted the warmth of love in return without hesitation.

I hold a special place in my heart for the incredible and loving people who enrich my life: Oscar, with his infectious laughter; Max, always ready with words of wisdom; Finn, whose boundless creativity never ceases to amaze me; and Ben, whose kindness and deep insight light up my days—along with Stef, who brought Max and Ben into my life. I am also deeply grateful to my parents, brother, and family, whose support means everything.

I also want to acknowledge my loyal friends who have walked with me for years and the new souls I've encountered on this journey. Your companionship and support enrich my life in ways words cannot fully capture. Thank you all for being such a meaningful part of my story!

To my dearest wife, Caroline,

Finding the words to express my gratitude and admiration for you is impossible. You are my North Star, a constant beacon guiding me through the turbulent seas of life. Without you, I would feel lost in the darkness.

You are the song that the morning brings.

Our journey together has been a beautiful tapestry woven with love and laughter, helping me become a better version of myself. Your mere presence calms my anxious mind. I am grateful for the shared moments and cherished memories that enrich our lives. I am happy to know we have so much more to explore together.

So, now and again, I look up to the evening sky, give the big guy a wink, and thank Him for such an exciting, turbulent, heartbreaking, joyful, hilarious, and beautifully imperfect little life thus far.

I'm eager to see what's next for this restless soul.

www.ingramcontent.com/pod-product-compliance
Lightning Source LLC
Chambersburg PA
CBHW030356130626
46549CB00004B/1520